List Cultures

List Cultures

Knowledge and Poetics from Mesopotamia to BuzzFeed

Liam Cole Young

Routledge
Taylor & Francis Group
LONDON AND NEW YORK

First published in 2017 by Amsterdam University Press Ltd.

Published 2025 by Routledge
4 Park Square, Milton Park, Abingdon, Oxon OX14 4RN
605 Third Avenue, New York, NY 10158

Routledge is an imprint of the Taylor & Francis Group, an informa business

ISBN: 9789462981102 (hbk)
ISBN: 9781041182160 (pbk)
ISBN: 9781003698937 (ebk)
NUR 670

Cover design: Suzan Beijer

DOI: 10.5117/978 9462981102

Table of Contents

Acknowledgements

A first book is a strange thing. It emerges from an intense solitude that, if one is lucky, is sandwiched by periods rich with dialogue, collaboration, and conviviality. I am grateful to have been so lucky.

Thanks are due, first and foremost, to the many readers of the many drafts of this project: to Bernd Frohmann, for his limitless hospitality and friendship, his extraordinary dedication as a reader, and his precise and unflinching editorial eye; to John Durham Peters, whose unique talent for making the familiar strange pushed this project where it needed to go; to Nick Dyer-Witheford, for provocations both intellectual and political; to the 'Recursions' series editors, Jussi Parikka, Anna Tuschling, and Geoffrey Winthrop-Young, for their support and careful stewardship; to Grant Campbell, Alison Hearn, Chris Keep, Susan Knabe, and Tony Purdy, for their insightful and incisive comments; to Kenneth C. Werbin, for his pioneering work on listing and security; and to the editors and anonymous peer reviewers at *Canadian Journal of Communication, Theory, Culture, and Society* and *Amodern*, where early sketches of this project appeared in 2013.

I am grateful for the friendship of Warren Steele, whose brave and brilliant answers to the impossible question of 'the meaning of technology' have shaped this research in ways too numerous to count. My thanks, also, to Chad Andrews, Michael Daubs, Atle Mikkola Kjøsen, Danielle Taschereau Mamers, Vincent Manzerolle, Henry Adam Svec, and Elise Thorburn for their friendship and formidable intellectual talents. Conversations and correspondence with this group were decisive in developing this book.

I have been lucky to develop as a thinker, writer, and teacher in spaces of robust but collegial intellectual debate; thanks to my friends, colleagues, and teachers at Western, Trent, Brock, and Carleton Universities for inspiring and sometimes infuriating me. I would also like to acknowledge the students I've had the pleasure of teaching over the years, whose enthusiasm and patience enabled me to test out many of the ideas contained in these pages. I am additionally grateful for the generous support of the Ontario Ministry of Training, Colleges, and Universities, and the Social Science and Humanities Research Council of Canada.

A book on lists wouldn't be complete without plunking down a heap of names, so I thank, for their company, ideas, and provocations, Luke Arnott, Jonathan Bordo, Zak Bronson, Lilianne Dang, Michael Epp, John Fekete, Scott Henderson, Hugh Hodges, Svitlana Matviyenko, Dilyana Mincheva, Liam Mitchell, Michael Morse, Bohdan Nebesio, Davide Panagia, Chris

Russill, Will Straw, Tiara Sukhan, Ira Wagman, and Darren Wershler. Thanks also to organizers and audiences at conferences and symposia including 'Network Archaeology' (Miami OH University, 2012), the Centre for the Study of Theory and Criticism's Theory Sessions (Western University), Trent University's 2016 MA in Public Texts colloquium, as well as the annual meetings of the Canadian Communication Association, the Document Academy, the International Association for the Study of Popular Music, and the Popular Culture Association of Canada.

Heartfelt thanks to my family—brother Matt, sister-in-law Jolene and their three precocious children, 'Sloane, Jone, and Bone'; sister Erin, brother-in-law Roger, and their gang of four, Kennedy, Grace, Matteo, and Isla; step-sister Catherine, sister-in-law Sarah and her partner Jona; and of course my parents, new and old: Lorette and Peter Bentley, Jim and Kim Young, Marilyn and Lorne Brack. Their collective support of this project and love of its author have known no bounds.

Last but not least: thanks to Katie, my partner and my buddy, who tops the list in every category. These pages testify to your belief and love, and to the warmth, honesty, and grace with which you greet each day.

Preface

'We like lists because we do not want to die,' quipped the late, great Umberto Eco. The occasion for this remark was the opening of his 2009 Louvre exhibition, 'The Infinity of Lists', a dizzying exploration of listing activities over the last 5000 years. Curating the exhibition compelled the Italian polymath—who knew more than a little about such matters—to claim the list as 'the origin of culture.'[1]

Eco was not the only literary figure with a fondness for the humble list form. 'Bare lists of words are found suggestive to the imaginative and excited mind,' wrote Ralph Waldo Emerson, whose work is littered with enumerations.[2] We also learned, upon her passing, of cultural critic Susan Sontag's self-described list 'compulsion'.[3] Curators of the born-digital Sontag archive at UCLA were baffled by the preponderance of lists on her hard drives: topics she planned (or hoped) to write about; listed records of correspondence (incoming and outgoing: who wrote what and when and to whom); pages of titles of films and images (viewing reminders? a canon of her favourite pieces? things to keep in mind?) and, of course, to-do lists, those gentle giants of administration that do so much heavy lifting for us, but whose burdens weigh us down.

Sontag's beguiling lists illustrate everything that this book is about. They show how a study of lists is a battle against entropy. When you start looking for lists, they are everywhere; when you start talking about lists, your eyes and ears are filled with suggestions and ideas. One's only recourse is to add these to a list of things to consult, to read, to think about. Sontag's archive shows that lists categorize, yet, at the same time, defy categorization. This is perhaps their essential feature. We typically think of lists as administrative: they organize thoughts, offer reminders (not always friendly), and help get things done. But they do so much more than this. Lists draw things together and allow us to forge connections between divergent items, placing them under a logic that is all our own. This seemed to be what so fascinated Sontag about the form. By making lists, she wrote, 'I *perceive* value, I *confer* value, I *create* value, I even create—or guarantee—*existence*.'[4] This is strong language from someone not prone to exaggeration.

Found lists, like those on Sontag's hard drives, are ruins. Like found photographs, they are tinged with melancholy and longing. They seem to swirl around death, poignantly marking absence or loss. We come across another person's shopping list only after it has been cast aside, having served its purpose or been abandoned mid-stream. What is a to-do list when it can no longer remind, organize, or program action? Having lost its ability to do, and absent of any doer, it is a trace of past action, a vestige of possibility never realized. Who was this person? What happened to make them abandon this list? Even when we know its author, a list draws us in. Sontag's are mysterious because they slice through traditional modes of classification and lack context or description. What did they mean to her? What was their purpose or function? How did she think about them? How did they affect her thinking? Such lists seem to speak from the void, provoking thought, grief, and wonder.

The list is a form that mediates boundaries between administration and art, knowledge and poetics, sense and nonsense. It operates in the realm of ontics, a realm that recent 'German' media theory presents as prior to, and thus constitutive of, such aspects of human culture and society as knowledge systems, rituals and traditions, forms of selfhood, even modes of being.[5] The archaeological record is filled with examples of human societies using lists to hold themselves together across space and time, from literary lists like Homer's catalogue of ships to complex algorithmic writing in computation, and the billions of inventories and to-do lists in between. Such listing activities are the infrastructure of culture, making lists an ideal object for media theory. They help us glimpse the techniques and technologies by which human societies administer, police, and imagine themselves. In so doing, lists invite us to return with fresh eyes to a 'civilizational' approach to media history developed in Canada during the middle decades of the twentieth century, and most closely associated with Harold A. Innis and Marshall McLuhan.

Listing—as Sontag, Emerson, Eco, and Homer understood—is immensely powerful. But what is the nature of this power? Where and how does it operate? From where comes our impulse to list? Is there something about this form that speaks to our current historical moment? In what ways have other cultures used lists? How can we even begin to ask these questions? At the onset of this project, I was not sure. So, taking inspiration from Walter Benjamin (who is always good for inspiration), I started collecting, observing, and speculating, with no destination in mind. This took me to many surprising places: from the Top-40 charts in pop music that spurred my initial interest to grain inventories of Ancient Sumerians; from the *florilegia* of mediaeval manuscript culture to modern bureaucracies; from Melville's cetological classifications to BuzzFeed listicles; from computer programming to Borges' infinite libraries. The list tells many stories. Some appear in these pages. Most remain as fragments in notebooks, lists to be rediscovered somewhere down the line.

Introduction[1]

'An inclusive list of media effects opens many unexpected avenues of awareness and investigation'
– Marshall McLuhan[2]

Start with five lists from recent headlines (in no particular order):

March 2014—the governments of the United States and Russia engage in a tête-à-tête over Crimea that revolves, largely, around lists. An executive order from US President Barack Obama 'black lists' eleven officials of the Russian government as well as 'any individual or entity that operates in the Russian arms industry, and any designated individual or entity that acts on behalf of, or that provides material or other support to, any senior Russian government official.'[3] In response, Russia releases a list of Americans no longer welcome for business, diplomatic, or leisure purposes. Neither list proves effective in addressing the immediate issue of Russia's annexation of Crimea, but both are economical nuggets of information easily digested by the 24-hour news cycle.

April 2014—changes to the *Canadian Navigable Waters Protection Act* (NWPA), proposed by Stephen Harper's Conservative government in its 2012 omnibus budget bill C-45, take effect. The NWPA—an Act in which the default status for Canadian waterways was environmental protection under common law[4]—becomes the *Navigation Protection Act*. Waterway protection is reconfigured under the new act around economic interests and enforced by a new 'List of Scheduled Waters'. This list denies protection to 99.7 per cent of Canada's lakes and 99.9 per cent of its rivers. Notable exclusions are the Kitimat and Upper Fraser Rivers, which lay along the path of the proposed Northern Gateway Pipeline. Notable inclusions for protection are cottage country lakes in British Columbia and Ontario, where 'powerboat owners will maintain unfettered navigation protections.'[5] Protection is now exception; exception is granted by the 'List of Scheduled Waters'.

November 2015—While campaigning for the 2016 Republican Presidential nomination, Donald Trump replies 'Oh, I would certainly implement that—absolutely,' when asked if the United States should create a database of Muslims in the country. He adds that he would employ 'good management procedures' to get Muslims entered into the database.[6]

October 2015—*The Intercept* goes public with its latest bombshell intelligence leak, 'The Drone Papers'. A whistleblower 'from inside the intelligence community who worked on the types of operations and programs described' suggests he was compelled to act after learning of kill-listing activities of the American government. 'This outrageous explosion of watchlisting—of monitoring people and racking and stacking them on lists, assigning them numbers, assigning them "baseball cards", assigning them death sentences without notice, on a worldwide battlefield—it was, from the very first instance, wrong.'[7]

October 2014—author Shaun Usher releases *Lists of Note*, a book that, he says, speaks to the 'depth of [hu]mankind's obsession with lists.'[8] The book contains poetic and quotidian lists from historical figures both prominent and obscure. Some notable inclusions: Galileo's 1609 shopping list; Albert Einstein's list of conditions for prolonging his marriage to Mileva Maric (1914); a list of objections given to Charles Darwin by his father about a proposed journey aboard the HMS Beagle (1831); and Johnny Cash's whimsical to-do list, most likely a love letter sent to June Carter-Cash.

These examples show how lists and rankings proliferate at every turn: online and offline, at work and at play, in politics and art, in 'high' culture and 'low' culture, in conversation and print. Shopping lists, bucket lists, no-fly lists; as Werbin writes, 'in lists we are.'[9]

Our relationship to the form is complicated. Though they shoulder heavy administrative and organizational burdens, we heap scorn on the use of lists in cultural or literary contexts: arguments about listicles degrading long-form writing, or bullet points leading to limited attention spans, are as ubiquitous as the lists themselves. We are told that 'best of all time' collections strip meaning and context from great works of art. Many a critical theorist has argued that list-like forms debase reason.[10] In spite of these reservations, we list on. Countdowns, rankings, and 'best of the all-time' collections are ubiquitous. The list seems almost paradigmatic of digital culture: the zeitgeist in a BuzzFeed listicle.

Why this explosion of lists, and why now? One's first instinct is to suggest it has something to do with huge increases in the volume and velocity of data flows—lists as a strategy of managing 'information overload'.[11] Certainly, both producers and consumers have turned to the form, producers to quickly communicate information, consumers to help navigate a perceived information deluge. Lists reduce noise in the channel (the most important condition for any successful communicative act according to Claude Shannon's famous 'Mathematical Theory of Communication').[12] There are political stakes to this information ecology. Political discourse and action

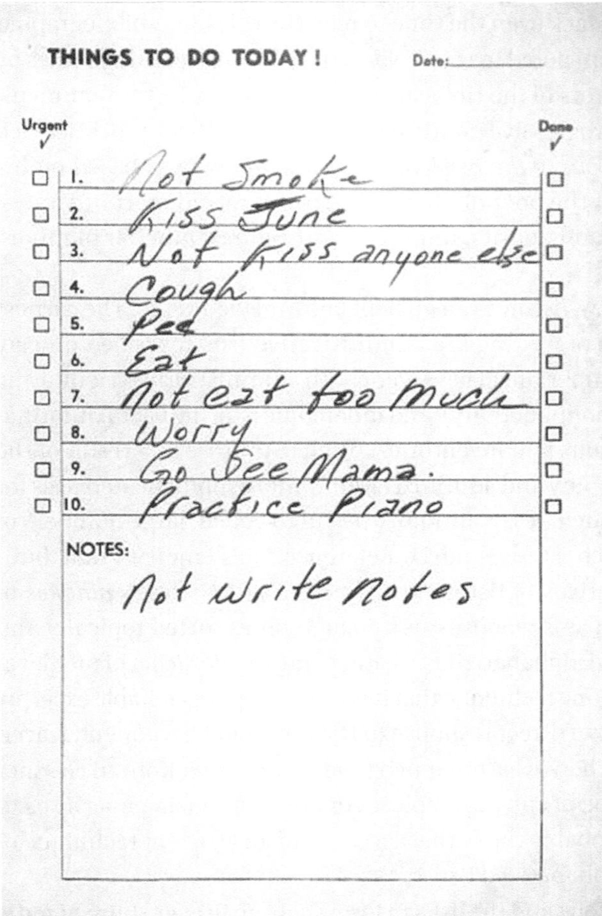

THINGS TO DO TODAY! Date:

Urgent ✓			Done ✓
☐	1.	Not Smoke	☐
☐	2.	Kiss June	☐
☐	3.	Not Kiss anyone else	☐
☐	4.	Cough	☐
☐	5.	Pee	☐
☐	6.	Eat	☐
☐	7.	Not eat too much	☐
☐	8.	Worry	☐
☐	9.	Go See Mama.	☐
☐	10.	Practice Piano	☐

NOTES:

Not write notes

Johnny Cash's to-do list, (date unknown).

are shaped by the communicative forms and processes available to citizens. In networked society, as Terranova and others show, the complexity of the world is broken down into a series of resolvable probabilities (yes/no, good/bad, us/them, important/unimportant, etc.).[13] These are contained in and delivered by communicative forms like lists. In this light, the list appears as an agent by which identities, institutions, economies, and governments are policed via neoliberal techniques of measure, enumeration, and data analytics.

But is the story so simple? Information overload is not unique to digital culture. We have been complaining that there is 'too much to know' since at least the early modern period (more probably since antiquity).[14] 'There are so many books that we lack even the time to read the titles,' bio-bibliographer Anton Francesco Doni noted in 1550.[15] Nor is the administration of bodies by lists new, as the horrors of the Holocaust and the French Terror remind us. And furthermore, progressive political movements use lists, too. Friedrich Engels's *The Conditions of the Working Class in England* was based on his 1842-1844 surveys of the poor of Manchester: disease and mortality rates, population growth and density, import/export figures, number of mines, etc.[16]

Though it feels new, listing is an ancient cultural technique. The earliest surviving examples of writing are administrative lists inscribed on clay tablets by ancient Sumerians. These were both administrative (facilitating trade and other economic activity), and mnemonic (storing useful information about transactions and inventories). Such lists arose as a result of the needs of public economy and administration.[17] More sophisticated uses for lists cropped up as societies of antiquity began to collect large numbers of texts in libraries such as Alexandria. Reference tools emerged that 'built on preexisting practices of list making (including Aristotle's *pinakes* of poets), sorting (such as Theophrastus's doxographies sorted topically and chronologically), and alphabetizing.'[18] Later came the *florilegia* of medieval scholars—a note-taking technique that involved compiling notable excerpts from other texts—as a direct response to the early modern lament, traced by Anne Blair, that there was 'too much to know.' In 1548, Konrad Gessner describes a technique of cutting up pieces of information on paper so as to re-arrange them, probably the earliest account of an efficient technique of generating many alphabetized lists.[19]

Listing as a technique and the list as a form show up in every bureaucratic apparatus conjured by modern minds and hands to address the needs of emergent institutions like the state and the corporation, and it haunts the work of every great thinker of bureaucracy and administration from Weber to Latour. Lists today are ubiquitous not only at the interface level of web aesthetics, but also in giving form to protocols and algorithms. In short, lists have been a part of every new media ecology and its corresponding 'flood' of information—from ancient administrative writing through early modern manuscript and modern print culture, to the analogue world of gramophone, film, typewriter, and into the digital code of network society. Clearly, preliminary hypotheses that regard it as either a corollary of network society's 'information overload', or as a surreptitious agent of neoliberalism, are not sophisticated enough to do justice to a form that exists in, or alongside, almost every inscription system on record.

How to explain this persistence? What can its varying historical functions teach us about the list's ability to survive shifts in ways of knowing? By collecting and materializing information, do lists create fields of knowledge? How do they structure the way data and knowledge circulate? What are the ethics of listing, a technique that has been complicit in the administration of human populations and in the 'disenchantment' of the modern world? Does list-making offer opportunities for challenging dominant systems of classification or ways of knowing? What is the role of the list in digital media environments, and in human artistic expression? Such questions guided my research, and this book exists because cultural and media studies do not yet have adequate tools to answer them.

Lists are important to media theory because they link familiar techniques of data organization and control with those that are much older. Lists offer a heuristic that allows us to see connections between digital media and the origins of writing. That they have received relatively little scholarly attention is surprising—an *aporia* perhaps indicative of a general trend in media studies to conflate layers of form, content, technique, practice, and habit under totalizing categories like 'media' or 'network'. Because they travel amongst and through media objects and networks, lists teach us about the way data become culturally inscribed as knowledge. Yet, lists are unique in their ability to interrupt the same systems of knowledge production and circulation that they seem, on the surface, only to enforce. This is a key point, and the crux of my argument: lists teach us about the systems of order that surround and enframe us because they simultaneously conceal and reveal, enforce and subvert the contours of such systems. Lists inscribe ways of seeing and knowing the world that they elsewhere make strange. Nobody understood this better than Borges, whose playful and beguiling creations teach us more about the classification and circulation of knowledge than thousands of pages of philosophy. From 'The Analytical Language of John Wilkins':

> These ambiguities, redundancies and deficiencies remind us of those which doctor Franz Kuhn attributes to a certain Chinese encyclopaedia entitled 'Celestial Empire of benevolent Knowledge'. In its remote pages it is written that the animals are divided into: (a) belonging to the emperor, (b) embalmed, (c) tame, (d) sucking pigs, (e) sirens, (f) fabulous, (g) stray dogs, (h) included in the present classification, (i) frenzied, (j) innumerable, (k) drawn with a very fine camelhair brush, (l) et cetera, (m) having just broken the water pitcher, (n) that from a long way off look like flies.[20]

We will return to Borges and his taxonomy in the latter stages of this book. For now, I set him aside in order to address one question in particular that looms over this project: what, precisely, *is* a list?

'What is a list?' or, are we asking the right question?

The list is hard to pin down. It can function variously as a communicative device, a cultural form, an operational mode of writing, a storage or archival device, a poetic form, and a mediator. Lists can be past, present, or future oriented; retroactive, administrative, or prescriptive. Lists are sometimes registers that index, and at other times metrics that rank and compare. Belknap's is a useful preliminary definition: 'At their most simple, lists are frameworks that hold separate and disparate items together. Lists are plastic, flexible structures in which an array of constituent units coheres through specific relations generated by specific forces of attraction.'[21] But so are sentences and paintings. Belknap's definition, if we are trying to pin down what exactly a list *is,* seems hopelessly open-ended, including everything from taxonomies, recipes, rankings, inventories, catalogues, lexicons, etc. He addresses this problem by distinguishing between pragmatic and literary lists. The former are quotidian lists of the everyday, enumerative containers that are concerned with the storage and retrieval of information and so do not mean anything, at least in literary terms. Literary lists, on the other hand, 'appeal for different reasons. [In them] we do not hunt for a specific piece of information but rather receive the information the writer wishes to communicate to us.'[22]

This distinction allows Belknap to offer a convincing case for what literary lists are and what they mean. But in limiting his focus to the literary he turns away from the majority of lists we encounter every day. How can we also account for lists in administration, a realm where they have dwelled for thousands of years? Furthermore, are literary and pragmatic lists so different? Another of Belknap's strategies can help with such questions. Just as he looks first at what lists *do* in literature before speculating about what they are or mean, so too must we look at what pragmatic lists do. Starting with an essential definition of what a list is or means—or even using these as animating questions—shuts down the generative potential of analysis. It locks the researcher into a trajectory that, in its quest for scientific accuracy, leads only towards negation—the list is *not* that, or the list is *only* this and never that. I propose a more generative approach that starts not with the question of what a list is or means, but rather asks what lists do: administratively, communicatively, epistemologically, even poetically.[23]

Media materialism offers tools required to pursue a functional history or genealogy of listing activities. With 'media materialism', I seek to capture a loose grouping of media-theoretical concepts and approaches including (but not limited to) media archaeology, theories of *Kulturtechniken* ('cultural techniques'), critical infrastructure and logistical media studies, as well as their historical antecedents in the 'civilizational' stream of media history pioneered by Harold A. Innis and Marshall McLuhan at the University of Toronto, c. 1930–1970. At a micro level, this grouping is interested in objects and texts not in terms of interpretation, meaning, or content, but rather in terms of the physical properties of surfaces and the techniques of inscription, transmission, and reception that structure them. At a macro level, media materialism is interested in the historically specific arrangements of spatial and temporal factors related to knowledge systems and information flows—what Innis first understood with the concepts of space- and time-bias.[24] I expand on this intellectual lineage, and my contribution to it, in Chapter one. For now, I will note that media materialism fills gaps in the currently dominant paradigms of what is called 'media studies' in Anglo-America. These are, generally, cultural studies approaches that emphasize textuality, subjectivity, and reception, on the one hand, and political economic approaches that emphasize systemic and institutional factors, on the other. This binary is crudely drawn but heuristic. It provides a useful orientation to an ongoing conversation into which *List Cultures* intervenes.

The arguments

This book develops four intersecting arguments. The first is disciplinary and methodological. It contributes to calls for contemporary media and cultural studies to more forcefully integrate media materialist approaches and concepts. Such approaches allow us to develop more accurate accounts of media networks and environments (contemporary and historical) than those that focus on use or ownership. Media materialism takes into account more than devices, institutions, texts, and audiences. It 'un-black boxes' the usual objects of media studies to illuminate forms, formats, techniques, protocols, programs, etc. that play crucial roles in the establishment and functioning of media-technological systems, but which are too often conflated under broad concepts like 'media' and 'network'. My contribution is to bring forward the 'civilizational' stream of media materialism, particularly its Canadian iteration, which brings much to current debates.

The second argument presents the list as a concrete example of what media materialism brings into view. Listing is a cultural technique that performs ontic operations that inscribe concepts and categories upon which technical systems and social institutions are built. As a form that is constitutive of certain kinds of knowledge, the list can tell us much about the material circumstances in which human beings enact thought and action.

The third and fourth arguments are about lists themselves. Argument (3) is that lists cannot be easily dismissed or endorsed. It is not enough to say lists are good or bad. Their complicated and sometimes contradictory operations—observed throughout this book—demand a precise tracing of how they function. Argument (4) proposes that the enduring presence of the list in our thoughts, texts, and programs arises from its unique capacity to negotiate tensions and paradoxes that have perplexed us for millennia. These include fear and desire, wonder and horror, entropy and order. The latter tension, which Eco describes as a poetics of 'etcetera' vs. 'everything-included', is particularly important to this project.[25] I will show that, on the one hand, the list's tendency towards 'everything included' (i.e. the drawing of borders) has led it to be harnessed by forces of rationality and governmentality that categorize and administer people, words, and things. On the other hand, the list has the capacity to negate such forces and open spaces for thinking beyond their limits. The poetics of etcetera can challenge the logic of everything-included; the paradigmatic AND, AND, AND of the infinite can displace the syntagmatic IF/THEN of the finite. This double function resonates with Jack Goody's dialectic understanding of lists, discussed in Chapter one (that they challenge the boundaries of knowledge that their borders materialize) and with Martin Heidegger's understanding of the relationship between art and technology, wherein the 'saving power' exists precisely where the 'danger' is most imminent (discussed in Chapter six).

These four arguments run parallel and often intersect. Studying the list does not offer us a convenient, Malcom Gladwell-esque insight into the nature of humanity forever and ever amen. Lists are not deterministic but heuristic. Through them we can map and compare shifts in ways of knowing. Tracing their operations gives us fresh insight into how we think, how we do, and how we imagine. They show us, if we know how to look, the ways that our rules and desires are encoded in various techniques of knowledge production and circulation, administration, and poetry.

Method and chapters

Because lists are ubiquitous and innocuous, it is difficult to bring them into focus. They are so woven into the fabric of our media and information environments that we do not often notice their presence. The list is part of what McLuhan called the 'ground'; the challenge here is to make it a 'figure'. One way to do this is to trace and compare list operations in a number of social, historical, and technical contexts. Rather than one argument about lists repeated over similar case studies (i.e. variations on a single theme), I have chosen to weave each of the four arguments above through case studies from different realms: epistemology, administration, logistics and computation, and poetics.

The arguments and case studies do not simply map onto one another. The popular music charts of Chapter two do not only teach us about cultural knowledge and history, nor do the computational lists of Chapter five teach us only about real time. Some tendencies are more evident in certain contexts than in others. Such differences emphasize that the list cannot be reduced to any single thing. I thus intentionally avoid judgement—lists as either good or bad, this or that, here or there—moving analysis beyond stock ideological critique. Such an approach, and the binary categories it relies upon, is not helpful in thinking about a form that has been in constant use for 5000 years. Of course there are ideological dimensions to lists—such an adaptable form of organizing and communicating information can and has been mobilized for various ends. But this kind of critique places too much emphasis on the content of lists at the expense of their operations. Latour's first rule of method is a good rule of thumb: instead of black-boxing the technical or material aspects of the list and then looking for social influences and biases, I seek to 'be there *before* the box closes and becomes black.'[26]

The list as an object attracts various methodological approaches. In addition to Latour, I borrow from the structural and institutional critique of communication studies and critical theory; the emphasis on inscription surfaces and techniques from media theory and documentation studies; and the close reading of literature and film studies. That these approaches can be productively combined speaks not only to how lists draw things together, but to the fact that, on their own, such traditional approaches are unable to account for the 'hidden' layer of list-like forms that travel through media networks, texts, and institutions, and which have many often-competing functions.

This research is equal parts synthetic, primary, and interpretive. It brings fresh eyes to familiar forms and proceeds as follows: Chapter one traces a brief history of 'list' as a concept, intellectual technology, cultural practice, and object of study. I expand on the challenges it poses to traditional interpretive approaches in media and cultural studies and sketch, with more specificity, approaches and concepts from media materialism that I find better suited for analysing lists and listing. I also foreground the modest contribution of *List Cultures* to this intellectual lineage.

Chapters two, three, and four re-read familiar histories through the lens of media materialism, following the list into seemingly disparate fields and historical moments. Chapter two builds on Bruno Latour's early science studies work to trace the list as a standardized format that structures the production, circulation, and reception of knowledge in popular music. It asks: what does the history of popular music look like if we view charts not as a political economic phenomenon, nor as a vector for exploring consumer subjectivity and identity, but as a cultural technique of categorization that structures the epistemology of a cultural field? I show how lists were present in this field from the beginning, and how institutionally-sanctioned lists, e.g. the 'charts', continue to inscribe borders and draw distinctions that enact categorizations and modes of classification. Popular music is a field where lists are particularly easy to trace, and where they receive a relatively unusual amount of critical attention. We can learn from this attention and export it to other realms where lists are no less present but much harder to observe.

Chapters three and four shift focus from the role of lists in making knowledge to their role in what Hacking calls 'making up people'.[27] We move from lists of words and things to those of number and human beings. Chapter three traces the list form in the emergence of fifteenth-century Italian double entry bookkeeping. Building on Mary Poovey's argument that double entry bookkeeping established a concept of 'fact' upon which modern empirical structures of knowledge were built, in Chapter four I connect this way of looking at words, things, and number to Nazi administration (which I describe metonymically as 'the Nazi census'). Luca Paciolli's series of interconnected lists established new categories of economy in the same way that Nazi registers inscribed new categories of personhood. Chapter four asks: what do we learn by reading Nazism as a modern phenomenon not at a philosophical level, as done most famously by Horkheimer and Adorno, but by looking at cultural techniques of paperwork? In doing so, we grasp how such techniques structure a particular way of understanding the world that is about logistics: the movement of people, things, and data through time and space. This 'logistical orientation' frames the earth and its inhabitants as material to be ordered according to human ends, what Heidegger referred to as *Bestand* ('standing-reserve'). Nazi listing techniques are a limit case study, included not to shock the reader or bring gravitas to this research, but again because its list operations are relatively easy to trace. There is a plethora of archival material and research on the subject. The familiarity of the historical event also shows us the power of re-reading history through the lens of media materialism.

Chapter five moves to the contemporary world, learning from the historical excursions of earlier chapters to explore how lists of code and protocol in computation are infrastructural elements of 'logistical modernity' (a term Benjamin Bratton uses in describing Paul Virilio).[28] Computational lists are elegant data structures that operate in real time to facilitate what is required of them: compression, calculation, and circulation. In this way, they can be connected to earlier case studies. Real-time operations of logistical lists make them a privileged operator at both code and interface level. Big databases are lists, as are algorithms, and their logic finds expression in data-mining techniques used in state surveillance and corporate-commercial sectors alike. A 'new media' corporation like BuzzFeed is a paradigmatic example of how list-protocols structure computational processes, interface aesthetics (e.g. listicles), and corporate organizations. Surprisingly, the time-critical dimension of logistical lists brings forth a connection to ancient, non-narrative modes of relaying the past. Real-time operations channel the chronicle and the epic, what Ernst calls modes of 'counting' rather than 'recounting'.[29] This moves lists beyond logistics and administration into the realm of poetry.

Chapter six picks up this suggestive thread, offering a more redemptive reading of listing. Using the words of Borges and Benjamin, and the images of Chris Marker, I show the list as an imaginative form that can explode the structures of order it elsewhere enforces. Such lists offer a unique space for what Heidegger understood with the concept *poiesis*. Lists here render the structures and limitations of modern thought uncanny, they intrude on modern historical and narrative time by channelling other, non-narrative times and affects, thereby preserving a heterotopian space for thinking 'other'.

I draw together this collection of divergent and seemingly arbitrary case studies to show how lists materialize connections, previously invisible, between realms, worlds, and historical moments, making visible a world of secret affinities. 'To write history [...] means to quote history,'[30] wrote Benjamin, lover of list and aphorism. Through quotation and enumeration, we interrupt the continuum of History, and it is in the spirit of Benjamin's listed scraps of observations, analysis, and quotation that the following is offered. Let us now explore some of the functions and poetics of a form that has resonated for over 5000 years in our programs and our imaginations, which are usually not so different.

1. History: Lists and Media Materialism

'"History is merely a list of surprises," I said. "It can only prepare us to be surprised yet again. Please write that down".'
– Kurt Vonnegut, *Slapstick*

The English word 'list' has a complicated etymology. Two related planes of usage converge to give us the modern sense of 'catalogue or roll consisting of a row or series of names, figures, words, or the like' (c. 1604).[1] Both come from the French *liste*, itself an adaptation of the Old high German *lista*. The first plane of usage (c. 1300) denotes 'border, edging, strip'. It later (c. 1450) came to more specifically describe the selvage or edge of a piece of cloth, or indeed any strip of cloth (such as those used to filter or drip a liquid). Extending out from cloth, the word came to describe, c. sixteenth century, any line or band conspicuously marked on a surface—a line in a man's beard, a stripe of colour, or a scar. The second and closely related meaning, that of boundary or border, was also widely adopted in the sixteenth century, e.g. the 'Primer of 1559': 'The miserable captives, which as yet be hedged in within the lists of death,'[2] or Shakespeare in *King Henry V*: 'Dear Kate, You and I cannot be confined within the weak list of a country's fashion: we are the makers of manners, Kate [...].'[3] From here come the 'lists' of battle. This second sense more forcefully implies lists as *containing* rather than the more general line or strip of earlier usage. But both early meanings of 'list', as border and as boundary, demonstrate that the term has always been used to describe various cultural techniques of collection and separation.[4]

Though form is clearly emphasized in this history of usage, much of the small but insightful literature on modern practices of listing focuses on content. Most argue the basic premise that lists establish or entrench configurations of power, dictating not just how and who may judge, but the very ontology of discussion; as Werbin notes, the list *serves*.[5] Others disagree, pointing to autobiographical lists as a site of emergent identities and subjectivities.[6] These latter remain focused on the performance of self that occurs through list contents, e.g. the expression of one's sophisticated taste and cultural capital through a personally-curated top-10 list. This emphasis on content over form, message over medium, arises from a general neglect of earlier, pre-modern practices of listing. Jack Goody's consideration of ancient listing techniques in terms of form, rather than content, helped him to theorize a dialectic dimension of the list. His thesis is that lists simultaneously challenge extant knowledge bases while also creating new ones. His 1977 Chapter, 'What's in a list?', offers, to date, the most sustained analysis of the formal dimensions of the list and deserves an extended commentary.

Lists appear with the onset of writing in Mesopotamia, c. 3100 BCE. Clay tablets inscribed with cuneiform script found in the area by archaeologists over the last two hundred years are mostly inventories and transaction records. Goody traces the impact of lists on these pre-alphabetic societies, arguing for their direct and profound effects on the shaping of 'modes of consciousness' and knowledge formation, and thus on the organization of both social life and cognitive systems.[7] He distinguishes three kinds of early lists: first, retrospective lists that are a kind of inventory of persons, objects, or events, such as a king-list. These can both sort and store data in the long or short term. Second are prescriptive lists (e.g. shopping lists) that serve as a plan for future action. These lists deal with information that is not often stored long term. Third are lexical lists, specifically those of the ancient Sumerians, which comprise 'a kind of inventory of concepts, a proto-dictionary or embryonic encyclopedia.'[8]

These lists are not oral, nor do they simply represent speech. They are an entirely different manner of collecting, storing, presenting, and thinking about data. 'The materialization of the speech act in writing enables it to be inspected, manipulated and re-ordered in a variety of ways.'[9] Because it materializes words and things visually—an ancestor of today's much-hyped data visualization—Goody sees the list as an inscription technique that distances itself and its users from earlier oral traditions and conventions. In other words, the list as a form facilitates 'modes of thought' and techniques of information processing, storage, and transmission that do not abide by the structures that govern the oral tradition.

> These written forms were not simply by-products of the interaction between writing and, say, the economy, filling some hitherto hidden 'need', but [...] they represented a significant change not only in the nature of transactions, but also in the 'modes of thought' that accompanied them [...] in terms of the formal, cognitive and linguistic operations which this new technology of the intellect opened up.[10]

While writing as storage 'permits communication over time and space, and provides man with a marking mnemonic and recording device,'[11] there is an equally important *processing* function of such writing, 'which shifts language from the aural to the visual domain, and makes possible a different kind of inspection, the re-ordering and refining not only of sentences, but of individual words.'[12] Ancient administrative lists decontextualize words and things from speech, and, in later cultures, from narrative, affording new configurations in the visual realm. 'Speech has no spatial aspect but writing has. With the introduction of writing existing knowledge may be put into other formats which may have considerable heuristic value.'[13] The writing down of a word allows it to be contemplated and manipulated in ways not possible in orality. Such a process enables the communication of a certain kind of knowledge over space and time, knowledge that has been *classified*. It also opens up new capacities for words, data, knowledge, and cognition. In this context, lists function as epistemological operators (a thread pursued in more detail in Chapter two). Goody's dialectical understanding of the relationship between listing and cognition shows that lists do not arise simply to fulfil the instrumental needs of human beings, but are active material agents in processes of writing, thinking, and acting.

Lists are an intellectual technology that affects human cognition and the organization of social life. Written lists are obviously different from oral modes of communication. They are also quite different from 'writing' as conventionally understood. In fact, listing probably has more in common with techniques of counting and exchange that preceded the appearance of writing in Mesopotamia than with narrative styles of writing that came after. The archaeologist Denise Schmandt-Besserat argued that Mesopotamian lists are material traces of a token system that was used for thousands of years to keep track of commercial transactions and inventories. As she recounts, in 1957 A. Leo Oppenheim discovered at Nuzi (north of Babylon) a hollow tablet inscribed with a list of 48 animals and containing 48 tokens corresponding to these inscriptions (c. 1500 BCE).[14] This discovery caused Pierre Amiet, Head Keeper of Western Antiquities at the Louvre, to reconsider a series of 50 hollow clay balls filled with tokens found near Susa, Iran c. 3300 BCE. Amiet realized these to be accounting devices of the same kind as Oppenheim's Nuzi tokens.[15] Schmandt-Besserat's fieldwork led her to discover similar tokens throughout the Middle East dating back to 8000 BCE, five thousand years before writing was invented. The shapes on many of these tokens, particularly those from 3300 BCE forward, closely match the shapes of the earliest signs of cuneiform writing. Her argument was that with urbanization came new stresses on the economic system, leading to expansion and changes to the previously-stable token system. Shifting labour markets and economic conditions corresponding to urbanization required a more robust system of record-keeping than tokens could provide. Thus came 'envelopes'—hollow clay balls that 'provided both a means of holding and protecting tokens and also a clay surface onto which the parties involved in a transaction could impress their personal seals.'[16] Due to the impenetrability of seals and the opacity of clay as a medium, the imprinting of each token onto the surface soon followed. This, for Schmandt-Besserat, was how writing came about: '[o]nce the tokens were impressed upon the outer surface of the envelope, their presence inside the envelope became superfluous. It was not long before the hollow envelopes were replaced by solid tablets into which the shapes of the relevant tokens had been impressed.'[17]

Three-dimensional tokens are transcoded or 'processed' into two-dimensional symbols on a surface for storage and transmission (a list is a more economical, malleable, and stable container than the earlier clay envelope and token system). This process of visualizing material things from the world is crucial to understanding the way lists function epistemologically. Raible calls such writing 'ideography' because it 'visualize[s] aspects of the content that have no equivalents in the sphere of sound.'[18] Krämer conceives of such writing as possessing a 'notational iconicity' (from the German *Bildschriftlichkeit*), a 'fundamentally visual-iconographic dimension' that enables it to be *operative* rather than semiotic or narrative.[19] As ideographic forms, lists loosen the knot that binds words to speech, visualizing words and things in a new way that allows them to be contemplated and re-ordered. When placed in a list, entries become data that can be manipulated—processed—in real time. The putting of words and things in relation to one another in a list allows for connections to be made that did not exist prior to the act of listing. The upshot is, as Goody understood, that lists simultaneously challenge extant knowledge formations, but also create new ones by inscribing certain modes of organization and classification (which amount to new ways of seeing and doing). Thinkers like Le Goff and Vismann argue this makes listing more than an intellectual technique and, in fact, constitutive of new modes of state and monarchical power. Imperial registries of thirteenth-century Europe, for instance, are 'more than nifty administrative techniques designed to economize on reading and writing; they were nothing less than the media technology for a state as a permanent entity.'[20]

Because lists are neither oral, nor entirely literary, they (along with other forms of ideography) illuminate the extent to which the conventional orality-literacy polarity, theorized in the classical media theory of Walter J. Ong and others, does not hold.[21] Primarily at issue is that the polarity rests on an idea of meaning that lies behind or within language in both its spoken and written forms. Pragmatic or operative lists do not 'mean' in this way. They possess neither an inherent narrative function, nor semiological units to be decoded. Lists reject conventions like prose and syntax. Meaning does not arise from grammatical structures of language because the latter do not factor in the construction of a list, which instead adheres to a different, non-grammatical structure. Certain visual and graphic qualities govern the creation of most lists—columns, rows, and techniques of ordering determine its form and the manner by which a list is written, or better, the way it is *filled in.* But these structures do not produce meaning, at least not in a phenomenological or hermeneutic sense.

Because ancient lists of the kind described by Goody and Schmandt-Besserat were primarily administrative, the only 'meaning' we can attribute to them is functional. Lists function to facilitate various forms of interaction between human beings (economic, social, political, etc.) while also standing as a record of the occurrence of this interaction. Lists make things happen while also registering items and transactions. Each administrative list of the Ancient Sumerians stands as a record of an event (e.g. an economic transaction), while its contents correspond to an item involved in the transaction (whether a chicken, a tool, a person, etc.). But there is no narrative here, nor are there syntactical rules inherited from speech governing the list as a written formation. As a result, for a long time these lists remained unread by modern scholars. In fact, they were *unreadable* due to a tacit assumption in early twentieth-century archaeology that Babylonian lists of the third millennium BCE were bits of narrative text. 'It was only after dropping the assumption that the strange signs conform to the logic of grammar, sentence, and line,' Vismann writes, 'that they were revealed to be accounting lists based on a nonsyntactic order.'[22] A window onto an entire world of non-narrative grammatology had opened. In this case, the format was the message.

Listenwissenschaft

Thus was born *Listenwissenschaft,* or, the 'science of lists'. This term was introduced by famous Assyriologist Wolfram van Soden in 1936 to describe a 'typically Sumerian psychological trait: *Ordnungswille* [will-to-order].'[23] This 'will-to-order' resulted, according to Van Soden, in the creation of lexical lists that mirrored the order of the world as it was established by the Sumerian gods. Since these lists were never codified into coherent doctrines or arguments, as in later Judeo-Christian written traditions, the scholarship of Van Soden and the other *Listenwissenschaftler* never went beyond 'the level of the lists.'[24] Most of Van Soden's theorizations have since been shown to be highly anachronistic, with his analysis of Sumerian *Ordnungswille* less a discovery of an ancient cosmology made manifest in cultural techniques of order than a reflection of the preoccupation of modern thinkers like Van Soden with ordering systems.

Most contemporary discussions of *Listenwissenschaft* occur in Judeo-Christian religious scholarship.[25] Swartz looks at the abundance of lists in blessing and curse texts in various traditions. He argues that such lists 'objectify the object of the practitioner's love or hate' and demonstrate his or her virtuosity and wide-range of knowledge. More broadly, they signal an important change in aesthetic sensibilities during late antiquity. This new aesthetic,

> in contrast to the classical age, privileged not proportion or narrative shape, but the interplay of individual elements arranged for dazzling effect. As a result, late Latin poetry abounded in artfully composed lists of distinct parts and elaborations of what was known as *leptologia*, the lavish description of details in the course of a poem or narrative. In this aesthetic, lists took pride of place.[26]

Swartz also points out that such lists feature both magical (i.e. poetic) and legal formulae. He cites the following fragment from the twelfth century:

> May curse and damage amputate their thighs. Amen.
> May murder and butchery slice up their bowels. Amen.
> May slashing and swelling blow up their legs. Amen.
> May weariness and cursing cut their feet. Amen.
> Let these curses come to all their limbs
> and all their sides, to perpetuate their illness
> and to make their flesh rot, until their name is obliterated,
> as is written in the Torah of Moses about them and those like them:
> Let the Lord never forgive them, as it is said:
> "The Lord will never forgive him" etc., one and all,
> and may each and every one of them
> be destroyed, swallowed up, mutilated, stabbed, thrown down,
> damaged, torn, impaled, chained,
> torched, left to die, injured, burned, uprooted,
> split, diminished, ruined, ignited, annihilated,
> hung, struck by all kinds of boils and pestilence.

17 And may all plagues affect him. In the evil hours
18 when the stern decrees go out,
19 that come newly to him, as it is said:
20 "The Lord strike you with consumption;" etc.; "The Lord will strike you with Egyptian inflammation" etc.; evil;
21 "The Lord will strike you with madness and blindness" etc. "and you shall become [a horror to the peoples of the earth];"
22 "Cursed shall you be in the city," etc. and all the rest of the curses
23 written in this book of the Torah, to eradicate
24 their name and memory and to eliminate them from the world.
25 Amen Amen Selah.
26 Cursed be they by the awesome, magnificent and fearsome one,
27 twelve hours a day. Amen.
28 Cursed be they by God, who dwells in the high heavens,
29 twelve hours each and every night. Amen.
30 Cursed be they by God, who authorizes every plague—
31 Eighty-eight thousand
32 eight hundred eighty-eight every moment.
33 Cursed be they by God, who is glorious in holiness,
34 thirty days of every month.
35 Cursed be they by God who is before him,
36 twelve months of every year.
37 Cursed be they by the one who established (that which is) above and below,
38 seven years of every sabbatical cycle.[27]

This list abstracts objects into words and draws seemingly incongruous items together to dazzle and terrify the reader or listener. It also conveys rules and principles, the power of which, according to Swartz, arises from enumeration, repetition, and prosody. His characterization of poetry and law as two sides of the same coin is extremely suggestive. It is a recurring theme of this book.

Scholarship on lists in Judeo-Christian texts and rituals foregrounds listing as a cultural technique that functions beyond the realm of administration. Interestingly, almost all theological scholarship on lists erroneously credits the term *Listenwissenschaft* to a theologian, Albrecht Alt, who must have picked up the term from Van Soden, but, to my knowledge, did not cite his work. Much of the Judeo-Christian tradition comes to us via texts and litanies that do not convey stories in the way the modern eye and ear are trained to receive them. Perhaps Alt was inspired to import Van Soden's

Listenwissenschaft into his theological studies because it offered at least a preliminary framework through which to understand the operations of such non-narrative modes of speech and, later, writing.

Research into *Listenwissenschaft* has only ever occurred on the margins of fields like Assyriology, Religious Studies, Anthropology, and Media Studies, and it usually looks only to ancient societies. The modern mind still consistently ignores non-narrative writing even though it is the vast majority of the writing that has occurred in modernity. Guillory argues that 'informational' writing, compiling e.g. memos and lists, stands in contrast to the way modern people think of their writing as always being either literary or scholarly/scientific.[28] This tendency to gloss over the banal realm of administration is reflected in the conventional orality-literacy polarity of classical media theory. This polarity cannot properly account for administrative forms of writing such as lists (but also tables, charts, diagrams, etc.[29]) because it does not account for any form of writing that is not simply a duplication or representation of speech. The speech bias in orality-literacy scholarship—evident to varying degrees in Innis, McLuhan, and especially Ong—probably stems from a tendency to over-privilege antiquity's orality, or perhaps from a preoccupation with the primacy of the Word in the Catholic tradition. Written forms such as lists (variously called ideographic, operative, pragmatic, or administrative) undercut this bias, because they literally bring into view an alternative, non-narrative syntax that runs parallel to, and is in constant tension with, conventional syntaxes (grammar, narrative, etc.). Until relatively recently, such writing was mistakenly reduced to non-meaningful noise in the channel. But as Kittler and others teach, noise is often as crucial to understanding the dynamics of a media discourse network as any other factor.

Administration

Most lists, in modern and ancient societies alike, administer. They are deployed in order *to order*: lists make sense of the world, they facilitate the development of knowledge and discourses, they organize experience. But such functions can be deeply contradictory. Illuminating the wider political and historical implications of the list addresses the extent to which it can and has served power interests, both in the acquisition of power and its retention. Lists were a privileged form mobilized in the name of the French Revolution—witness Condorcet's assurance to provincial administrators that '[e]ach hour that you consecrate to this work, each line that you inscribe in the register, is a step forward for the Revolution [...]'[30]—but also in the name of its subsequent terror—chief of the General Police Bureau Augustin Lejeune, asked by Robespierre to draw up a list of accusations against those deemed 'good for the guillotine,' writes, 'I shuddered reading this list, I brought it home with me, I lifted up a paving stone, and buried it, determined to perish rather than allow it to reach its destination.'[31] While Lejeune's act of destruction may, in this instance, have saved lives, Ben Kafka shows that more often than not such lists—which categorized citizens of the Republic as 'moderate', 'aristocrat', or 'counterrevolutionary'—had bloody consequences.[32]

These examples show the list to be particularly amenable to the control of individuals and populations. Techniques of self-administration are internalized as lists of things to do or not. Max Weber famously described the checklists used by conscientious Puritans to supervise their own states of grace.[33] Or H. Vaughn, even earlier: 'When the light comes, list thy deeds.'[34] Benjamin Franklin, as he describes in *Autobiography*, made extensive use of lists in his quest for methods of self-improvement.

> [...] I included under thirteen names of virtues all that at the time occurred to me as necessary or desirable, and annexed to each a short precept, which fully expressed the extent I gave its meaning.
>
> These names of virtues, with the precepts, were:
>
> 1. TEMPERANCE. Eat not to dullness; drink not to elevation.
> 2. SILENCE. Speak not but what may benefit others or yourself; avoid trifling conversation.
> 3. ORDER. Let all your things have their places; let each part of your business have its time.
> 4. RESOLUTION. Resolve to perform what you ought; perform without fail what you resolve.
> 5. FRUGALITY. Make no expense but to do good to others or yourself, *i.e.* waste nothing.
> 6. INDUSTRY. Lose no time; be always employed in something useful; cut off all unnecessary actions.
> 7. SINCERITY. Use no hurtful deceit; think innocently and justly, and, if you speak, speak accordingly.
> 8. JUSTICE. Wrong none by means of doing injuries, or omitting the benefits that are your duty.
> 9. MODERATION. Avoid extremes; forebear resenting injuries so much as you think they deserve.
> 10. CLEANLINESS. Tolerate no uncleanliness in body, clothes, or habitation.

11. TRANQUILLITY. Be not disturbed at trifles, or at accidents common or unavoidable.
12. CHASTITY. Rarely use venery but for health or offspring, never to dullness, weakness, or the injury of your own or another's peace or reputation.
13. HUMILITY. Imitate Jesus and Socrates.[35]

Externally, lists establish or reaffirm social categories and relations by placing human subjects next to one another, inscribing or creating relations between diverse subjects. Lists are important to regimes of biopower, a concept Foucault developed to describe the ways that life itself came to be the subject of power; as Hacking describes, 'it was not simply individual living persons who might be subjected to the orders of the sovereign, but Life itself, the life of the species, the size of the population, the modes of procreation.'[36] Foucault points to the emergence, in the late seventeenth century, of an entire matrix of administration devoted to the observation, collection, calculation, and analysis of data about 'populations' and 'territories' (themselves new categories): demography, evaluations of relations between resources and inhabitants, analysis of wealth and its circulations, and so on. Biopower, in short, 'designate[s] what brought life and its mechanisms into the realm of explicit calculation and made knowledge-power an agent of transformation of human life.'[37] To study biopower, Foucault proposes an 'ascending' analysis that looks first at 'infinitesimal mechanisms'. By starting with these mechanisms, 'which each have their own history, their own trajectory, their own techniques and tactics,' we can then 'see how [they] have been—and continue to be—invested, colonized, utilized, involuted, transformed, displaced, extended, etc., by ever more general mechanisms and by forms of global domination [...].'[38] Lists are such 'infinitesimal mechanisms' and their role in the administration of populations demands attention. This topic is the focus of Chapters three and four; for now, I offer only a few introductory remarks.

Although historically many forms of rule have made use of census taking and other population administration techniques, clearly the most hyperbolic and macabre extension of such techniques are found in Nazi Germany. By reducing human beings to an entry in a registry and abstracting bare life into numbers and figures, such tactics served not only to dehumanize subjects, but also to 'transport them to a new reality—namely, death.'[39] Werbin argues that the integral role of the list in the Nazi installation of what he calls 'massively organized information' cannot be understated. With the onset of Nazi governmentality, lists were redeployed as 'critical support technologies' and 'juridical-disciplinary mechanisms.'[40] These ultimately:

> came to constitute a unique new way of seeing and doing in their own right: involving fracturing 'threatening populations' from 'healthy populations.' The list was at the heart of these schisms that marked modern Nazi governmentality—healthy || diseased; Aryan || Jew; us || them—serving the delimitation and policing of abnormal cases in populations; installing *caesuric* social fractures.[41]

The crucial point is that because the list is so flexible, so innocuously woven into the fabric of the world that we pay it no mind, lists are easily mobilized for political ends. Its *caesurae* delineate populations so they may be administered and policed. In this way, lists are Hannah Arendt's banality of evil materialized: components of a system of administrative protocol that prevents any 'conscientious functionary' from being able to act, even if they wish to. At least, so they are wont to claim while on trial: 'You might ask why [...] we signed in this way documents with which we were not familiar. I respond: By absolute necessity, by the physical impossibility of doing otherwise[,]' claimed Carnot, deputy of the Terror's infamous Committee of Public Safety, a full 165 years before Eichmann in Jerusalem.[42]

This ethical dimension raises a whole host of questions that have been given careful treatment by others.[43] Some of these questions will be pursued at greater length in Chapters three and four. Suffice it here to say that highlighting ethical questions around listing activities shows these activities and this form to be deeply implicated in rationalism. Lists can quite clearly be a friend to the disenchanting bureaucratic apparatus sketched by Max Weber,[44] the instrumental reason so vehemently attacked by Horkheimer and Adorno,[45] or the mechanization of knowledge feared by Harold Innis.[46]

But before lists are about power, they are about data operations: processing, storage, and transmission; calculation, compression, circulation. Vismann argued that lists in the domain of the law 'do not communicate, they control transfer operations [...] individual items are not put down in writing for the sake of memorizing spoken words, but in order to regulate goods, things, or people. Lists sort and engender circulation.'[47] In this view, the list is strictly a medium of transfer; its storage capacity is only ever temporary because there is no need, nor any desire to preserve a list once the act or event that it facilitates has occurred. Therefore, its orientation is always towards the present. At the same time, Vismann notes, lists prefigure files and thus govern the inside of the file world. Files are process-generated algorithmic entities, and the process generators are 'list-shaped control signs.'[48] Lists prescribe any file's movement through space and time: file notes issue commands for the next movement or event of a file's existence—to where or to whom the file should travel, at what time, by which means, etc. Each executed command triggers the next. Over time, these notes accumulate, one after the other, preserving a listed record of a file's 'life'. There is a triple function here: lists administer while also archiving and prescribing. They are not simply present based, but can record the past and program the future. Lists are here algorithmic sets of actionable instructions that determine future trajectories; they anticipate the operational writing of digital computation (a thread pursued at length in Chapter five).

Though Vismann's work masterfully sketches lists in relation to data transmission and processing, we must not overlook storage. Bibliographic lists, for instance, were probably the most important document in early modern libraries, providing not only a register of a library's contents, but also a means of orienting visitors.[49] Registers—whether of books or files—ascribe *addresses* to material items in the world, a practice 'designed to account for units that threaten to disappear among countless masses.'[50] Such practices are undertaken explicitly with the future in mind: 'detailed and exact written procedures are needed to guarantee the logistical architecture of the library beyond the fluctuations of a term of office.'[51] Krajewski demonstrates that written lists are not quite flexible enough for the registration needs of an ever-changing library collection. Erasability is a necessary precondition for an up-to-date register, and so various techniques are developed to better equip registries for absorbing new entries, such as the cut up method and later the card catalogue system.[52] Keeping the capacity of lists for storage and address in focus ensures an analysis of the list does not stray into a mode of critique too fixated on its tendency to be co-opted by forces of rationalization, and thus on whether lists are good or bad.

This brief history shows that lists simultaneously carve out knowledge, erecting its barriers through inclusion or exclusion according to specific criteria. But, as Goody emphasizes, embedded within any list is a challenge to the very knowledge formation it erects. This challenge is implicit in the list's constant display of its exclusionary nature, observable in its inscribed, formal attributes. As he notes, the list:

> has a clear-cut beginning and a precise end, that is, a boundary, an edge, like a piece of cloth [...] it encourages the ordering of the items, by numbers, by initial sound, by category, etc. And the existence of boundaries,

external and internal, brings greater visibility to categories, at the same time as making them more abstract.[53]

Through its visible borders, the list wears its principles of organization as an exoskeleton, always observable but often unnoticed. Listing always involves choices, which are imminent in form and beg us to question them. Certain thinkers have explored this tendency, primarily in the aesthetic realm, as a 'poetics' of the list.[54] Eco in particular sees the list as possessing a unique capacity to collect the world; it is suggestive of what he calls the '*topos* of ineffability,' an aesthetic gesture towards the infinite, the unknowable, or the not-yet-known that is meant to stimulate the beholder's imagination.[55] John Durham Peters is also fond of this disseminative capacity of lists. He describes their function in his own writing as a 'battle against [his] own finitude' and a futile attempt to 'catch the cosmos.'[56] A recent exhibition on lists at New York's Morgan Museum suggests this dimension of lists and list making has continuing resonance in artworlds.[57] Chapter six examines such list poetics more closely.

Media materialism

How to give an account of a form that so defies classification? As mentioned above, focusing on what the list is may be less useful than focusing on what it does—how it functions in relation to techniques of inscription and representation, historical configurations of power/knowledge, and media-technical conditions of processing, storage, and transmission. Media materialism, I argued, offers tools for such an analysis—but what are they?

It is tempting to frame this book as a media archaeology of the list. Media archaeology re-emphasizes the historical and material dimensions of media that are often glossed over by conventional approaches to 'new media'. Though there is 'no general agreement about either the principles or the terminology of media archaeology,'[58] Huhtamo stresses both its cyclical nature and its concern with 'the 'excavation' of the ways in which [various] discursive traditions and formulations have been 'imprinted' on specific media machines and systems in different historical contexts, contributing to their identity in terms of socially and ideologically specific webs of signification.'[59] For Wolfgang Ernst, media archaeology is a kind of epistemological reverse-engineering that 'makes us aware of discontinuities in media cultures as opposed to the reconciling narratives of cultural history.'[60] Media archaeology de-emphasizes the human subject as central figure of historical and technical change, seeking instead to unearth the 'nondiscursive infrastructure and (hidden) programs of media' that structure what it is possible for humans to think and do.[61] Following Kittler,[62] Ernst argues that the contours of these infrastructures are shaped by the media-technical conditions of possibility that obtain in any given historical moment; these are, namely, the means by which data is processed, stored, and transmitted. While thinkers like McLuhan and Virilio have convincingly demonstrated the extent to which such medial conditions structure perception, Ernst goes a step further in arguing that they also delineate *cultural* data such as history and memory. Because media measure, process, and so structure time, they are the true archivists of pasts both human and non-human.

But media archaeology has its limits. Critiques of the 'cold gaze' and technicism of anti-humanist thinkers such as Ernst and Kittler are well documented.[63] The crux of this critique is that certain strands of media archaeology fetishize, or at least mistakenly elevate, mechanism, machine, and code at the expense of the equally material received knowledges and embodied techniques—practical, philosophical, institutional—that inform the technical development of media. Media archaeology may have been too quick to adopt the Kittlerian model (adapted from Foucault) of understanding technical development in terms of sudden rupture, rather than slow sedimentation. Beyond this, too often the media devices and objects of media archaeological analysis seem simply to drop from the sky; as Parikka notes, they 'might be important to give us history (as conditions of knowledge) [but] seem themselves surprisingly without history and outside time.'[64] Conceiving of media as the a priori of history denies that they are developed in specific institutional, political, industrial, socio-economic, cultural, and technical constellations, as, for instance, Sterne shows.[65] Gitelman offers a similar critique of the German *milieu* from which media archaeology emerged, noting its tendency to sacrifice empirical and historical specificity in the name of grand theories of everything.[66] She urges media analysis to resist the urge to frame media objects or systems in such general terms—to speak not simply of 'the telephone' or 'the computer', but specifically of e.g. telephones in the 1890 rural United States, or tablet computers in 2012. Beyond these critiques, we must note the relative paucity of sustained attempts to politicize media archaeology or to integrate it with, for instance, historical materialism and political economy. Parikka has advocated that such syntheses are urgently needed in the field.[67] Research is currently underway towards these ends. Monea and Packer argue that attending to Foucault's distinction between 'archaeology' and 'genealogy' will invite approaches more explicitly attuned to analyses of power and politics.[68] Non-Foucauldian models exist. Harold Innis, for instance—a foundational though rarely discussed intellectual precursor—was trained as a political economist and developed a method, 'dirt research', that is, in many ways, media archaeology *avant la lettre*.[69] Finally, the dubious politics of media archaeology's father figure, Friedrich Kittler, are well documented (if slightly overblown).[70] Still, there is clearly a tendency in media archaeology to bracket politics and humans at the expense of machine and code.

Such limitations are not the primary obstacles in adopting a media-archaeological approach to lists. These are instead conceptual and methodological. Media archaeology is primarily about tinkering and taking apart—going 'under the hood' of media to understand the technical processes and mechanisms that make them work, begging the question: how to go under the hood of a list? When one excavates a digital computer or a radio, one finds a whole host of complex mechanisms and entities at work (minute inscription tools, silicon chips, circuit boards, electric cables, wheels, fans, etc.), each of which has a complex developmental history.[71] But is it possible to similarly 'excavate' a list? If so, what do we find? In order even to address this question, we first have to acknowledge that every list is contained within some medium, in an echo of McLuhan's famous dictum. The constitutive elements of a paper list, for example, are not necessarily mechanisms or 'things in the world,' but inscriptions, indexical marks, traces of handedness, practices of writing, ways of framing and organizing data. We find lines, boxes, words, and numbers that have been processed into the symbolic field and inscribed on the medium of paper using various techniques and tools. These are quite different from the elements unearthed in much of the more radically mechanistic media archaeology. We see that the constitutive elements of such a list are not necessarily operative in time as those in digital and analog media are, but are spatially oriented in relation to whatever medium contains them. A paper list is a series of marks that materializes a technique of spatial data organization. These elements do not move through time nor space on their own (as, for instance, a spinning mechanism does) but only via other media (a list never exists outside the medium in which it dwells). It is not the list that moves through an office, but the paper on which it is written. It would be more correct to say that the list is itself an entity that is excavated by a media archaeology of paper. In other words, instead of thinking of the list as a medium, how can we think of it as something that moves in, through, and across various media, as something that gives us a sense of the 'mediality'[72] of any given media environment?

Jonathan Sterne describes such operations in his discussion of formats. I follow Sterne in developing an approach not primarily concerned with media as such, but with formats and their more general precursor: forms. According to Sterne, a format such as MP3:

> denotes a whole range of decisions that affect the look, feel, experience and workings of a medium. It also names a set of rules according to which a technology can operate [...]. This specification operates as a code—whether in software, policy, or instructions for manufacture and use—that conditions the experience of a medium and its processing protocols.[73]

Format is a precise term that describes a form that has been institutionally or technically standardized. Sterne traces the long history of experimentation with, and failure of, various forms and modes of audio compression that prefigure the appearance of the standardized MP3 format. Standardized administrative or epistemological lists are formats. Lists in art and literature are forms. The necessity of this distinction will become evident in later chapters; I point it out here to remind us that a given format is but one possible instantiation of a form. By fashioning an approach to the list at the level of form and format, I hope to carve out a similar path on the terrain of writing to the one Sterne does using MP3 on the terrain of sound formats and technologies.

This book also takes inspiration from Sterne's speculations on the possibility for a 'general history of compression' that 'could easily extend back to the invention of the point and the number zero, the codex and the scroll form of the book, the wheel, and perhaps even some kinds of ancient writing and number systems.'[74] We have already seen that lists are present at the onset of writing. The list has continued to play an important role in more modern processes of compression. 'As people and institutions have developed new media and new forms of representation, they have also sought out ways to build additional efficiencies into channels and to economize communication in the service of facilitating greater mobility.'[75] What are ancient Sumerian grain inventories, 1960s *Billboard* charts, or everyday shopping lists (whether on paper or smartphone) other than attempts to streamline and economize, to remove redundant data from a channel or medium, to compress? There may be no other mode of inscription that has performed this compressive function more consistently and robustly than the list. Fashioning such an approach to the study of lists involves thinking in broad strokes about writing as a medium, envisioning inscription surfaces like paper as channels, with limited bandwidth, which transmit data over space and time. In this view, the list is a format that compresses data and maximizes the efficiency of paper's bandwidth.

Sterne's format theory 'focus[es] on the stuff beneath, beyond, and behind the boxes our media come in'[76]—the very same impulse behind media-archaeological methods. The family resemblance arises from a shared indebtedness to Michel Foucault's archaeologies of knowledge. Looking beyond and inside the black boxes of media leads, logically, towards both the 'cold gaze' technicism of radical materialists like Ernst and Kittler, and also the 'other side' of German media analysis—with which Sterne's format theory resonates strongly—an approach focused on *Kulturtechniken* ('cultural techniques').

Cultural techniques[77]

Theories of cultural techniques emerged around the turn of the millennium in response to Friedrich Kittler's controversial establishment of media as the technical a priori of the human sciences. To sum up this move in one sentence: Kittler updated Foucault, 'the last historian or first archaeologist,'[78] so as to account for an archive comprised not only by writing and discourse, but by film, sound recordings, and typewritten matter. No discourse without pens and paper, no governmentally without files, but also no state policing without photography, no surveillance without film and video.

In Kittler's wake, the concept of media proliferated, eventually becoming over-extended and totalizing. Media theory, post-Kittler, was increasingly troubled that important considerations about what precedes media devices and networks, even media as a concept, had been pushed aside in the fevered dream of 1980s media analysis, with its proclivity for lost media stories, devices, and white male engineers. The claim was that too much baby had been thrown out with the bathwater in the rush to, in Siegert's words, replace the Critique of Reason with a Critique of Media.[79] Siegert, Vismann, and others like Thomas Macho, Sybille Krämer—even Kittler himself—sought a way to escape this blind alley, to loosen the problematic knot the media concept had become. They did so by rediscovering a late nineteenth-century agricultural concept, *Kulturtechniken*, which described procedures like irrigation and draining, straightening river beds, or constructing water reservoirs.[80] The *Kultur* of *Kulturtechniken* is a far cry from the 'culture' concept we are used to using in Anglo-America to describe either the 'best that has been thought and said' (Arnold) or a 'whole way of life' (Williams). The culture of cultural techniques has to do with cultivation, nurturing, or rendering habitable. These are, after all, the etymological roots of the word (the Latin *colere* means to tend, guard, cultivate, or till).[81] So this is culture in the sense of doing, handling, working; it has to do with hands and bodies, tools, the drawing of borders, and the processing of distinctions.

Imported from agricultural science into media theory, cultural techniques are by Siegert's definition 'conceived as operative chains that precede the media concepts they generate.'[82] This approach starts not with totalizing concepts like 'media', 'network', or 'power', but instead,

> places at the basis of changes in cultural and intellectual history inconspicuous techniques of knowledge like card indexes, media of pedagogy like the slate, discourse operators like quotation marks, uses of the phonograph in phonetics, or techniques of forming the individual like practices of teaching to read and write.[83]

Theories of cultural techniques hold that these techniques—in which tool, body, and act converge—delineate and assemble broader spatio-temporal infrastructures of societies. This approach is therefore less interested in emphasizing devices, objects, or systems (in the way that early German media analysis did) than in observing the ontic operations that process the distinctions at the core of any society, such as those between inside and outside, subject and object, nature and culture, matter and form, etc.[84] As Vismann puts it, '[c]ultural techniques define the agency of media and things. If media theory were, or had, a grammar, that agency would find its expression in objects claiming the grammatical subject position and cultural techniques standing in for verbs.'[85]

Theories of cultural techniques focus on operators like doors, abacuses, musical instruments, maps, and index cards, which precede and generate concepts like inside and outside, number, tone, or territory. The study of cultural techniques holds that operators are not simply passive objects to be used or activated according to the whim of an acting (human) subject. Media and things supply their own rules of execution—we do not choose how to open or close a door, it does not present us with an open horizon of possibility. As anyone that has encountered a 'Norman door'[86] knows, we must act according to the rules set out for us by the door: push or pull, open or close. The door has agency of a certain kind. It delineates what is possible *to do*. Thinking of a door in this way also shows that the picture of agency we usually work with, as reserved for acting human subjects, is insufficient.

As Vismann reminds us, in an echo of Latour, '[c]ertain actions cannot be attributed to a person; and yet they are somehow still performed.'[87]

Another famous example from the literature on cultural techniques is the plough that draws a furrow in the earth to mark the threshold of a city that will be built.[88] Inside this space will be order, law, custom, exchange; outside will be chaos and barbarism. The furrow, and the door or gate that will eventually replace it, is a cultural technique of hominization: inside is the space of the human, outside the space of the beast. Entire moral, political, ethical worldviews are built upon such distinctions; they are the fabric with which social orders are woven. According to Vismann: 'the agricultural tool determines the political act; and the operation itself produces the subject, who will then claim mastery over both the tool and the action associated with it. Thus, the *Imperium Romanum* is the result of drawing a line—a gesture which, not accidentally, was held sacred in Roman Law.'[89] Property still works like this. Ownership only comes to exist after the drawing of a boundary, a line on a map. In this way, Vismann can claim the furrow of the plough as the cultural technique not just of property or ownership, but also of sovereignty itself.

Theories of cultural techniques are not interested in the content or meaning of media or things, historically the focus of Anglo-American media and cultural studies, but in ways of doing—counting, measuring, collecting, observing, playing, confessing, listing—that engender systems of knowing and modes of social organization. 'Media' as we understand them (devices like gramophones, telegraphs, and computers) communicate and order by encoding non-sense into sense (and vice versa) through the recording or transmission of signals, or the translating of data into alphanumeric characters. Cultural techniques are the parasitic third, neither sense, nor non-sense, but that which engenders the distinctions and operations required for media to do their communicative and ordering work.[90]

One should note that the German re-discovery of cultural techniques brings us back not only to nineteenth-century German agricultural science, but to understandings of culture and technology from the Anglo-American tradition that similarly grasped relations between humans, tools, and environments as dynamic feedback loops. Lewis Mumford wrote in 1934 of the 'cultural preparation' for the coming of 'the machine' (with 'the machine' he meant to describe not just devices but 'the entire technological complex', embracing 'the knowledge and skills and arts derived from industry or implicated in the new technics, and [including] various forms of tool, instrument, apparatus and utility as well as machines proper').[91] Mumford traces the cultural preparation for the machine back to the thirteenth-century appearance of the mechanical clock, and indeed to the even earlier techniques of measuring time employed by Benedictine monks from the seventh century (with Benedict's addition of a seventh canonical hour to the devotions of the day, 'some means of keeping count of them and ensuring their regular repetition became necessary').[92] A few decades later, Raymond Williams traced the etymology of the word 'culture' from its familiar metaphorical uses to its origins in agriculture and animal husbandry.[93] Though he used different language (that of his disciplinary training in Economics), Harold Innis's early-career studies of the fur trade and cod fisheries frame Canadian history in terms of cultural techniques, infrastructure, and logistics: the movement of things, people, and data. These studies go far beyond conventional economic histories. They give careful attention to techniques of cultivating land for extraction of staple goods, and the way such techniques draw distinctions (in maps, settlements, trade routes, fixed capital, etc.).[94] In later works, Innis extrapolated, seeking to understand the way such techniques and distinctions produce different civilizational 'biases' towards space and time.[95] More recent work in Anglo-America continues in this vein, though it has not yet coalesced as a coherent theoretical 'movement'.[96]

These Anglo-American and German approaches exist within what Peters sees as a fourth, minor tradition of media studies that 'ponders the civilizational stakes of media as a cultural complex.'[97] It has received less emphasis in the last thirty years than the dominant streams of media and communication research, which Peters schematizes as: (1) textual and interpretive, (2) social and explanatory, and; (3) historical and institutional (forming a 'media studies triangle' of text, audience, and industry).[98] The more elusive fourth stream has to do with understanding the way that the biases of dominant media shape the character of civilizations, marshalling social, political, and institutional life towards certain tendencies: spatial conquest, as with Rome and its parchment administration, or temporal endurance, as in monumental ancient Egypt.[99] Innis's great insight was to suggest that an understanding of large-scale civilizational issues can be derived by observing both the granular techniques of e.g. memory and preservation, administration, or communication, and the larger knowledge practices that structure these realms (aside from 'bias', his most well-known concept is probably 'monopoly of knowledge').

Innis was after something like a theory of civilizational cultural techniques. The tradition of which he is a part offers us tools to grapple with issues of infrastructure and logistics, which is where most of the above approaches brush up against one another. It also provides a way out of entrenched battle lines that dominate media and cultural studies, particularly in Anglo-America. Theories of cultural techniques reject the common practice of beginning analysis by deploying a pre-existing framework, such as 'cultural studies', 'semiotics', or 'political economy', in order to unmask the world of illusions. Cultural-technical analysis looks at such frameworks as historically contingent knowledge formations, constituted through specific ways of seeing and doing that are related to the way the world is measured, collected, recorded and observed. The epistemological and discursive contours of traditional approaches can and should be subjected to the same analysis and critique as their objects of study. As Latour teaches, concepts, like technologies, often function as black boxes.[100] Theories of cultural techniques ask: what are the core categories and concepts that enable cultural studies or political economic analysis? What are ontic operations at the heart of concepts like identity, subjectivity, representation, or the body? On what distinctions and material surfaces do they rest? What are the cultural techniques of exchange, circulation, value, or class? How would it change our analysis if we did not start with these concepts but looked first at tools and techniques that produce them?

This book shows how quotidian forms like the list are heuristics for understanding such 'civilizational' questions of order, knowledge, and being. Listing is a cultural technique that precedes a whole host of media networks, from Ancient Sumerian clay tablets to contemporary computer code. A border is drawn around certain items, inscribing order on a field of possible data. What is included in a list vs. what is excluded is a basic distinction upon which rests all kinds of second-order operations, speculations, and actions that comprise media networks of trade and circulation, whether in early modern Europe or on Wall Street in 2016. Listing engenders a proto-binary code: included is to one and yes as excluded is to zero and no. Once the distinction is drawn, it goes out in the world; it becomes encoded in media objects and protocols that cannot function without this basic distinction. There are major political stakes in such operations: the form of the protocol determines how computation unfolds; how a person is listed can determine his or her fate. These and other issues will arise in the case studies that follow.

2. Epistemology: Pop Music Charts and the Making of a Cultural Field[1]

'I've been around the world several times;
now, only banality still interests me.'
– Chris Marker, *Sans Soleil* (1983)

This chapter examines the function of lists as epistemological operators[2] in popular culture and mass media. Its animating question is: how does the list structure the production, circulation, and reception of cultural knowledge and information? The goal is to demonstrate that lists are constitutive of fields of knowledge, and, as such, delimit communication and social action in and around these fields. I have chosen popular music charts as a case study because of their privileged status in that field. But first, a few notes on the historical role of lists in the formation of knowledge.

What is the relationship between lists and knowledge?

Any list forges connections between its contents—even if just the basic fact of being placed together—that did not exist prior to the act of listing. This can be for the purposes of suggesting the infinite in a poetics of 'etcetera'. It can also be for more pragmatic purposes, as in the documentation of science, knowledge, and 'everyday life'. In both cases, the list is aimed at reducing entropy, allowing us to help combat or even 'become superior to that which is greater than us.'[3] 'Utilitarian' lists are more about doing than showing, but it would be a mistake to write them off as essentially less complex than lists used for aesthetic purposes.

Focusing on utilitarian lists shows the important role that interstitial forms of writing play in historical shifts in ways of knowing and acting in human societies. Such forms of writing are typically overlooked. They enter into relations with other nodes in media-technological networks (whether human or non-human) that have implications for knowledge production and dissemination. Latour and Serres suggest that the goal of analysis should be to trace these relations.[4] An example is Goody's account of the prescription, a documentary form that emerges from the writing down of medical 'recipes' in the third millennium BCE. Prescriptions began as a solution to a simple storage problem—a wish to preserve and share information over space and time. Once put down on paper, however, a process of trial-and-error is enacted on the information. Subsequent users of the prescription can add or subtract to it as deemed necessary. Such a process enhances knowledge about the human body and its treatment, Goody suggests, and he points to it as a kind of proto-scientific method.[5] The key point is that administrative forms of writing, which arise out of practical, everyday problems of storing and sharing information, inaugurate processes that affect the trajectory of human thought and action. They have a kind of agency in not merely facilitating, but actively contributing to such processes. Such epistemological factors only come into view when we broaden our understanding of writing beyond the grammatical, semiological, or conventionally historical to encompass interstitial entities like lists.

Goody's analysis of the prescription shows an understanding of human knowledge, society, and history that is not about inventions, inventors, nations, or spirits of ages determining the unfolding of history; rather, he emphasizes the unintended consequences and implications of material documents and the documentation of everyday life. The repetition of such acts of administrative writing (in lists, prescriptions, recipes, experiments, transactions, etc.) comes to influence the way written statements are conceived and documented. Such acts of writing become future-oriented in their preservation of data or information to be used later, and therefore enable ancient societies to break free from the perpetual-presentness of homeostasis.[6] This is achieved not only by the capacity to preserve the past (as might be conventionally thought) but also to affect the future.

Latour discusses the ability of those who possess knowledge or information about the world to affect the future in relation to his concept 'centres of calculation'. Historic centres of calculation such as eighteenth-century empires of the European continent emerge after cycles of accumulation bring (in addition to material wealth) information about the world back to a certain point. Once it allows those who occupy the point to act on the world from a distance (in space and in time), the point becomes a centre of calculation. Cartography, for instance (which arose as a field only once its cultural techniques of measure became standardized) enabled empires of conquest to first know the world and then to act on it from a distance in future expeditions. Latour's example is the French explorer Laperouse, who collected information about the East Pacific and transported it back, first to his ship, then to Versailles. This knowledge allowed future expeditions to know what to expect of the area in question, thus freeing them up to collect different kinds of information beneficial to the King. Fewer material resources and less intellectual labour needed to be devoted to cartography by subsequent expeditions. Latour's point is that we do not often examine the techniques and forms invented to collect, preserve, and transport data from field to centre, which he calls 'immutable mobiles'.[7] Goody's prescription is just such an inscription technique: information from the outside world is collected, listed, and stored within it. The prescription then allows whoever possesses it to act on the world and affect the future; it preserves this knowledge, and carries it forward through time.

The purpose of this brief example is to show that Latour's extensive work on the material means by which institutional knowledge arises is of use in broadening our understanding of how utilitarian lists participate in such processes.[8] Using Latour's language, listing draws things together and places them in relation to one another. As visual forms of information, lists show us previously unseen things. Connections are forged and relations become traceable. Lists help to accelerate and make more efficient the collection of data in cycles of accumulation, thereby facilitating the ability of any point to become a centre of calculation. Lists are part of the stuff from which the social, the cultural, the political, and the economic, are assembled and preserved. And by turning our analytic eye towards them, we begin to see that they are not simple forms after all.

By combining and stabilizing data so that it can be mobilized as knowledge, lists are constitutive of epistemology. Take an example mentioned earlier, the *florilegia* of the Middle Ages. While this technique of information organization emerged initially as a personal list of things worth remembering about a text, Blair notes that authors of *florilegia* quickly began to share and disseminate their lists, which served to establish and spread awareness of a kind of 'canon' in any given field.[9] Blair's work shows that these arise not simply because of the way lists formally organize information, but also because such lists circulated easily. More than mere summaries, *florilegia* stood as concise value judgements about a text in which the 'best' or 'most important' passages were isolated and emphasized. These hierarchical lists of individual judgements circulated as authoritative documents regarding important sources and passages. They rested on the authority and erudition of their authors, who used the list form to do the laborious work of institutionalizing and legitimating knowledge. Frohmann demonstrates that such documentary practices do stabilizing work, preceding and enabling concepts such as 'information'. Documents become 'informing' only once they acquire the cache of the 'social and pedagogical disciplines that maintai[n] them.'[10] He argues we should not understand information as an ontological 'substance' to be sought, gathered, and translated into meaning (i.e. knowledge) by the human mind. Information instead emerges as the end result of documentary practices. As a concept that engenders knowledge, 'information' arises out of cultural techniques of data organization and documentation.

Florilegia show lists as epistemological operators on emergent fields of knowledge and discourse communities during the Middle Ages. Those practices cannot be simply imported to a contemporary *milieu*, since '[d]ifferent times and different places exhibit different kinds of documentary practices and different kinds of institutions.'[11] But *florilegia* do share a family resemblance with contemporary cultural listing activities such as found in the field of popular music. Lists congeal as 'knowledge' its various components: songs, artists, moments, and memories are abstracted as data in a variety of lists that function in field-specific ways. Through this form, collective archives and canons emerge, commodity circulation is measured, taste is made, and mastery of knowledge is performed. The process of knowledge formation arises from the exceptionally hard work of coordinating and stabilizing many networks of observation, experimentation, commentary, citation, classification, and the like.[12]

Popular music lists

There is a long-standing relationship between popular music and lists. Over the course of the twentieth century, sales charts and year-end top-tens came to structure the field in a variety of ways: as a summary of industrial and market tendencies; a snapshot of musical preferences and taste; a marketing device; a communicative format linking producers, critics, and consumers; and an active archive of social musical experience. Such list functions are an important yet often overlooked component in the documentation of popular music history. More recently, with the rise of iPod, iTunes and streaming music services like Spotify, the user- or algorithmically generated playlist has become perhaps the dominant interface of contemporary musical experience.[13] Meanwhile, collaborative knowledge projects, such as Wikipedia, enable and encourage the unquestioned use of lists to prop up aesthetic claims. Finally, most of the lists in recent critical and popular music discourse are more overtly historicist and experientially ambitious than traditional sales charts or top-tens. These import what Straw calls the 'sequenced revelation' of radio and television countdowns (e.g. 'Top of the Pops') to reverse and transform the 'static verticality' of traditional charts like *Billboard*'s 'Hot 100'. Examples include *Rolling Stone's* 'Top 500 Albums of All-Time' or *Pitchfork* online magazine's 'P2K: The Decade in Music'. These are often adorned with artist portraits or video which 'expand the visual field of the chart and nudge it closer to the status of the image gallery.'[14]

By observing lists in this realm, several important considerations come to light. We can draw an important distinction between, on the one hand, the list as a format that does crucial epistemological work and, on the other, the act of listing as a cultural technique of comparison that structures and, to borrow Latour's term, assembles the social activity of the field. This distinction is between institutional lists—sales charts, top-tens, playlists, etc.—that materially measure, trace, and map the field (storing and processing its data), and what I will call 'memory' lists—subjective and participatory lists that are about taste and lived experience, among other things.[15] The ubiquity and importance of these to contemporary popular music and culture, readily observable with every web-browsing session, demonstrate that lists are not simply administrative, but rather are bound up in a much broader network of collective memory work. On both ends, institutional and participatory, lists process the distinctions and inscribe the categories through which the 'selective tradition' of culture, to borrow Raymond Williams' phrase, is generated.[16]

First, I outline the emergence of institutionally sanctioned charts as a standardized communicative format. This history shows the important role of charts in establishing 'popular' as a category of music, and the list as a crucial intermediary through which economic and institutional discourse pass. The upshot is that listing as a cultural technique comes to also structure social music experience. In this chapter's second half, I test the proposition that such listing practices can undercut institutionally sanctioned lists by analysing Bob Mersereau's *Top 100 Canadian Singles*. The analysis shows that any subversive potential is severely limited by the fact that such memory work is delimited by the borders of the list format, and serves only to mimic the historicizing function of institutionally-sanctioned lists.

Rise of the chart[17]

The company that did the most to popularize the chart originally had nothing to do with music. *Billboard Advertising* was founded in 1894 as a trade paper for the bill posting industry, 'a monthly resume of all that is new, bright, and interesting on the boards.'[18] A few years after its inception, the paper began running advertisements for circuses, carnivals, vaudeville and other live entertainment. Demand for the magazine in burgeoning entertainment industries was so great that by 1901 *Billboard* appeared on newsstands in almost all major American cities. Coverage of motion pictures began in 1909, with radio following in the 1920s. By 1913, *Billboard* marketed itself as 'The Show World Encyclopedia' and had achieved global circulation.[19]

Since the late 1950s, *Billboard*'s 'Hot 100' has been the paradigmatic popular music chart, but its prehistory is murky. *Billboard* itself points to the first, unofficial 'chart' as its 1913 listings of 'Popular Songs Heard in Vaudevil [sic] Theatres Last Week' (in New York, Chicago, and San Francisco).[20] This claim is contested by scholarship on charts, which points variously to *Melody Maker*'s honours list from 1928,[21] *Variety* magazine's amalgam of the publishers' charts,[22] or its monthly best-selling records chart[23] (both established in the 1920s). *Billboard* published the 'Network Song Census' in 1934, followed by a series of radio 'Hit Parade' programmes from 1936 onwards. In 1940 came its 'first fairly accurate tabulation of popular music sales,'[24] but the 'Hot 100' did not take its recognizable form—a listing of the most popular songs in a given week in descending order of popularity—until 4 August 1958. Ultimately, though, the question of origin is irrelevant. What matters is how quickly and broadly this technique spread, how universally it was accepted, and how unquestioned it came to be as a metric and a communicative device.

Early twentieth century charts were adopted from preexisting industry listing practices. They started with *fin-de-siècle* travelling road shows and vaudeville as a way for sheet music publishers to promote their best-selling songs. These charts were alphabetical lists that publishers carried from show to show, using them to drum up interest from potential customers.[25] It is often forgotten that publishers, not artists or composers, were at the centre of American popular music prior to phonograph and radio technology. The saleable music commodity was sheet music and, prior to recorded music and copyright, charts were one of the most effective ways to generate compensation and profit. The publishers' lists generated interest, competition, and artificial scarcity amongst their commodities. Such charts allowed publishers to inscribe market parameters on paper. They also materialized the power of publishers over performers and composers; the only data points listed beside a song on these charts were title and publisher, nothing of performer or composer.

When these charts migrated into trade papers like *Billboard* (c. late 1920s), whose tepid interest in music was heating up, they were aimed not at consumers but industry insiders. The consumer appeal of charts was as yet undiscovered and thus unexploited. Structural dynamics of the popular music industry at the time led trade papers and publishers to believe there was little point in circulating charts to consumers. These were: (1) the dominant commodity being sheet music, which demanded musical proficiency and thus ensured a limited market size; (2) the tight control over the production, circulation, and distribution of the sheet music commodity by publishers, which resulted in; (3) songs being extremely slow, both to market and to circulate. A hit song would typically spend around three years on the industry charts. This slow turn-over rate enabled publishers to anticipate demand and maintain stock effectively.[26]

In an ill-fated attempt to combat the rise of radio and phonography in the early 1930s and encourage more playing of their product, sheet music producers flooded their once tightly controlled market.[27] This increase in the number of songs on the charts necessitated an increase in information per listing. Where once only the publisher and name of song had been listed, now both number of radio plugs and artist names were included. The latter helped audiences differentiate between songs, and inscribed performers into the very fabric of the charts. 'Artist' became a category on paper as distinct from performers' previous status as invisible hired guns with no material presence on the charts. With their increased stature and recognition came eminently reasonable demands from artists for compensation and proprietary rights.[28] Broadcast Music Inc. (BMI) was established in 1939 by a consortium of independent radio stations as a lower cost alternative to the American Society of Composers, Authors, and Publishers (ASCAP), which had hitherto enjoyed a monopoly over license agreements.

Competition in copyright and performing rights pushed music publishers out. In addition to song title, artist, number of radio plugs, charts now included information about the copyright agency, rather than publisher. Competition amongst copyright agencies also offered artists an enhanced role in the industry, though this was not without its drawbacks. The accelerated turnover rate of hit songs led to a new formal feature on charts: 'previous chart position'. This addition installed a backward-looking dimension to the charts that had previously not existed. Inscribed on the charts now was an imminent archive of performance, a new metric of status. The demand to chart high and long also established what Hakanen understands as a new valuation of music: star image of artist and recent performance of song over aesthetic quality or merit.[29] The ranking system (previous charts had been alphabetical) framed the artist star image as saleable commodity. The star image continues to drive popular music business and artistry.[30]

The expansion of music commodity metadata (title, artist, copyright, chart position, radio plugs, etc.), the acceleration of song turnover, and the emergence of the artist as saleable music commodity all occurred first on paper. Each of these factors contributed to the segmentation of audiences into categories themselves: 'the music business began to conquer and divide audiences into manageable parts.'[31] It did this on and through the charts. Anand and Peterson go so far as to suggest that *Billboard*'s appearance of statistical objectivity and its politically neutral tone saw its charts become a major resource for competing parties seeking to consolidate recorded music into a culture industry during the mid-twentieth century (e.g. phonograph machine companies, song publishers, radio networks, Hollywood studios, labour unions).[32]

Cultural techniques of categorization

The cultural technique of listing, adopted by travelling sheet music publishers for economic and administrative needs, establishes an epistemological framework in which the popular music field comes both to know itself and be known by its consumers. This framework's paradigmatic format is the chart. Well into the recorded music era, charts served primarily business interests by providing empirical data to demonstrate the successes and failures of publishers and labels, acts, producers, etc. 'By the end of the 1940s record stores, publishers and music licensing agencies, record industry and broadcasting trade magazines, industry tip sheet, and jukebox distributors all generated lists of their most popular records.'[33] Charts still provide—or at least did until recently— an easy metric for industry decisions regarding investment and labour costs. 'A huge amount of money is therefore spent in order that the industry can constantly feel its own pulse and test the market.'[34]

While the weekly top-40 charts appeared simply to represent consumer choice and taste, the prehistory sketched above shows how deeply encoded publisher interests are in the format itself. Listing was a cultural technique that prefigured media concepts and networks we now think of as natural. When, for instance, mass circulation of recorded music and radio began to alter the terrain of popular music, the shorter half-life of hits had more to do with the concerted (and doomed) attempt by publishers to flood the market and move more units of sheet music than with fickle consumer tastes arising from increased choice. More 'hit' songs on the sheet music charts established accelerated turnover rates that would survive into the more expanded, commercial chart system of the 1940s and 50s. Even the category of popular itself, Hakanen argues, was established via the chart system of the pre-recorded music era—not by consumer choice or taste, but by publishers' dictum.[35] What was popular on the early charts was what publishers said was popular—whether their lists of 'best sellers' were based on actual units sold or units they *wanted* to sell is impossible to say. What is certain is that the rules of the game were already set when charts congealed in their recognizable 'top-40' format and began to be targeted directly to consumers, c. 1940–1960.

The widespread adoption of the term 'popular' to describe genre, style, and also a new category of fan, occurred via the charts. The shift in the 1930s towards a chart system more explicitly aimed at consumers was to a large degree the result of publishers coming to understand that their charts had inscribed a new taste community that was beginning to self-identify with the music contained therein. The 'low' culture of the proletariat existed on the charts in contradistinction to bourgeois 'high' culture that went unlisted.[36] Hakanen argues that these new categories established pillars by which the 'lonely crowd' of mid-century America attempted to categorize itself. '"Popular" comes to describe the audience as it delivers itself to the market.'[37] More than a mirror of an extant category, the charts are a separate construction of the *perception* of popularity. There is an intersection of two senses of the word 'popular' in its establishment as a category of popular music. Whereas with early sheet music charts the term was used to describe what was 'widely favoured' or 'well liked' (even if this was not empirically verifiable), over time a second meaning was integrated. Widely favoured 'low' popular music literally *came into view* via the charts, establishing a set of shared visual markers with which, Hakanen argues, a new taste community could imagine itself. In identifying itself with the popular music charts, this new proletarian taste community reclaimed the pejorative sense of popular as 'low' or 'base', injecting back into the word a sense of 'folk' or 'of the people'.[38] This was a restricted field of democratic cultural activity, the borders of which were defined by the charts. Charts channelled vectors of personal identification towards non-class based categories of genre and taste. It is beyond the scope of this chapter to pursue this question further, but the connection to class is suggestive.

Parker shows that when song metadata are abstracted and fitted to the templates of the charts, divergent musics and artists become standardized and thus more suitable for direct competition. Formal or generic distinctions disappear when songs appear on the pop chart, and the flattening of differences ensures songs and artists must compete with one another for chart, and thus market, supremacy. 'Within the market-place there is only competition on the basis of assumed equivalence; any differences are reduced to differential calculations about exchange value.'[39] The logic and values of capital are encoded in the structural attributes of popular music's paradigmatic format. 'Exchange value of the object has become the relationship of a song to other songs.'[40]

In an effort to create or maintain a competitive edge, insiders used the charts to establish new subgenres of music and consumer categories. *Billboard*'s chart ecology has expanded continuously since the 'Hot 100' appeared in 1958. The majority of chart distinctions have been drawn according to generic and geographic borders. Today, the chart ecology is split into four broad categories: 'Overall Popularity', 'Genres', 'International', and 'Web'. 'Overall Popularity' includes seventeen charts,[41] while 'Genres' has nine major hubs with sub-charts and ten 'Additional Genre' charts. These are in addition to ten international charts and four Web charts.[42] *Billboard* is nothing if not invested in classification. These efforts to redraw chart and genre boundaries, particularly in the digital age, are part of a broader effort by industry to combat the imperialism of pop charts it created by adopting techniques like niche marketing. Distinctions drawn by these smaller 'sub'-charts create new spaces for contra-identification, for going against the grain of the pop charts. For instance, the 'Alternative' chart (a sub-chart of a sub-chart, Rock) creates new value for the consumer by taking away the competition of the 'vulgar' conventional pop genres. Alternative songs are given their own space to compete amongst themselves, rather than against the crushing mass of 'vapid' pop. Consumer identification via negation, and thus a new consumer profile, is enabled by distinctions drawn on charts between genres, and by borders drawn around style and brand. Consumers believe this to be an 'organic' distinction arising from their tastes and preferences. In fact, the category exists on the chart before anywhere else. Genre categories migrate from institutionally-sanctioned publications, and the formats they contain, into suburban bedrooms. The key point is that the logic of the charts persists; more charts only strengthen the hold they have on the field.

As new categories were established on the charts, new concepts were required to describe, for instance, 'crossover' songs that moved across genre and taste communities.[43] Such marketing terms are cloaked in the veneer of objective description and rest on the assumption that the charts are extant ontological structures. What we have seen, however, is that while a song may move across lists or amongst categories, this activity is arbitrary rather than empirical, epistemological rather than ontological. When industry insiders draw borders around categories, any song or artist can be made to move to any chart or position. Such activity cannot be said to be anything other than furthering the economic interests of the gatekeepers that compile the lists or hold the copyrights. The marketing function of charts and their categories is also made obvious by the fact that, though music single sales (and music sales generally) have fallen precipitously over the last 50 years—to such a degree that RIAA sales thresholds had to be scaled back in 1989—the 'Hot 100' remains the most widely circulated and discussed music chart. Finally, the marketing function of charts is expressed by the circular logic in which charts purport to communicate only empirical data about sales and radio play, yet radio playlists, and to a certain extent consumer choice, are derived from songs already on the charts.[44]

The various practices of listing outlined so far show it to be a cultural technique that inscribes new categories for social, cultural, and economic life. Lists process the distinctions upon which categorizations that come to structure the popular music field are drawn. This structuring format, the chart, creates a focal point around which taste communities are articulated. Charts organize economic activity by allowing industry insiders to inscribe market parameters on paper, and to observe in almost real time consumer behaviour. The appearance of empirical objectivity masks the logic of the market; the interests of producers are baked into the format itself. Charts are a particular epistemological organization of popular music that is presented as normal, empirically verifiable, and true. Echoing Siegert's pithy phrase, 'the map *is* the territory,'[45] we might say that the chart *is* the field.

Another rule of the game established by the charts is the frequency with which popular music information is circulated. Through charts, a spatial form, the field comes to organize itself around the week as the primary unit of time. Fans and industry alike are always looking to the next week, the next hit, the next chart. This constant updating of the charts survives to the present day. Though it is impossible to say conclusively, weekly charts likely emerged as the standard (as opposed to monthly or yearly charts) due to the aforementioned desire of industry insiders to have constant a finger on the pulse of the business. There is no evidence this had anything to do with consumer behaviour or preference.[46] But whatever its origin, the weekly rhythm of charts imposes both a backward-looking archival impulse and a perpetual forward momentum on the field. Charts are a means by which the present is frozen for posterity, a current snapshot of what is hot or not. As mentioned, the 'previous position' column frames this present as part of a longer trajectory, either rising or falling. Straw sees this as 'transfor[ming] the often erratic commercial life of a musical commodity into a curve of ascendant and descendant popularity, so as to endow that life with the legibility of both narrative and tabular form [...].'[47] Such a frame structures the reader's judgement of an artist and a song's performance, and elicits speculation about this entry's future trajectory—is it headed towards the summit of the #1 spot, or the abyss of the chart's bottom edge?

In charts, many times converge and become standardized according to its logic of competition: collated pasts, anticipated futures, and what's hot now in 'real time'. Charts freeze the present as part of an ongoing archiving of popular music history, creating a 'stockpile' of information that prescribes the future.[48] According to Straw, '[t]he curve of a song's rise and fall endows its lifecycle with the romance of individual success and ultimate exhaustion, while the hierarchical verticality of the chart conveys the sense of all songs sitting in momentarily stable relationships within a homogenous historical moment.'[49] Time is rendered spatial, materialized as data on a page. Insiders can base marketing decisions that affect future song performance on such data, while fans can rely on the charts to provide knowledge about music they have not directly experienced. '[C]harts seemingly allow for knowing about the music's performance, rather than knowing the performance of music.'[50] At the same time, this archival impulse is in constant tension with the enduring ephemerality of charts.[51] The spectre of entropy and etcetera haunts any given chart. The essence of a chart is that it is finite and disposable; the next chart is always on the horizon. The order a chart inscribes now will dissolve and be replaced by Sunday. Charts go on, but *this* chart will not. In this way, a chart is precisely the kind of 'information' Peters describes, whose 'value is given in relation to time (its freshness or staleness) and its accuracy. New "information" does not enlarge or transform old information, but makes it obsolete.'[52] Charts fetishize newness because they never allow consumers to stop looking at the present in terms of the future. 'Continual watchfulness [as] a precondition for the acquisition of valuable pop knowledge.'[53]

The constant negotiation of this tension between everything-included and etcetera accounts, I argue, for the enduring appeal of the charts. 'Top 40 charts operate as an ordered, finite way of making sense of the vastness of mass culture.'[54] A weekly chart draws a border around a network of actors, events, objects, commodities, sounds, etc., which are in constant circulation and are impossible to empirically *know* as a totality. The borders of the chart create a format by which audiences and industry insiders can understand their field as a field—past, present, and future. 'Everything' is included, but, of course, 'everything' is only some things. 'Charts give value, channel, and select things that otherwise have none, that would float undifferentiated.'[55] Categories and taste communities are articulated, economic decisions are made, and histories are written according to the borders a chart draws.

The field of popular music is comprised by objects, actors, and processes; categories, concepts, and metrics. The charts, and thus the list, are crucial to the articulation of this field.

Memory lists

The above history of the charts paints a fairly bleak picture of listing in the cultural field. Charts serve the interests of economic and cultural capital to perpetuate the status quo. Some research rejects this view, arguing that pop music charts are embedded in complex processes of collective memory work, 'engaged simultaneously in the remembering and forgetting of music.'[56] Others suggest it is not enough to dismiss charts as pure ideology, that 'determinist' political-economic analyses can be countered by demonstrating the role of lists in mediating subjectivity and agency. Parker views the charts as a space of play, suggesting that—in contrast to producers who live and die by the economic stakes of the charts—consumers enjoy charts as they enjoy sports tables, as a form of bounded recreation.[57] To play a game, you must accept its rules. Charts are attractive because they have clear structural rules within which participation and play can occur. They provide a shared reference point, 'a terrain around which judgments can be made,' and so stand as a site of cultural meaning making. '[Charts] are a contested sign, but one that has a strong residue of preferred meanings that help to construct understandings of the music they contain.'[58] We might hospitably extend this argument by conceiving of listing as a cultural technique that allows consumers to exert agency on the popular music field. Fans author their own lists in reaction to institutional lists such as the *Billboard* charts, or critics' top-10 lists. Michael Berube argues that such listing serves an important critical function that complicates conventional understandings of popular culture fandom.[59] Anna Poletti adopts a similar understanding of listing in zine culture, as a format by which the self is performed: taste, life narratives, and cultural capital are articulated in personal lists that challenge hegemonic institutional culture. Poletti sees listing as the deliberate use of pop music's paradigmatic format to subvert hegemonic culture and articulate one's outsider status.[60]

Implicit in these more forgiving analyses is the idea that charts function as a way to negotiate the tension between chaos and order. They are cartographic tools that decrease entropy in the popular music archive. Charts, according to Straw, reconcile conflicting impulses to, on the one hand, tabulate the increasingly discrete and distributed units of popular music reception and circulation (songs, plays, views, clicks, and other 'impressions') and, on the other hand, to organize this material into coherent cultural narratives.[61] In doing this work of distillation and organization, list making and list reading are access points for fans into a musical conversation. Fans exercise their critical faculties and challenge the status quo by redrawing the borders of the field using the same format as official institutions. They carve out different histories and canons. The result is a proliferation of lists and rankings with a more overtly historical tenor. They compare and rank according to importance or influence not only songs, artists, or albums, but also urban scenes, genres, fashions, even historical moments.[62] Their will to history echoes Huyssen's description of a cultural 'turn toward memory [which] is subliminally energized by the desire to anchor ourselves in a world characterized by an increasing instability of time and the fracturing of lived space.'[63]

We might see the historical claims in these memory lists as symptomatic of a general shift away from traditional evaluative and comparative criteria, such as the aesthetic or empirical, and towards subjectively adjudicated significance. William Brooks famously conceived such a shift as being from taste to tastelessness:

> Surrounded as we are by vast amounts of musical debris, we can invent rules, screening procedures, to help us choose what to study. And by exercising a modicum of ingenuity, we can invent rules that leave our opinions out, rules that select and reject music automatically according to criteria which are peripheral to musical 'value'. By means of such rules, I might select, for instance, only those records that made *Billboard*'s Top-ten lists between 1945 and 1955, or only the records owned by my grandfather, or all those issued in 1960, 1970 and 1980 with pictures of women on the cover, or all 45s released last May whose titles begin with C, I or A. As long as the rules are inclusive and unambiguous, they will operate virtually autonomously; there will be no need for me tastefully to assess the musical content of each recording. To this extent such rules allow me to choose bits for my history 'objectively'—though 'arbitrarily' is probably a better word.[64]

Hakanen puts it more pithily: 'Being eclectic or understanding of other tastes no longer requires knowing the actual cultural product, only its ranking system.'[65]

Such memory work occurs in an 'indeterminate' domain that 'stands at the point of intersection of 'public' history and 'private' memory.'[66] Cultural lists of the kind we find in pop music find resonance with their readers in precisely their ability to occupy this space. They compile 'public' artefacts (the songs, artists, moments, etc. that together make a shared popular music history) and at the same time encourage the music fan and list reader to pore over their own personal histories. Lists encourage the reader to contemplate their own direct memories of the objects themselves (a memory of attending a performance, acquiring a record, etc.), as well as those memories that are accompanied by musical objects (the 'soundtrack to our lives'). By distilling popular culture, and specifically popular music, to a manageable scope, lists help to create mass audiences that cross national and linguistic boundaries. Frow attributes such a function indirectly to the list: he sees Georges Perec's *Je me souviens* ('I remember'), an extended list of personal-public memories, as rousing the reader to compose something similar, 'a technology so easy to use that the effect of the book is, irresistibly, to drive the reader to produce parallel sets of memories, to construct for themselves that public domain of private memories that the book sets in play.'[67] For Frow, whether we like it or not, shared collective experience occurs through objects and documents that are ready to hand, be they in commodity form or otherwise. It has always been thus. Charts and lists collect and present the raw materials that compose a collective history.

Such accounts are moderately compelling but limited. Countering a political economic analysis of charts with one based on individual experience misses the point. Material properties of lists perform the same structuring functions in both subjective and institutional cases. Charts function as 'institutions of consecration; functioning as a template for comparing, valuing and ordering pop artists while simultaneously governing music industry agents in their struggles to move songs up places and thus signal their success.'[68] Charts set the rules of the game, they limit what epistemological, commercial, and social activity can occur within the parameters they establish. The play engendered by charts is bounded by the homology 'between charts and the economic and social structures that surround them.'[69] Charts embody the central values of consumer capitalism, so play of the kind Parker describes is ultimately superficial and solipsistic. We all play games of different kinds and find different ways to articulate identities; I am not sure what makes the list an especially notable form through which this activity is pursued. The types of play lists engender serve conservative functions, as Lovink describes in a more recent cultural context.

> It is not enough to draw up lists of counter-classics in an attempt to resist national campaigns to canonize cultural and scientific heritage. The

> reactionary call for national canons, heard worldwide in so many different contexts, is a clear response to the unheard explosion of untamed commentary and the loss of authority of the artist formerly known as author.[70]

Arguments about the transgressive lists of individuals arise from a tradition of media and cultural studies scholarship that, in reading human engagements with culture, looks for items that 'subvert' the logic of X (where X could be capital, patriarchy, racism, technological determinism, etc.). These and other evils in the world need opposing, but participatory culture and semiotic *bricolage* do not get us very far. In this case, even those charts that appear to be offering a unique site of identity construction are in fact abiding by the same structures of the institutional charts they seek to subvert. This has less to do with top-down ideology than it does with the way charts on paper draw distinctions and determine categorizations from the bottom up. The structuring function performed by the list format is more notable than the social activity it engenders: how the list delimits the exercise of critical faculties, the authoring of life narratives, and play. It is not that charts are ideological. Ideology implies illusion or false consciousness. Charts instead materialize the conditions of possibility for subject positions and knowledge related to popular music. There is no pure realm of organic music fandom and culture that is corrupted by the charts. The very category 'popular' is an effect of the widespread adoption of the charts. Subject positions—even those that 'subvert' convention—are articulated using the raw material provided by the charts. We do not need to turn to concepts like play or counter-hegemony to 'save' the charts; we need to develop conceptual tools to understand how they operate and what they do. We need less about essence and meaning and more about function.

Un-black boxing a list

The following analysis of Bob Mersereau's *Top 100 Canadian Singles* will allow us to understand more clearly how a contemporary cultural list functions. This phase of the argument rests on the idea that the list as a format became inscribed via administrative and economic purposes (as described above) before travelling out in the messier world of culture. While these lists may appear to be less hegemonic, more open to play, in fact the material properties of the list format perform the same structuring functions on memory work as institutional lists. To more forcefully argue my point, this section turns away from officially sanctioned charts. It offers a close analysis of a list with a family resemblance to those just described and is similarly embedded in wider networks of subjective and collective memory work. *Top 100 Canadian Singles*[71] is a 'collectively authored' archive of Canadian music, an alternative canon that offers a snapshot of what people 'really think'.

In compiling the list, music critic Bob Mersereau employed a method of first polling a committee of over 800 Canadians that he describes as follows:

> Many are directly involved in the daily creation, sales, promotion and broadcasting of Canadian music. There are famous musicians, well-known media people, managers, record company employees, reviewers, writers, deejays, retailers, roadies and club owners. And there are also lots of just plain fans who love Canadian music and make it a part of their daily life.[72]

From each committee member he solicited a ranked top-10 list of singles defined as 'songs that had been released as singles, whether to the public for sale or to broadcasters in some sort of medium for airplay.'[73] Mersereau has not divulged exactly how the results were tallied or what formula or point system was used to amalgamate the individual lists, other than to suggest the results were run through a statistical formula.[74] This committee format allows the list to offer what he describes as a 'consensus', rather than simply a subjective ranking of his own picks or a critics' poll.[75] The critical environment by which a list is authored is reconfigured. We move away from the single author or publication and towards an ostensibly more democratic 'Canadian consensus'.

We can see in this claim of consensus for *Top 100 Canadian Singles* something Latour observes in scientific discourse: the process by which many voices are deployed to strengthen an argument or truth claim. Latour calls this the 'context of citation' of a given piece, the marshalling of voices in favour of an argument.[76] Mobilizing a battalion of jurists allows Mersereau to avoid being critiqued for his own critical judgements (since his method does not incorporate them). No single person can be blamed or celebrated upon the reader's (dis)agreement, since blame or praise must be diffused over 800 jurists. The method also means the list appears not to offer an argument or judgement. This is not the case. The list appeals to the authority of 800 voices to make an implicit argument that it is representing something worth knowing: a snapshot of Canadians' opinion about their musical past. Mersereau is explicit in his rejection of his own status as an authority and that of music critics, emphasizing strength in numbers rather than prestige or expertise. The list is shielded: a paper with few sources is easily attacked, while one that draws on numerous voices is much more difficult to refute.[77] The truth of this list appears in numbers and statistics. In order to challenge its claims, the contrarian would need to examine each juror list to determine its meeting of proper criteria, the accuracy of the statistical methods of amalgamation, etc. These data are anyway not available, but if they were, the task would be monumentally time-consuming.

One might argue that the connection between such a list and the discursive process Latour describes in the scientific field is tenuous, since the individual lists Mersereau solicited are based strictly on opinion, and opinion is not forced to abide by any objective standard of truth. True enough. But the description of 800 jurists as a consensus shields what the list actually does, how it acts on the field of which it is a part: it streamlines Canadian music; it incorporates certain artists, genres, and eras at the expense of others; it defines Canadian music as *something*; it inscribes the list itself as a viable or legitimate form through which to organize and communicate information about the field of Canadian music; and finally, it enacts and demands a mode of engagement with music that is neither empirical (based on e.g. units sold), nor aesthetic (based on e.g. formal attributes), but is based on comparison. Further, it is comparison according to a specific logic and a set of criteria that are dictated by the compiler of this list. The definition of Canadian music used—'the only real entry qualifications were that the performer had to be technically Canadian, no matter where he/she lives now or came from'[78]—runs contra that of Canadian content (CanCon) laws and therefore allows for the inclusion of works that might not meet the criteria of the latter (e.g. much of Bryan Adams's work, a Canadian artist notoriously excluded by CanCon because of his song writing partnerships with non-Canadians).[79] By reconfiguring the epistemological terrain, these implicit criteria affect the way audiences think about Canadian music and cultural history.

While the list may initially spark debate about its method, legitimacy, or relevance, these factors over time become black-boxed. The list might be used in the future as a historical document, something that Mersereau acknowledges. 'The history of a lot of these songs just wasn't available in bookstores. [...] I was looking for a reference book and I guess, in the end, I just went "Well, I guess I'm going to have to write it".'[80] The list's context of citation (its assembled consensus) grants it legitimacy based on the number of contributors, which may allow it to be used in the future as a historical document or at least as a signpost that frames the conversation around

Canadian music. A list that is ostensibly present oriented—a 'snapshot' of how Canadians think about music at this particular moment—is also past oriented in its implicit historicizing ambition. Yet, it is also future oriented in that it seeks for itself legitimacy as a historical document to be used down the road. The incorporation of many voices makes this list's ability to act as it does much stronger than if Mersereau had authored the list himself, or even with a small number of music critics.

Mersereau takes pains in the introduction of the book, and in virtually every interview conducted while promoting it, to note, 'none of you will completely agree with the final one hundred chosen. Art is arbitrary—we knew that going into the project,'[81] or '[n]o list can be definitive [...] This is a snapshot of tastes and preferences in 2009. The 2010 list would be substantially different.'[82] Such statements anticipate readers' objections to the list's contents in advance, a tactic common to all rhetoric, scientific or not: 'thanks to this procedure, the text is carefully aimed; it exhausts all potential objections in advance and may very well leave the reader speechless since it can do nothing else but take the statement up as a matter of fact.'[83] While Mersereau encourages disagreement with the list, his series of statements and method of presentation effectively ensure that there is little dissent regarding the decision to organize, frame, and communicate this information in such a format. Readers are distracted by content and do not question the logic of the list—how it frames their thinking about Canadian singles and prescribes a specific, hierarchical path through the archive of all available Canadian music. The list ensures what Latour calls the 'captation' of the reader by exerting 'subtle control of the objectors' moves.'[84]

While readers are captive, objects—in this case, musical objects—are dominated. Latour shows how objects and/as data come to be 'dominated by sight', in that 'at one point or another, [objects] all take the shape of a flat surface of paper that can be archived, pinned on a wall and combined with others.'[85] Data points are frozen in visual forms such as lists, tables, charts, or diagrams in order that they can better be controlled from a distance. *Top 100 Canadian Singles* mobilizes, stabilizes, and combines data points about Canadian music, crystallizing them as knowledge and as history all in one place. In order to be placed on the list, musical objects—in this case, singles—are translated into units entirely unrelated to the formal, technical, or affective dimensions of music. These units are stabilized and mobilized by their collection and incorporation into the list, and combined together to become a document. This document is preserved in a stable form that can be transported with great ease and can be used in various ways. It can be compressed to 100 entries on 100 lines, reducing noise in the channel.

It can be combined or compared with other music lists such as Mersereau's *Top 100 Canadian Albums*,[86] or *Rolling Stone* magazine's '500 Greatest Songs of All Time'. These operations are similar to Straw's description of the chart, which

> with its multiple overlaid narratives of success and failure, becomes an efficient transmission device by reducing these narratives to the barest of informational tokens. The light weight of this information, relative to the weighty expressive substance of the music itself, allows the chart to be copied, displayed, and summarized across multiple media forms (blogs, newspaper articles, the walls of music shops), where it both represents and constructs the field of musical popularity.[87]

Few other formats allow for such a seamless drawing together of many discrete units dispersed over time and space—57 years separate the earliest entry (Hank Snow's 1950 'I'm Movin' On') from the latest (Feist's '1234' and Wintersleep's 'Weighty Ghost' from 2007). This list creates 'optical consistency' between its divergent units.[88] It slices across traditional modes of classification (whether genre based, time based, etc.): time is condensed, regional differences are flattened, genre categorizations do not hold. We glean new kinds of knowledge. Connections are forged between songs or artists that alter our perception of pop music categorization. This list tells us, for instance, that the 1970s, with 43 entries, is the decade most resonant with Mersereau's jury. We can then think about what we learn from such information, i.e. try to ascertain how or why this is the case, perhaps drawing on historical events such as the enactment of Canadian content rules in 1971. Visualization allows us to do certain things we could not do with this information previously—whether this is to debate the merits of the list or think about the hows and whys of certain patterns it contains.

A list such as *Top 100 Canadian Singles* is not a neutral intermediary. It is constitutive and acts on the popular music field, delimiting how the field is thought about, discussed, historicized, and canonized. All popular music lists draw things together to act on the field from a distance. *Top 100 Canadian Singles* constructs an archive of Canadian music that makes a series of historical claims, e.g. that the objects it contains should be privileged in the history of Canadian music. Since this historical record is constantly being constructed and contested, the list becomes a viable historical document. Latour's conceptual tools aid in clearing the ground for understanding the functionality of a list: how it comes to be, how it is made to circulate, what kinds of activity it enables or negates, i.e. what it does.

Conclusion

The chapter offered a history of institutional charts and a close analysis of a collectively authored 'memory' list, demonstrating that the same structuring functions of the list are operative in each register. Two key functions were emphasized: (1) the cultural technique of listing inscribes borders that enact categorizations and modes of classification. These structure epistemological fields and the social action that occurs around them; and (2) lists black box the imperatives that feed into their creation (such as criteria of inclusion/exclusion). Popular music was taken as a case study because its ubiquity of lists makes the format relatively easy to trace. Popular music is also a contingent, contested field. Its lists are worn as an exoskeleton, and they invite us to question the categories and histories of the field. The case study also brought into focus the proclivity of lists for making a difference, making things happen, which will be further explored in Chapters three and four.

I end this section with a generative thesis to complement the above diagnostic critique. We have seen that lists facilitate social activity, even if these modes of practice are bounded by the borders drawn by the list format. It is easy to dismiss 'bounded critique' as ultimately futile when it is viewed in isolation. But might bounded critique serve a more productive function when exported to realms where lists are less obviously contested? The critical engagement with lists in the cultural realm—however limited—acknowledges and makes use of the dialectic aspect of lists described by Goody. By calling into question critics' lists, sales charts, or historicizing lists like *Top 100 Canadian Singles*, critical audiences reveal lists as structures that simultaneously erect borders of knowledge formations and call into question the very borders they draw. Perhaps there are certain ways of thinking about and crafting cultural lists that can be politically useful. At minimum, they galvanize attention to the layer of seemingly banal paperwork that does so much work for political and economic interests. Formats and techniques matter, and we would do well to bring the same types of precise analysis that cultural lists garner to some of the less obvious instances in which governmentality is articulated on paper. These will be explored in subsequent chapters.

3. Administration I: The State, the Fact, and Double-Entry Bookkeeping

'And Satan stood up against Israel, and provoked David to number Israel. And David said to Joab and to the rulers of the people, Go, number Israel from Beersheba even to Dan; and bring the number of them to me, that I may know *it*.'
– 1 Chron. 21: 1-2 (KJV)

In the following two chapters, I want to show that lists operate not only in fields of knowledge related to cultural production, commodity circulation, and self-identification as outlined in Chapter two, but also in establishing administrative apparatuses that police and observe subjects. We move from observing the role of lists in making knowledge to what Hacking calls 'making up people',[1] from lists of words and things to lists of numbers and human beings, from cultural economies to protocols of governmentality. Listing is again conceived as a cultural technique of order and enumeration that processes the distinctions and *caesurae* that establish systems of categorization and classification. However, my problematic expands to encompass broader political questions. This is done with an eye towards understanding the role enumerative listing plays in establishing new ways of seeing the world, and thus new arrangements of power/knowledge. Serious ethical and philosophical stakes emerge that demand investigation, particularly regarding the role of lists in controlling populations and subjecting human beings to power. Animating questions of these chapters are thus: how does the list operate when human beings are its entries? How does one see the world through lists of people? More broadly, what is the relationship between listing and modernity?

In pursuing these questions, I develop a genealogy of the list as a cultural technique of 'logistical modernity'.[2] Circa 1500, a new way of approaching and understanding the world emerged. This orientation found extreme expression in the mid-twentieth century with the Nazi attempt at a totally administered society. We should conceive of this orientation not simply as modern, but as logistical. Under its rubric fall three privileged processes associated with modernity: compression, calculation, and circulation. Certain values, institutions, protocols, and systems emerge in the modern period to facilitate these processes: rationality, efficiency, speed, and bureaucracy, to name a few. Compression, calculation, and circulation are a nest of mutually-reinforcing processes that find expression in modern institutions (e.g. bureaucracy) and values (e.g. rationality). These are, I argue, primarily about logistics. In pointing to these features of modernity as 'privileged', I follow thinkers such as Ellul, Mumford, Berman, and Harvey, who outline in various ways how modern societies organize themselves around compression, calculation, and circulation.[3] Harvey, for instance, talks about successive waves of 'time-space compression',[4] Foucault of the shift in the role of government from disciplining subjects to facilitating new '*milieux* of circulation',[5] Mumford of the fracturing of experiential time into discrete units to be calculated and saved.[6] While they focus on different modern phenomena—the emergence and history of capitalism, of 'governmentality', of the machine—each describes processes that are logistical. They are processes geared towards the movement of people, things and data through time and space. My argument is that the cultural techniques of making modern people and institutions both inform and are informed by an understanding of the world in terms of compression, calculation, and circulation. Rather than a philosophy or ideology that sprang forth fully formed, the logistical orientation was articulated in a long history of modern administration, information, and paperwork. These fields and concepts are not a priori historical constants, but emerged only through the adoption of certain cultural techniques of order, such as listing.

These chapters contribute to an extensive literature on Nazi administration that situates it within a long trajectory of modernity. I add a degree of granularity to broader projects that explore this relationship at a philosophical level, such as those of the Frankfurt school,[7] or, more recently, by Baumann[8] and Herf.[9] Such studies connect Nazism specifically and fascism generally to certain modern modes of thinking (e.g. instrumental reason) in order to ensure these events are not reduced to the status of historical anomaly. I offer concrete case studies that show how such modern modes of thinking are articulated on paper and how they circulate. By extension, I show how ways of thinking become encoded into a logistical apparatus that reduces the world, as well as the objects and people which inhabit it, to what Martin Heidegger calls *Bestand*—a standing reserve of material to be ordered, exploited, and calculated at will.[10]

I show how this orientation emerged from an epistemological arrangement that pre-dated Nazism by at least three hundred years. This arrangement privileged calculation, compression, and eventually circulation. Within its conditions of possibility certain fields, concepts, and categories emerged to facilitate such processes: statistics, number, and induction among them. But these fields and categories did not emerge with epistemological authority fully formed, as if there were some a priori truth-value inherent in number or statistical calculations. They rest instead on an 'essential facticity' granted to them on the authority of what Mary Poovey calls 'the modern fact', which is a historically-specific epistemological structure.[11] What we find when we bore down to the granular level of 'facticity' are lists: the double-entry bookkeeping techniques of fifteenth-century Italian merchants. Double-entry lists are a cultural technique that grafts trust and truth onto number, preparing the ground for the modern fact.

Lists are not simply a surface level 'output' of Nazi logistics (e.g. deportation lists), but are also an architectonic form of the epistemological 'undergrowth' of Nazism. Put another way, the way of knowing the world that produces the Nazi census rests on the authority produced by the cultural technique of listing. At the same time, the census produces a proliferation of lists that establish categories used to order the world and its inhabitants. The list is a hidden operator that simultaneously produces and justifies the logistical orientation. From this orientation springs apparatuses of security that enable logistical operations—the movement of the people and resources of the world (*Bestand*) through space and time— required by the Nazi regime.

In this chapter, I offer an abbreviated history of modern administration, in particular emphasizing the emergence of information and statistics as the 'lifeblood' of the modern state. Particular emphasis is given to the role of lists in the emergence of the modern fact, and the subsequent spread of empirical modes of knowing such as statistics. In the next chapter, I consider the Nazi census as a radical expression of the logistical orientation. I explore how human beings are subjected to power via the list form, showing how Nazi lists enacted *caesurae* and drew borders that encouraged a view of the world and its inhabitants solely in terms of logistical operations: calculation, circulation, compression. 'Everything-included' lists are here read as a paradigmatic form of such an orientation, which Heidegger described with the concept *Bestand*.

This is not a deterministic argument about lists. They are one of many techniques in the matrix of administration conjured by modern minds and hands. Recall that cultural techniques are practices and processes that exist before the concepts and systems they generate, the 'verbs' in a grammar of media theory that operate on objects and people. I have chosen the list because it is a useful heuristic that shows how cultural techniques of order and enumeration establish categories and concepts that comprise the epistemological a priori of political and ideological worldviews. Not all lists inevitably lead to fascism. The form also played a substantial role in *defeating* Nazism—it showed up as lists of Red Army divisions, of allied bomber targets, or of rations in Britain. The form also helped people flee the Reich, e.g. Oskar Schindler's famous lists. I take the totalizing lists of the Nazi census as a case study for two reasons: (1) Nazism was an attempt at a totally administered society; because it used a lot of lists, the form is relatively easy to trace. Such limit cases are useful because, in them, we can easily spot phenomena and develop tools for their analysis. We can then export such tools to other *milieux*, where the object or phenomenon in question is more difficult to trace. (2) Limit cases are generative of controversies that push us to see what they miss; the question of 'counter-lists' only emerges in the shadow of an analysis of totalizing lists.

Administration

With the emergence of the modern state came the administrative apparatus we call 'bureaucracy'. Since at least Weber, critics of the modern project have been vocal about the alienating and de-humanizing tendencies of bureaucracy. It is cliché by now to note that well-intentioned bureaucrats forge the bars of the Iron Cage. But there is nothing essentially modern about administration or bureaucracy. Human societies have administered themselves as far back as our inscription systems allow us to remember. As is usually the case, the techniques prefigure the concept, likely by several thousand years. The Latin *administrāre* was a combination of *ad* (to; near) and *ministrare* (attend, serve, furnish).[12] By the time Tertullian used it in the late second or early third century CE, the word carried a variety of meanings: 'to be a helper, assist, to minister (to), to operate, work, to perform, carry out, conduct, to hold or perform the duties of (an office), to manage the affairs of, to manage (an estate), to bestow (on), to dispose of,' also 'to dispense (a sacrament)' in post-classical Latin.[13] For hundreds if not thousands of years, 'administer' has been a flexible concept used to describe practices of management and order.

While administration is nothing new in language or habit, what did change in the modern period was the scale and presence of administration—its elevation to the status of science, its migration into every aspect of human social life, and the largely unquestioned role of its techniques as arbiters of truth.[14] Administration in the modern period became synonymous with bureaucracy. Administration describes processes, bureaucracy a system that, crucially, became an object of study itself. As we learned in Chapter one, administrative forms like lists stand at the advent of writing. Early administrative lists were conceived as present-based media of transfer, non-standardized administrative supports rather than objects to be managed, systematized, or studied themselves.[15] Such lists were representative of the items they contained, the events they recorded, or the hands that inscribed them, but they were not a form to be studied on their own terms. Modernity is a story of the abstraction of such techniques and forms in the process of establishing administration as a science to be codified and disconnected from the world of its practice. A new field of administrative knowledge emerges floating, cloud-like, above the humans who perform its mundane tasks and are captured by its forms: bureaucracy. This abstraction has to do with two major factors: (1) the recalibration of time and space in the modern period, e.g. compression, and; (2) the epistemological rise of number as a mode of what Mary Poovey calls 'disinterested representation',[16] e.g. calculation.

Thinkers from Mumford and McLuhan to Berman and Peters tell the story of modernity as one of space and time, previously sutured to Gods and monsters, emerging as experiential human categories to be mastered.[17] Mumford argues, for instance, that the eternal time of the ancient mystics and the pre-Benedictine Christians—steadily eroded after the advent of calendars, clocks, and towers—is annihilated completely by the modern time of the clock.[18] Meanwhile, the horizon of space expands in the modern period to such a degree that human perception of the world actually shrinks, a process pithily described by McLuhan with his concept of the 'Global Village'.[19] The world comes to be understood as something more abstract than what is available through the phenomenological experience of an individual human body.[20] Yet, with the aid of modern techniques of order and representation it concomitantly becomes something fundamentally knowable. Continuing a process underway since the advent of writing,[21] new media technologies enable human communication and dissemination to break free from their physiological and existential constraints. David Harvey understands the modern historical trajectory as a series of successive waves of time-space compression, 'processes that so revolutionize the objective qualities of space and time that we are forced to alter, sometimes in quite radical ways, how we represent the world to ourselves.'[22] The central paradox of modernity is that enhanced mastery of space and time brings equally intense feelings of instability. The 'conquering' of space and time results in a world that, lacking discernible experiential contours, feels ephemeral and strange. With order comes entropy. Robust techniques of measure bring 'information overload', and all that is solid melts into air.

A vast array of processes produces this modern malaise. My interest is in the tensions and paradoxes (and attempts at resolving them) produced by the shift towards the measure of knowledge and experience in discrete, quantifiable units. This shift establishes an imaginative framework in which concepts and entities previously thought whole become subject to human manipulation. Space and time are fractured from human bodies and broken down into constitutive units that can be counted, shuffled around, conquered, or lost. New dimensions of natural phenomena previously unthought or black-boxed become knowable and manipulable. As Herbert Butterfield describes, in the modern period, Europeans put on a different kind of 'thinking cap'.[23] The effects of that cognitive wardrobe change still structure our imaginative, conceptual, and argumentative framework. A new way of seeing the world and conceiving of our place in it emerged, premised on concepts and categories previously minor or non-existent. According to Hacking, 'truth, objectivity, evidence, information, probability, proof, experience, experiment, wonder, curiosity, ignorance, classification. These are the ideas with which we organize our reasoning.'[24]

To tell the story of how a quantifiable and calculable world became thinkable, we need to look at the surfaces on which such abstractions occur. Modernity's compression of space-time is made possible not only by the array of new media technologies brought on through industrialization (i.e. the telegraph and railway), but also by innovations in paperwork. Administrative writing has often been dismissed as ancillary to the great modern projects of literature, science, and technology. Recent scholarship has offered a much-needed corrective.[25] John Guillory convincingly demonstrates that the vast majority of modern thought occurs not via the modes of writing modern people fancy themselves to be doing most of the time, literary or scholarly/ scientific, but via the banal genre he calls 'informational'.[26] Informational writing–memos, lists, diagrams, communiqués, etc.–is about administration. It allows modern people to get things done. It facilitates the movement of people and objects through space, the preservation in time of a written record of events, and the organization of institutions into hierarchies. Informational writing establishes a rhythm or order by which things unfold, programming future actions based on past results and present needs. It is thus, for Guillory, modernity's paradigmatic mode of writing.[27]

Informational modes of writing are about compression and efficiency in communication, which becomes more akin to processing. Guillory shows the evolution of writing in modernity as a move from *copia* and the performative fireworks of rhetoric towards writing that breaks free from conventional syntax and narrative.

> When new genres of writing emerged with the aim of transmitting information, new techniques of economizing transmission were called forth by that aim. These genres did not rely only on a method of using fewer words to do the same job. The standardized form, for example,

> discarded the connective tissue of sentences and paragraphs altogether in order to transmit information in a new way: by dividing up the page into fields, by offering boxes to fill or check rather than sentences to write.[28]

Guillory sees degeneration in such developments. The modern imagination is colonized by a new discursive mode, exposition, which deals with science and information and is driven by a principle of economizing attention. This results in a regressive shift from argumentation to exposition, reason to number. The logic of argument is displaced from *inventio* (the 'finding' of arguments) to *dispositio,* or arrangement. 'Arrangement—organization itself—came to constitute the logic of transmission for expository writing.'[29] Arguments and conclusions are implicit in the order or presentation, i.e. those items at the top of the list are self-evidently the most important. Bullet points fire 'self-evident' facts that require no elaboration or explanation.

Bracketing Guillory's judgement about the relative merits of classical rhetoric versus the perils of modern informational writing, the shift in emphasis towards exposition is indicative of modernity's space-bias. Critics of the period generally agree that it is marked by a transition from an era that focused on time—whether durational or serial—to one focused on space.[30] The hands of the clock spatialize time, as Mumford famously demonstrated. Guillory's work allows us to map this 'spatial turn' at the level of paperwork. It shows that the relationship between paperwork and space is not only about facilitating the movement of people and things through space. It is also about the way techniques of order organize items on the page. The *format* in which data is compiled and presented shapes the way it is conceived and used.

The ubiquity of informational writing in modernity is related to a deep and arguably constitutive connection between such modes and the emergence of the modern state. The Peace of Westphalia (1648) is oft-cited as a foundational moment of the modern state system.[31] With its connection to maps, treaties, signatures and the drawing of borders, Westphalia might be considered something of an 'informational event'. We need not make such a broad claim. It is clear that in the wake of the Peace states turned inward. No longer at perpetual war, they began to take internal account of themselves. New ideas emerged about the nature of the state, its subjects, and the relationship between the two. 'Political society was founded by a speech act; the social contract was an oral one. Parchments and papers appeared once it became necessary to establish the specific modalities of subjection.'[32] Clanchy shows that state power had been consolidated through the collection of numerical information as far back as the thirteenth and fourteenth centuries.[33] However, this mode of power had been largely dormant until the end of the eighteenth century when its intensity was increased.[34] This new system produced new desires and needs for order and reference, which were not minor matters. Ben Kafka notes that a survey from 1770 estimated there were some 5700 document depositories across France, 'most of them jealously guarded by feudal, monastic, and municipal authorities wary of the state's tendency to withdraw their privileges and then offer them back at a premium.'[35] It was becoming apparent that 'strength in number' applied not only to the battlefield. The notion that power resided with control over archives, dormant since the Roman period,[36] re-emerged, but with a crucial insight that this was true only when archives had some semblance of order, some capacity for reference. A flowering of modern systems of reference and classification followed. Thus, in the modern period, came what Hacking describes as an 'avalanche' of numbers.[37] An effect of this avalanche with far reaching consequences was the increasing subjection of administration to reason and rationality in the pursuit of science. The systematization of administration was in large part an attempt to institutionalize number and calculation as 'assurantial technologies' of the state.[38] Statistics arose as a second-order realm of informational techniques to do just that.

Statistics and number

Ian Hacking offers, to my knowledge, the most comprehensive analysis of statistics as an epistemological phenomenon. For Hacking,

> [s]tatistics has helped determine the form of laws about society and the character of social facts. It has engendered concepts and classifications within the human sciences. Moreover, the collection of statistics has created, at the best, a great bureaucratic machinery. It may think of itself as providing only information, but it is itself part of the technology of power in a modern state.[39]

Statistics becomes thinkable only in the context of what Hacking calls the 'erosion of determinism and the taming of chance' during the modern period.[40] He claims that between the end of the eighteenth century and the close of the nineteenth, 'chance' emerges as a legitimate category for understanding the world. For hundreds of years, humans had lived in a determined world. The determinant agent may have changed from time to time, from God or the past to the laws of nature, but the truth of a determinant arrow guiding human affairs was unquestioned. Nietzsche's 'death of God' was about the retreat of determinism. It was not only a matter of humans taking the place of God. As determinism receded, chance—in the sense of indeterminacy, contingency, or unpredictability—filled the void. Chance became an agent of history to be 'tamed'. Here, again, is the tension between order and chaos, everything included vs. etcetera. Chance, an undetermined world, was the foundational assumption of sciences and scholarship seeking to measure the contours of the world through number. Statistics grow from this epistemological ground.

The role of listing in statistics is so obvious and taken-for-granted that it might seem too trite to mention. But the form is present from the beginning, such as with Charles Babbage's call in 1832 for the publication of books of numerical constants: 'The learned societies of Paris, Berlin and London were to take turns, every two years, in producing a list of the numbers known to mankind.'[41] We see here the list present at the onset of the 'avalanche of numbers, the erosion of determinism and the taming of chance.'[42] These developments were commensurate with the establishment of measure as a basis of empirical knowledge (e.g. facts). The result was a world with 'too many numbers to leave the Galilean and Newtonian world intact.'[43] Lists deliver statistical figures to eyes, but they are also a precondition for the processes of compiling and calculating numbers that result in such figures. They deliver the raw material by which statistics, as a way of knowing, is forged.

Statistics is an 'assuriantial' technology of power in that it provides stability to the social order. In order to legitimize its rule through surveillance, to guarantee capital investment and colonial risk-taking, and to ensure the overall health and docility of its subjects, the modern state needs statistics. But how and why does this way of knowing enable the state to function in such a way? A short answer is that it does so by measuring the contours of the state and announcing it as a material entity to be policed and optimized. Peters recalls that, in the eighteenth century, statistics was 'the name for the comparative (and often, competitive) study of *states*.' In relatively short order, it became 'the science of making imperceptible aggregates perceptible in numerical arrays.'[44] He connects the rise of this science to the expansion of the scale of modern nation states. As borders extend outwards and populations swell, administrators and citizens alike are posed with the problem that the state is 'out of sight and out of grasp.'[45] Statistics compress the state down to a visual entity that is more manageable both imaginatively and administratively. 'And so, statistics arose as the study of something too large to be perceptible—states and their climates, their rates of birth, marriage, death, crime, their economies, and so on—and secondly, as a set of techniques for making those processes visible and interpretable.'[46] The 'cultural preparation' for statistics, to borrow Mumford's term, occurred with what

Kafka identifies as the French Revolution's fundamental transformation of the 'culture of paperwork'. The latter involved 'the emergence of a radical new ethics of paperwork, one designed to sustain a state whose legitimacy was founded on the claim to represent, at every moment, every member of the nation.'[47] The 'personal state' of patronage and monarchy became the 'personnel state' of bureaucracy and the Republic.[48]

There is a mutually constitutive relationship between statistics and the state. But how did this realm of knowledge come to achieve the empirical veracity and epistemological strength required to function as an assuriantial technology? If the authority of the state resides in its archives and the statistical figures they contain, where does the authority of statistics come from? It is, after all, not a field of knowledge that has always been with us. Nor did it emerge fully formed as an arbiter of truth. Rather, statistics comes to function as an assurantial technology not just because its figures materialize the contours of state, but also and primarily because they are considered *factual*. Statistics is the process of collecting, compiling, and calculating empirically verifiable facts. But what is a fact? Where do facts come from? Are they epistemological or ontological? Such questions are addressed by scholarship that sheds light on the degree to which the concept of the fact is itself historically specific.[49] To understand the authority of statistics and the state power they legitimize, a few words are needed about the emergence of the modern fact.

Facts

We think of facts as if they have always been with us, that they are things out there in the world for human beings to discover through our tools of empirical observation and analysis. This is not so. Mary Poovey's *A History of the Modern Fact* offers a rigorous account of how 'the fact' as an epistemological unit silently took hold of the modern mind. Facts became the unseen, unquestioned guarantors of truth and knowledge in the modern period. Systematic knowledge, once the bastion of rhetoric and argumentation, became impossible without facts. The realm of facts is one dominated by numerical representation. Poovey is interested in the way that 'numbers acquired the connotations of transparency and impartiality that have made them seem so perfectly suited to the epistemological work performed by the modern fact.'[50] Her work can aid in understanding the role played by cultural techniques and documentary formats in the emergence of the modern fact—the epistemological unit upon which statistics, informational writing, the modern state and its apparatuses of security all rest.

Poovey participates in the complication, by Science Studies, of a conventional narrative about the history of science that associates a 'scientific revolution' from about 1500CE with Francis Bacon's scepticism. That narrative proposes that emergent modes and fields of inquiry focused on the observed and the particular eroded the authority of ancient and medieval approaches to studying the world. The reality of this epistemological shift is not so simple. Frohmann, for instance, contrasts the modes of documentation employed by continental natural philosophers (based on 'Aristotelian conventions for articulating natural knowledge'), on the one hand, and those employed by English members of the Royal Society (based on the Baconian 'practice of building knowledge from the certified occurrence'), on the other.[51] Continental natural philosophers adopted Aristotelian conventions such as the literary device of the geometrical *problema* (involving the presentation of empirical observations as axioms) and the technique of multiple repetition (the presentation of empirical observations as typical, as things 'everyone knows'). British modes of documentation instead involved an elaborate presentation 'designed to put the reader on the scene, to have the reader perform a *virtual witnessing* of the event occurring in the laboratory,' as well as a modesty of presentation that spoke to both the gentlemanly manner of the experimenter and the 'Baconian nondogmatic attitude appropriate to inductive and probabilistic, rather than demonstrative and axiomatic, assertions of natural science.'[52] Frohmann participates in a refutation of the idea that there was any single rupture we can point to as a 'scientific revolution' or a specific figure upon whom to grant revolutionary status.[53] He argues that epistemological changes are traceable only through modes of documentation.

Poovey adopts a similar approach. Instead of focusing on Bacon and the 'rupture' caused by his insights, she links the emergence of modern fact to double-entry bookkeeping. This was a cultural technique of documentation that existed well before the epistemological changes and discourse that came after Bacon. Double-entry bookkeeping was a 'variant of the modern fact [that] appeared in a writing practice that did *not* participate in epistemology we associate with modernity.'[54] Double entry was a technique of mercantile, informational writing—a 'low' cultural form established for both practical and symbolic purposes. As possibilities for trade and exchange expanded and commercial exchange became increasingly mediated by currencies, merchants needed a new technique of keeping track of their accounts. Double-entry bookkeeping was an ingenious solution to this practical problem. It compressed complex commercial transactions into numbers and letters organized in a systematic way on pages and in books. It established an indexical account that ostensibly corresponded the events, objects, and actors involved in exchange. Such an index allowed merchants and purchasers to keep track of their capital reserves. The latter are translated by this technique into objects and cash, credits and debits. Double-entry bookkeeping freezes the spaces and times of commerce, materializing the fact of the event and the truth of one's holdings. It is a cultural technique that processes distinctions and performs 'ontic operations': transactions, objects, events, and values are encoded on paper according to a new symbolic system that is not oriented to scientific inquiry or literary representation but to the administration of trade and exchange.

Double-entry bookkeeping was much more than an indexical mnemonic technique; these, as we have seen, are as old as writing itself. It also fulfilled more than pragmatic administrative needs. Poovey shows that merchants sought, with double entry, to enhance the reputation of their trade by making their trust- and credit-worthiness imminent on the page. They did this by appealing to the authority of rhetoric, which had over the course of the centuries migrated from oral speech into writing.[55] Merchants sought to prove that their trade was not usurious but honest. The double-entry ledger made this case by 'following certain stylistic conventions: its contents were concise, orderly, and systematic, and its details were (presumably) faithful to the facts.'[56] Clean lines and organizational prowess—evident in individual books, and in the double-entry system—displayed and in a way programmed the moral rectitude of the merchants. They no longer had to prove themselves through rhetorical performance or even social reputation. The evidence of their honesty before God, a precondition for creditworthiness before wealth, was right there on the page.

Evidence of trustworthiness rested on the apparent transparency, accuracy, and precision of accounts, the truth of which could be easily calculated. If his books were balanced, it could be reliably assumed that the merchant in question embodied the same traits.

We see with double-entry bookkeeping the process by which a cultural technique standardized format and system, producing effects that 'exceeded transcription and calculation.'[57] These effects were social, proclaiming the honesty of merchants as just described, and epistemological, 'mak[ing] the formal precision of the double-entry system, which drew on the rule-bound system of arithmetic, *seem* to guarantee the accuracy of the details it recorded.'[58] The systematic nature of double entry is crucial, Poovey emphasizes, because it establishes protocols for writing that transgress the economy of knowledge production and circulation that had previously enjoyed a monopoly. With standardized rules anyone can write in the ledger, merchant or employee. Accuracy of writing in the system is guaranteed by rules all writers must follow. Writers become interchangeable relays—if the system is to function properly they cannot deviate from protocol.

Double-entry bookkeeping is framed and structured by the list format. We talk about bookkeeping in terms of number and 'the books'. These are important descriptors. But to focus only on these aspects is to ignore the fact that entries in a ledger stack up on top of one another to produce a larger, listed structure. 'The books' is a convenient placeholder to describe an ongoing series of mutually constitutive lists. In each of the four books that comprise an individual's double-entry system ('inventory', 'memorial', 'journal', 'ledger') the items, events, amounts, creditors, and debtors are listed according to some organizing principle (usually temporal). The final, authoritative *ledger* is a double list that stands as a guarantor of truth because of its ability to literally settle all accounts. Furthermore, double-entry bookkeeping displays the tendency towards *brevitas*—compression—that would become hegemonic in modernity.[59] Through a complex series of transmissions—from the inventory, through the memorial and journal, to the ledger—the information noted about an initial commercial exchange is steadily compressed down from prose into number.[60] Details from the memorial's relatively complex initial entries deemed excessive are shed in each translation. They are compressed to a format more amenable to calculation. The final entry written in the ledger achieves brevity, simplicity, transparency, and equivalence. These categories acted as guarantors for the credibility and moral rectitude of the merchant—a format to make the beauty of God imminent on paper.[61]

Bookkeeping is essential to the emergence of the modern fact for Poovey because, though it sought legitimacy for itself according to the prevailing epistemological conditions of the fifteenth century—namely, God's determining will—it actually served to undercut those conditions. By doing so, double entry prepared the ground for the emergence of a new kind of knowledge rooted in the transparency and 'disinterestedness' of number. We see another instance of Jack Goody's dialectic, wherein the formal properties of lists call into question the very limits of knowledge their borders enact. Poovey shows how double-entry bookkeeping stood as a model for natural philosophers of the eighteenth century of disinterested knowledge that was not beholden to the vicissitudes and pageantry of rhetoric. New ways of guaranteeing the essential truth or falsehood of an event, a claim, or an object were established: observed particulars, numbers and the calculations they enabled, and so on. Poovey's work shows, according to Hacking, that an 'essential facticity' was present in modes of commerce that pre-date, by a wide margin, the new sciences of the seventeenth century where the

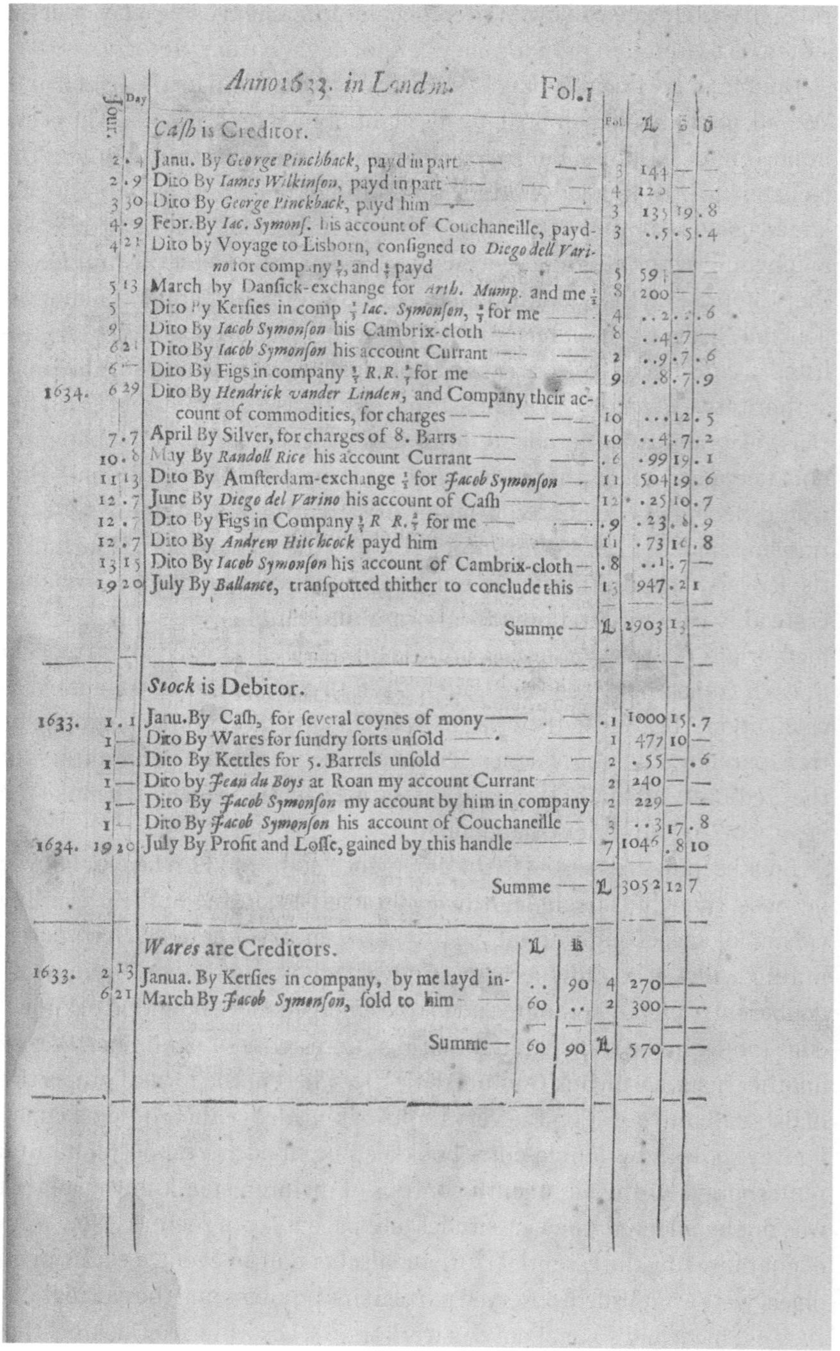

Anno 1633. in London. Fol. 1

	Jour.	Day		Fol.	L	S	D
			Cash is Creditor.				
	2	4	Janu. By *George Pinchback*, payd in part	3	144	—	—
	2	9	Dito By *James Wilkinson*, payd in part	4	120	—	—
	3	30	Dito By *George Pinckback*, payd him	3	135	19	8
	4	9	Febr. By *Iac. Symons.* his account of Couchaneille, payd-	3	5	5	4
	4	21	Dito by Voyage to Lisborn, consigned to *Diego dell Varino* for company 1/3, and 2/3 payd	5	59	—	—
	5	13	March by Dansick-exchange for *Arth. Mump.* and me 1/2	8	200	—	—
	5		Dito By Kersies in comp 1/3 *Iac. Symonson*, 2/3 for me	4	2	[illegible]	6
	9		Dito By *Iacob Symonson* his Cambrix-cloth	8	4	7	—
	6	21	Dito By *Iacob Symonson* his account Currant	2	9	7	6
	6	—	Dito By Figs in company 1/3 *R.R.* 2/3 for me	9	8	7	9
1634.	6	29	Dito By *Hendrick vander Linden*, and Company their account of commodities, for charges	10		12	5
	7	7	April By Silver, for charges of 8. Barrs	10	4	7	2
	10	8	May By *Randoll Rice* his account Currant	6	99	19	1
	11	13	Dito By Amsterdam-exchange 1/2 for *Jacob Symonson*	11	504	19	6
	12	7	June By *Diego del Varino* his account of Cash	12	25	10	7
	12	7	Dito By Figs in Company 1/3 *R R.* 2/3 for me	9	23	8	9
	12	7	Dito By *Andrew Hitchcock* payd him	11	73	16	8
	13	15	Dito By *Iacob Symonson* his account of Cambrix-cloth	8	1	7	—
	19	20	July By *Ballance*, transpotted thither to conclude this	13	947	2	1
			Summe	L	2903	13	—
			Stock is Debitor.				
1633.	1	1	Janu. By Cash, for several coynes of mony	1	1000	15	7
	1	—	Dito By Wares for sundry sorts unsold	1	477	10	—
	1	—	Dito By Kettles for 5. Barrels unsold	2	55	—	6
	1	—	Dito by *Jean du Boys* at Roan my account Currant	2	240	—	—
	1	—	Dito By *Jacob Symonson* my account by him in company	2	229	—	—
	1	—	Dito By *Jacob Symonson* his account of Couchaneille	3	3	17	8
1634.	19	20	July By Profit and Losse, gained by this handle	7	1046	8	10
			Summe	L	3052	12	7

	Jour.	Day	*Wares* are Creditors.	L	lb	Fol.	L	S	D
1633.	2	13	Janua. By Kersies in company, by me layd in-	..	90	4	270	—	—
	6	21	March By *Jacob Symonson*, sold to him	60	..	2	300	—	—
			Summe	60	90	L	570	—	—

Fol. 1.) *Anno.* 163¾. *in London.*

	Jour.	Day		Fol.	£	s	d
			Cash is Debitor.				
	1	1	Janu. To Stock, for ſeveral coynes of mony	1	1000	15	7
	5	27	Febr. To *Jacob Symonſon* his account Currant	2	328	10	11
1634.	9	22	April To *George Pinch-back*, received in full	3	9	11	2
	10	8	May To Figs ³⁄₅ *R. R.* and ²⁄₅ for me	9	525	—	—
	12	22	Dito To *James Wilkinſon*, received to clear a truck	4	102	16	1
	14	23	June To *Diego del Varino* his account of Caſh	12	25	10	7
	14	—	Dito To Profit and Loſſe, gained by *Diego's* fruits	7	13	4	—
	14	2	July To *George Pinch back* received by his Aſſignment	3	485	6	5
	16	11	Dito To *Iacob Simonſon* his account Currant	2	28	1	7
	16	20	Dito To *Randoll Rice* his account Currant	6	284	16	8
	16	20	Dito To *Andrew Hitchcock* received in part	11	100	—	—
			Summe	£	2903	13	—

	Jour.	Day		Fol.	£	s	d
			stock is Debitor.				
1633.	1	1	Janu. To *Iacob Symonſon* his acconnt Currant	2	150	—	—
1634.	19	20	July To *Ballance*, for conclude carried thither	13	2,902	12	7
			Summe	£	3052	12	7

	Jour.	Day		L	R	Fol.	£	s	d
			Wares are Debitors.						
1633.	1	1	Janu. To Stock, reſting unſold	60	90	1	477	10	—
1634.	17	20	July To Profit and Loſſe gained			7	92	10	—
			Summe	60	90	£	570	—	—

'Creditor' and 'Debtor' from Richard Daffore's *The Merchants Mirror* (1651). Princeton University Library.

relationship between the fact and trust is most often located.[62] Poovey shows that trust was sutured to the modern fact well before the seventeenth century. Trust was the crucial element in the keeping of accounts and the generating of their empirical facticity. In double-entry bookkeeping the transparency of number enables trust in the merchant that keeps clean and ordered books. Variants aimed at achieving knowledge both systematic and 'true to nature' emerge from natural philosophy's emulation of double-entry bookkeeping's essential facticity.[63] These included experimental moral philosophy, conjectural history, political economy, and statistics. Each of these, but particularly statistics, was developed as 'a technology for evading questions about induction in passing from facts to statesmanship.'[64] For the purposes of this study, we must bracket the philosophical problem of induction, which Hacking pursues with characteristic precision.[65] It is enough to say here that, (1) statistics is only possible in a world governed epistemologically by facts, and; (2) statistics, as a way of knowing the world, sutured the gap between the observation of particulars and generalizations based on probabilities. We can thus return to statistics proper, in order to discuss further how the field congealed as a science of abstract measure with an intimate relationship to the modern state. This relationship offers a point of entry into conceiving of what I earlier called the 'logistical orientation', and the Nazi limit case study, more specifically.

Statistical figures appear as a species of Guillory's informational writing—observed particulars through which systematic knowledge and governmental policy can be built. They are more precise than rogue data points, but still lack the requisite human interpretive schema to count as codified knowledge. By filling the gap between the particular and the systematic, the molecular and molar, statistics becomes installed as the connective tissue of the state as an abstract entity. Peculiarly, by filling such spaces-between statistics atomizes people, abstracting them as 'units'. Statistical figures are a medium by which people are simultaneously drawn together—whether as a 'population', 'income group', or otherwise—and discretized into entries that can be shuffled. Before these new categories and facts take their place in the minds of politicians or on the pages of newspapers, they are inscribed on paper in lists and charts.

In an early essay, Peters demonstrates statistics as a symptom of alienating tendencies in modern informational culture.[66] Though his thinking has evolved since then, many of the insights of the essay remain relevant. It outlines, in broad strokes, how the collection of statistical figures and their later analysis and administration in a bureaucracy become both the means and the ends of the modern state. Statistics establishes the contours of a state and the categories by which its people are able to conceive of themselves in relation to their 'imagined community'.[67] It offers a new imaginative grammar rooted in empirical measurement and number, a mode of understanding very different from those rooted in religion, literature, or philosophy. In the space cleared by the rise of the modern fact, empirical data becomes hegemonic, enabling statistics to 'make up people' and nations. Statistical data profess to be apolitical and ahistorical, simply waiting 'out there' to be uncovered and compiled. But this claim masks the extent to which statistical figures and 'information' are epistemological units measured into existence by bureaucratic institutions and machinations that require them to function. No bureaucracy without statistics, but no statistics without bureaucracy. This is one of the most essential feedback loops of the modern period. A bureaucracy collates, compiles, and analyses statistical data into 'information', which requires further techniques of order and yet more statistical methods of analysis. It is not surprising that this administrative realm of bureaucracy, information, and statistics has been a site of so much consternation in modern literature and philosophy. 'Bentham's Panopticon, Weber's Iron Cage, Kafka's Castle—since the beginning of the modern era, these buildings have darkened our skyline.'[68]

Peters argues that part of the reason statistics and, more broadly, information, are alienating to the modern mind is precisely because they abstract experiential dimensions of space and time from the human body:

> People who, thanks to statistics, 'see' something intellectually they could not see sensually, are put in a curious position. They know something that they can never experience for themselves. They have a kind of knowledge that no mortal can have. Statistics offer a kind of *gnosis*, a mystic transcendence of individuality, a tasting of the forbidden fruit of knowledge [...] This new kind of knowledge—knowledge that absolves individuals from the claims of *deixis*, of existing at one place and at one moment—is of course none other than information. Information is knowledge with the human body taken out of it.[69]

Though ostensibly about the observation of empirical particulars, statistics participates in the general tendency towards abstraction in the modern period. According to Poovey, '[o]ne effect of efforts to generate systematic knowledge was the production of a set of abstractions, which rapidly became the objects of these sciences. These abstractions, which include 'society,' the 'market system' (then 'the economy'), and 'poverty,' now constitute the characteristic objects of the modern social sciences, including the sciences of wealth and society.'[70] We thus circle back to see the extent to which techniques of administration and paperwork contribute to the existential malaise of modernity identified at the outset of this section. The facticity of statistics is rooted in a practice, double-entry bookkeeping, that facilitates compression, calculation, and circulation. These are categories of value that emerge with modernity's recalibration of space and time. Such are the great desires of the modern mind, but, as we shall see in Chapter four, their pursuit can have horrific consequences.

4. Administration II: The Nazi Census and Making Up People

> 'Theoretically, the collection of data for each person can be so abundant, and even complete, that we can speak at last of a paper human who represents the natural human.'
> – Methorst and Lentz, Directors, Reich Inspectorate for the Population Register (1936)[1]

This chapter explores the Nazi administrative apparatus as a limit case study of the modern trajectory traced above. I show how various aspects of Nazi administration embody the modern compulsion for compression, calculation, and circulation. This tripartite schema is the operative logic of the Third Reich and results in an orientation towards the world that is logistical.[2]

With their book *The Nazi Census*, Aly and Roth shed light on a hidden administrative history of National Socialism that had a direct and profound influence in shaping and implementing the Holocaust as an historical event. Their extensive archival research addresses a blind spot in conventional histories of the Third Reich, the fact that 'hardly anyone has ever [...] questioned how people were reduced to an entry in a *registration,* or how bureaucratic abstraction de-humanized individuals and transported them to a new reality—namely, death.'[3] In rare instances that statistics and other techniques of administration appear in histories of the Reich, they are typically regarded as secondary to, either, ideas in the minds that dreamed up the camps, or ideological positions that materialized as Nazi state policy. In such cases, administration is reductively conceived as a tool by which humans translate their ideas into reality. Or it is dismissed as the detritus of a vast mythic-ideological apparatus articulated via more conventional, literary forms of writing and rhetoric.[4] The infrastructure of Nazi administration—including fields like statistics and forms like lists—is elided as noise in the archival channel from which conventional narrative and causal histories of the Third Reich are written. Edwin Black points to Raul Hilberg's *The Destruction of European Jewry* as a paradigmatic example that, though it outlines the bloodshed and violence mandated by bureaucrats, pays little mind to the specific practices, forms, and methodologies that structured such decisions. 'In fact, the crucial minutiae of registration are barely mentioned in any of thousands of books on the Third Reich.'[5] Black further notes that there is no mention of the IBM Hollerith punch cards (the object of his analysis) in any of the precise studies of the camps or the psychologies of their creators, such as Softsky's *The Order of Terror*, Gonen's *The Roots of Nazi Psychology*, or Kogon's *The Theory and Practice of Hell*.[6]

Lists are everywhere in Nazi administration. Most obviously, deportation lists transported of Jews and other 'undesirables' to camps. But Nazi administration also had an elaborate system of lists built into census taking and statistical methods that established subject positions—making up people—that could be observed, calculated, and transported. Registration lists proliferate. These kept track of information about residency, previous convictions, motor vehicles, and immigration patterns of the population.[7] Lists of those with hereditary illnesses appeared by 1934, followed by those of 'Jews in the Reich', and 'Gypsies', both in 1936. In 1939, the Ministry of the Interior and the *Reichsführer-SS* urged that the compiling of lists of 'names of foreigners, members with non-German ethnic backgrounds, Jews, and mixed Jews' to be the highest priority.[8] By 1939, there was even a list of 'Jewish First Names'. Those whose names were not on the list were required to sign their marriage licences as either 'Israel' or 'Sarah'.[9] Perhaps the most famous and macabre of all Nazi lists was the inventory included in the report prepared for Himmler in 1943 on the status of the 'final solution of the Jewish question'.

> Listing activities that pre-date the Third Reich prepared the ground for the Nazi census. Individual German states introduced censuses in the wake of post-Napoleonic administrative reforms. Prussia started counting in 1816 and the German Tariff Club began in 1833 [...] The first general all-German census, conducted by the Imperial Office of Statistics, took place on December 1, 1871, shortly after the German Reich was founded.[10]

Over time, these techniques evolved beyond simple head counting. The counts of 1916, 1917, and 1919 were geared towards the administration of the war effort and the post-war period, focusing on food rations as well as employment and business registration. In 1925, an 'economic and social-statistical evaluation' was conducted that relied heavily on the 'household list', a questionnaire that identified members of a family and their relationship to the head of the household. In addition to previously used categories like age, birthplace, gender, occupation, and place of residence, new categories were incorporated to identify the mentally and physically 'fragile'.[11] The questionnaire for the 1926 count was even more detailed. The new National Socialist government carried out in 1933 plans for a more comprehensive census that had been deferred since 1930. This census would serve an architectonic role in the Nazis establishing unique administrative, juridico-legal, and security apparatuses over the next twelve years.

Most notable about the 1933 census is that it signals a shift in the way census data was conceived. The shift was from a diagnostic and cartographic orientation towards the past and present to a predictive and analytical orientation towards the future. Statistical data would now be used to calculate, for instance, optimal birth rates amongst populations of 'biologically valuable' women.

> The meaning of this [family statistical] survey for the evaluation of marital fertility is of great importance [...] Old methods of population statistics are inadequate because they limit themselves to determining what 'was' and what 'is.' One has to move beyond answers of the past and present and adopt a biological perspective.[12]

Later, in the run up to an even more expansive census planned for 1939, the Cologne edition of the official Nazi newspaper *Völkischer Beobachter* proclaimed 'it is the duty of every fellow German (*Volksgenossen*) to answer every single question completely and truthfully. Each comrade has to be conscious of the fact that he will give the Führer and his colleagues the basis for future legislation for the next five to ten years.'[13] The 1939 census was conceived as the 'opening balance sheet for the Greater German Reich' and it included an additional card that was specifically geared towards identifying and registering 'foreigners and persons of non-German ethnic backgrounds.'[14] Primary among these non-German persons were Jews. The information gleaned from this additional card enabled the Security Service to establish a 'Reich file for Jews and mixed Jews,' something it had been working towards for years with little success. The additional card also aided the military's goal of 'optimiz[ing] the "deployment of people" in the war [by putting] together a register of persons, categorized by occupations (those for which people had trained but which they did not necessarily practice), that would cover the entire Reich.'[15] We see in this re-orientation of statistical data towards the future—a stockpile to be analysed and used later—a vision of the world that is logistical.

The 1939 census was geared at producing the crucial item for the Nazi recalibration of the Reich, the *Volkskartei* ('register of the people'). 'By establishing a people's registration (*Volkskartei*)', Göring proclaimed in 1938, 'we will achieve complete supervision of the entire German people.'[16] This complete registry—a perfect, everything-included inventory of inhabitants in the Reich—would enable the optimal deployment of resources towards the goal of establishing the Thousand Year Reich.

> First, we would need to collect data and to scientifically examine and evaluate the conflicting material. Second, there would need to be a scientific analysis and evaluation to suit the practical considerations. This is necessary in order to get the most reliable and complete material for the purposes of resettlement and the strengthening of German culture.[17]

The proper location of resources in space and the most efficient circulation rates in time could be calculated using the data from the *Volkskartei*. We see here the familiar modern desire for total knowledge, recalling Peters's discussion of statistics as *gnosis*.[18] Population and territory are abstracted to become a completely graspable, usable resource to be manipulated and re-ordered according to human desires.

> The registry will be of particular importance for the defence of the Reich, insofar as it registers not only military draftees but also the entire population. In the event of war, the population in its entirety can be mobilized, with every individual used according to his or her abilities, only if the *Volkskartei* provides incontestable proof of the existing age groups available for this purpose. The actual purpose of the registry is for registration. The goal is directly achieved if the registry has been established and the place of residence and changes in personal status are entered on an ongoing basis.[19]

The human being is transformed into a node in a network of action, an object to be calculated, compressed, and circulated.

The *Volkskartei* project was implemented all over Germany and its conquered territories. The card proved, until at least the end of the Blitzkrieg in the winter of 1941–1942, 'an excellent tool [...] in peace or, above all, in war, for quickly and efficiently targeting particular groups of people on the basis of their abilities, and directing them to achieve specific goals.'[20] This movement of humans-as-material is logistical. Also important to note about these more elaborate systems and structures of administration is that they had evolved from being primarily about indexing and measuring, as, for instance, the 1925 census had been, to being primarily about retrieval. Such systems are not simply about creating and guarding an archive, but being able to put the archive to use, to release its data out into the world so that the latter can make things happen. We see here that the modern predilections for compression and calculation are being marshalled towards circulation, about which much more will be said below.

The Nazi census of 1938 and its antecedents demonstrate the development of an increasingly sophisticated system of data collection, sorting, and counting. It was a system that provided the raw data for second-order analysis and policymaking. A uniform Reich registration system was not enough. Individual registers were means, not ends. The goal was to create a system that was 'more than an address book', which

> provided an indispensable foundation for the work of the numerous officials who worked in the Reich middle management staff in the cities and various regions; thus, ultimately, it provided a foundation for the entire Reich. The Reich Postal System, the Reich Office of Statistics, the Reich Office for Urban and Rural Planning and the Reich Family Office, the Criminal Police, and the Gestapo could not afford to work with incomplete data.[21]

As its creators liked to say, 'the Reich Registration Order is a beginning, not an end.'[22] 'The end' would be pursued through the mobilization of this data in statistical analysis.

Calculation: Nazi statistics

National Socialism was as much an epistemological event as it was military, political, or otherwise. It attempted to 're-wire'[23] or re-calibrate the imaginative, conceptual, and material life of Germany. 'At the vanguard of Hitler's intellectual shock troops were the statisticians.'[24] The field of statistics was conceived as an essential force in the 'work of building Germany,' according to Friedrich Zahn, then President of the German Statistical Society, '[i]n its very essence, statistics is very closely related to the National Socialist movement.'[25] The field was perceived as an intellectual approach that corresponded to the militarism of Nazi cultural, political, and economic life. According to Zahn, 'besides physical fitness, a firm character, and a rigorous approach to science, [Hitler] demands soldiers of politics, economics, and also of science.'[26] Zahn, and the Statistical Society he presided over, were only too happy to occupy this position.

> [Hitler's] regime demands clear results in a wide range of areas and great flexibility, which for the most part can only be provided by statistics. In

> using statistics, the government has the road map to move from knowledge to deeds, from advice to action, in order to succeed in its enormous task of building society.[27]

Reinhard Heydrich (chief of the Security Service, the Reich Criminal Police, and the Gestapo) encapsulates the crucial role of administration and statistics in remaking the world in the Aryan image when he explains that the 'combat mission for the administrative sphere,' the task of 'securing the idea,' was not something that could be realized through 'superficial scanning but rather by fundamentally grasping and registering reality.'[28] The 'reality' to be grasped was that of long-standing racial prejudices given new life by the brazenness with which they were disseminated under National Socialism. The 'special count' of Jews in the census of 1933 (a separate census conducted in addition to the general one), for instance, materialized and thus 'objectified' known prejudices. Data collected in the count signalled that Jews were 'primarily active in trade,' as furriers, jewellers, etc., and also that they had a 'predilection' for academic pursuits.[29] It emboldened the Bavarian Ministry of Economics to conclude that 'Jews shy away from hard work or work that is not as profitable. They have also infiltrated the upper strata of economic and professional activities.'[30] Statistical figures and analysis act as a means by which to ground racist views about Jews and other persons, previously rooted in 'common sense', as objective knowledge. Statistics' claim to objectivity is granted by the apparent veracity of the 'facts' contained in Nazi registries.

The tracking of Jews had been occurring in Germany for at least 60 years prior to the establishment and rise of National Socialism. Beginning in 1875–1876, state registry offices had documented every change in an individual's marriage status and also his or her religion. These changes included 'Jewish baptisms' and 'mixed marriages'. These registers were reviewed starting in 1933 by the Nazi *Rechsstelle für Sippenforschung* ('Reich Office for Family Research'). The latter also began to systematize and collate church registers that went back even further. In 1936, 'more than 150 work comrades' created a filing system for the Berlin Evangelical Community's baptismal books from the period 1800–1874. The result was the 'largest church book registry in the world' that Aly and Roth argue

> provided a model for the overhauling of registry systems in churches in other urban areas that acted in the service of denouncing 'non-Germans.' Without this type of registry, the state offices would have had a much more difficult time legitimating the terms 'race Jews' and 'mixed Jews.'[31]

Cultural techniques of listing precede the categories and distinctions upon which Nazi race policy and disciplinary structures are built and legitimized. When baptized in the waters of statistical analysis, data contained in church registries become 'indicative' of certain categorizations such as 'Jew' and 'undesirable'. These data become numerically verifiable and thus the conclusions drawn from them can be considered factually true. Data visualizations soon followed, which further enhanced the truth claim of categories created from Nazi statistical aggregates. There was a remarkable proliferation of charts, maps, tables, graphs, and lists as the Nazis found efficient means to create a stockpile of facts ready-to-hand and easy to deploy in rhetoric, writing and in policymaking. These data were disseminated internally to the party and externally to the public. Examples included a graph that compared the composition of the Jewish population with that of the *Gesamtbevölkerung* ('total population') in terms of employment categories (domestic services; holders of public office; trade and transportation; industry and manufacturing; agriculture and forestry),[32] or a map of the distribution of 'Jews' and 'mixed Jews' (*Die Juden und Jüdischen Mischlinge*) culled from the 1939 census.[33]

As we have seen, statistics was not an invention of the Nazis. Since at least seventeenth-century probability theory, there have been robust intellectual debates around statistical data and analysis. Nor is statistics, as a field, essentially evil. Hacking notes that statistics had been used to bring about tangible benefits for vast swathes of European populations. 'One may suspect the ideology of the great Victorian social reformers and still grant that their great fight for sanitation, backed by statistical enquiries, was the most important single amelioration of the epoch.'[34] What marked the Nazi statistical approach apart was that it developed and made extensive use of techniques that isolated unique subsets of the population at both the group and individual levels. Previously, statistics had been a matter of measuring the contours of a territorial totality under the rule of a sovereign. The field measured 'states and their climates, their rates of birth, marriage, death, crime, their economies, and so on.'[35] It was incredibly difficult, if not impossible, to track an individual within the statistical totality. Any delineated sub-fields were based primarily around geographical space (regions or towns). Integrating the atomized and jealously-guarded regional archives of post-Revolutionary France, for instance, was a huge challenge.[36] The Nazis changed this situation, incorporating techniques by which to first *identify* individuals, then *track*, and finally *move* them through space and time. As early as 1932, a new method for 'individual statistics' was appearing on the horizon that would be taken up by the Nazis and exploited to the furthest extent. It was described at the time by Swiss researcher Arnold Schwartz:

> The method is based on the repeated statistical observation of the same objects while maintaining their individuality. What was overlooked in the past, namely, individual destinies, are now in the spotlight of the statistician [...] Instead of taking a ball out of the 'urn of nature' from time to time and then returning the ball to the urn with others, now those balls are marked before they are returned. After some time has elapsed, one can very carefully check to see how many of those marked balls are still there, how many have been destroyed in the mixing process, and how many have been added. One checks their weight increase and decrease, not just their color.[37]

The human being was *made* as a calculable object.

Nazi statisticians built on the work of their predecessors in the Reich statistical office to develop techniques that more accurately and comprehensively measured the contours of German territory and populations. The goal was to find ways to more easily identify, differentiate, and track groups and individuals of various kinds. 'The only way to eliminate any mistakes,' wrote Dr. Karl Keller, 'is the registration of the *entire* population. How is this to be done? The establishment of mandatory personal genetic-biographical forms [...] Nothing would hinder us from using these forms to enter any important information which can be used by race scientists.'[38] To sort and reshuffle vast swathes of data in ways previously impractical or even impossible, Reich statisticians turned to a machine developed for the US Census Bureau's 1890 census by German expatriate Hermann Hollerith.

Compression: Hollerith punch cards

As Edwin Black recounts, the US Census Bureau was in a period of transition when Hollerith joined its ranks. The existing system of enumeration and compilation was slow, inefficient, and limited in scope. It involved, first, distributing questionnaires that asked only very general questions—a glorified headcount more than a census proper. For archival and reference purposes, collected answers were transferred from questionnaire forms to small cards. These cards were then cross referenced and filed accordingly. Time-to-completion for census taking was extremely long, usually a decade or more. Census frequency was established at ten years, so preparations were typically well underway for the next census before counting the one previous had even been completed.[39] As America expanded in population, size of territory, and complexity of governance, improvements to this system were sorely needed. Thus, Hollerith entered the US Census Bureau during a period of experimentation, innovation, and opportunity. He attacked these problems head on.

The Hollerith machine, which first appeared in 1894, improved on card-based census tabulation techniques by combining them with mechanical components found in automata such as French looms, music boxes, and player pianos. The latter all used punched holes on cards or rolls to automate gear mechanisms that produced motion or sound. Hollerith generated the idea for his machine after observing a train conductor who, in order to police against ticket re-use, would punch a unique pattern into each ticket corresponding to the appearance of each passenger. These holes noted physical characteristics such as height, hair colour, size of nose, and clothing.

> Hollerith's idea was a card with standardized holes, each representing a different trait: gender, nationality, occupation, and so forth. The card would then be fed into a 'reader.' By virtue of easily adjustable spring mechanisms and brief electrical brush contacts sensing for the holes, the cards could be 'read' as they raced through a mechanical feeder. The processed cards could then be sorted into stacks based on a specified series of punched holes.[40]

The cards established formal parameters for a system of classification. Choices were made as to what criteria to include in the census questionnaire based on what could be punched into the card. Each card was limited in the number of hole-categories it could contain. A way to increase the bandwidth of the cards, however, was to encode information into numbers. Rather than having a rudimentary one-question-per-one-hole equivalence, 'this code is based on the decimal system and translates terms such as persons, achievements, dates, and the like into numbers. The catalogue of possible answers is then calculated and the applicable identification number is punched in the card.'[41] Rather than reducing the questionnaire to simple binary, yes || no, questions—as might be expected in a rudimentary process of quantification—automating the compilation process preserved or even enhanced the complexity of questions, while reducing tabulation time by over 85 per cent. A diverse array of answers contained in boxes across myriad census forms and cards are compressed onto a single surface. The bandwidth of this surface is economized by encoding data into a system of numbers and columns wherein difference is marked through the punching of holes.

The technology soon took off. Hollerith's machine proved a boon for both his personal fortune and a growing American state desperate for information about its internal machinations and populace. Having convinced the US government to enter into a licence agreement (rather than a sale) and secured patents for both the machine and the specialized cards it required, Hollerith's company reaped considerable financial rewards. His Tabulating Machine Company would eventually be sold to notorious venture capitalist, war profiteer, and 'father of trusts', Charles Flint.[42] Flint folded Hollerith's company in with three other seemingly unrelated manufacturing firms he had acquired: the International Time Recording Company (which manufactured time clocks to record worker hours), the Computing Scale Company (which sold retail scales with pricing charts attached, as well as a line of meat and cheese slicers), and Bundy Manufacturing (which produced small key-actuated time clocks).[43] This assemblage was named the Computing-Tabulating-Recording company (CTR), and it gives us a glimpse into the peculiarities of *fin-de-siècle* American capitalism, as well as the increasing importance of proto-information communication technologies (ICTs) that were engineered to solve problems of data processing, storage, and transmission. CTRs machines were what Peters calls logistical media: devices and techniques that serve to abstract, order, organize, and compute human space-time.[44] Flint's combining of these three seemingly divergent realms of manufactory—time clocks, retail scales and slicers—testifies to the convergence of modern desires for compression, calculation, and circulation into logistical operations and media that involve the efficient movement of people, things, and data through spaces and times.

Eventually, Flint would lose a power struggle in his own company to the man he hired to manage it, Thomas J. Watson. Watson re-christened CTR as 'International Business Machines', a name change that would launch IBM towards its future as one of the most notorious corporations of the twentieth century. Watson and IBM were complicit in National Socialism, of this there is no doubt. He not only aggressively marketed the machines to the Reich, but also devoted significant resources to tailoring the punch card system so as to fulfil the Nazis' precise requirements.[45] The Hollerith machine was attractive to the Nazis not simply because of Watson and IBM's willingness to fine-tune the system according to their needs, nor only because it streamlined and automated processes of enumeration (thus speeding up the rate at which humans could be counted), but also because it was a system capable of calculations and rudimentary data analysis. As Black notes, Hollerith's system could do more than count people.

> It could rapidly perform the most tedious accounting functions for any enterprise: from freight bills for the New York Central Railroad to actuarial

> and financial records for Prudential Insurance. Most importantly, the Hollerith system not only counted, it produced analysis. The clanging contraption could calculate in a few weeks the results that a man previously spent years correlating.[46]

In Nazi usage, this involved

> the awesome sorting and resorting process for twenty-five categories of information cross-indexed and filtered through as many as thirty-five separate operations—by profession, by residence, by national origin, and a myriad of other traits. It was all to be correlated with information from land registers, community lists, and church authorities to create a fantastic new database. What emerged was a profession-by-profession, city-by-city, and indeed a block-by-block revelation of the Jewish presence.[47]

Cultural techniques of data collection, collation, and analysis converge to produce a classification system by which individuals can be listed, sorted, and moved as logistical objects. Extant techniques of listing, such as found in church registries, were accelerated by technical innovations like the IBM Hollerith punch card system, and by the enhanced profile, mandate, and resources available to institutions like the Reich Office of Statistics. It is important to emphasize, again, that the robust administrative apparatus these elements combined to create did not appear out of the ether. The Nazi census and IBM Hollerith punch card technology all had baked within them the logic of statistical methods developed during the nineteenth century. Such methods, as we have seen, rest on an epistemological framework derived from even older cultural techniques, the listing of double-entry bookkeeping. As a cultural technique that processes the 'ontic operations' that stand before modern facticity, the list is constitutive of Nazi statistical methods. The latter provided the enumerative and calculative infrastructure of the Nazis' attempted recalibration of the world in their image. The lists of the Nazi census not only embody the modern compulsion for compression, calculation and circulation, but also draw the distinctions and categories on which Nazi military and social policy was based. Such policy was increasingly fixated on the racial re-engineering of the population and the total logistical mobilization of the Reich. This epistemological framework, what I am calling the logistical orientation, materializes via a system of administration that involves census lists, statistics, and Hollerith punch-card technology.

The work of Aly and Roth and Black on statistics and Hollerith technology, respectively, foregrounds the modern technologies and techniques of paperwork that collect, compile, analyse, and disseminate so-called facts and so-called knowledge that serve to justify ideological or political positions. In so doing, these thinkers correct a blind spot in histories of the Third Reich that gloss over the role of administration. They help us to see what is ignored by histories that focus only on people and their ideas—whether they are 'great men' of the Nazi leadership or the functionaries of its bureaucracy. Through they do not use the term, both projects show the Nazi administration to be a matrix of cultural techniques that process the regime's foundational distinctions and categories. They focus not simply on the camps themselves, but show us the epistemological undergrowth that enables categories of 'undesirables' to be observed, policed, and administered before they arrive in camps. None of this occurs solely in the mind; without hands and paperwork, such a project could never have been attempted.

Though Aly and Roth discuss the 'rise of statistics' in the Third Reich, but they do not spend much time considering the much longer history of statistics as a field of knowledge. Statistics is not an invention of National Socialism. It had established a cachet of empirical veracity for at least one hundred years prior to Hitler's rise. The danger of ignoring this longer history is that statistical figures appear as either a) nothing more than tools to be bent to the whims of a dominant power, or b) determinant agents that will inevitably produce fascism. Neither of these positions is tenable. To dismiss only the *use* of statistics by the Nazis denies the crucial structuring function that systems of thought have on human affairs and the unfolding of history—a mistake made all too often in the analysis of technology in general. But to wholly renounce statistics as a field of knowledge and inquiry is to ignore that their collection and analysis have yielded unquestionably positive results for a great many human beings during the modern period. Perhaps the reason that this inadequate binary emerges out of Aly and Roth's important work is because they conflate too much under the categories of 'statistics' and 'administration'. They use the term statistics to describe a loose constellation of impulses, practices, techniques, and material forms that together comprise the Nazi administrative apparatus. But statistics is not simply the collection and compilation of information. It is far more than counting, as Hacking has shown and this analysis contends.[48] Statistics is a particular series of epistemological claims that rest on concepts and categories derived from distinctions processed by cultural techniques.

Black's work adopts a similarly broad concept of statistics, though his close analysis of the Hollerith machine does at least add a degree of granularity that helpfully shows us more about how statistical information is compiled and sorted. His analysis, however, also fails to ground the Hollerith machine in a longer historical trajectory. He offers a few preliminary remarks about the development of the Hollerith machine that predates the Nazis by about 50 years, but does not link the emergence of this machine within the broader intellectual *milieu* of modern thought. The latter is an essential component of the story because it was the intellectual and conceptual space within which the problems of 'statistics' emerged in the first place—what Hacking describes as the 'taming of chance.'[49] The modern nation—comprised of a citizenry (or at least a population), encompassing a spatial territory, operating according to new juridical-legal and economic orders—posed a fundamentally new set of administrative problems. Statistics was a modern, not necessarily fascistic, solution to these issues. The danger of missing this essentially modern dimension of Nazi administration is that texts such as *The Nazi Census* or *IBM and the Holocaust* will be read—against their authors' wishes—as framing Nazism as either a historical rupture that established a fundamentally new trajectory of 'post'-modern biopolitics or, worse, as simply an anomaly of history.

Circulation: Apparatuses of security

Kenneth C. Werbin intervenes in these debates to avoid such a reading. He shows explicitly that fields of knowledge like statistics and technologies like punch cards rely upon other 'critical support technologies,' like lists. For Werbin, the list *serves*. It is a 'political technology that serves juridical-legal mechanisms, disciplinary mechanisms, and apparatuses of security' by exercising 'force in the delimitation and policing of the movement of "threatening elements" circulating in uncertain *milieus*.'[50] Werbin integrates the list form into histories of the Reich by showing them to stand

> not only [as] a way of *seeing* and *doing* law, discipline, circulation, and security under the Third Reich, but also a way of operationalizing the fracture of threatening populations from general populations in the constitution or regimes of truth about the battles between 'us' and 'them'.[51] (p. 3, emphasis in original).

By delimiting 'threatening' or 'diseased' populations to be policed, lists for Werbin enable the Nazis to first conceive of and later attempt to bring into being a healthy German *Volk*.[52]

This was not simply a programme of classification. Werbin's analysis shows that the 'juridical-disciplinary mechanisms' and 'apparatuses of security' that comprised Nazi governmentality—underpinned by lists, statistics, and proto-computational punch cards—established what Foucault calls a *milieu* of circulation. Foucault develops the latter concept to describe the shift in modern power from sovereign, to disciplinary, to governmental.[53] The seventeenth- and eighteenth-century administration of towns is paradigmatic of this shift, an expression of the 'taming of chance,' given its tendency towards the reduction of uncertainty and unpredictability. With an infinite and indefinite series of events (plagues, famines, attacks, etc.) and an indefinite series of elements both fixed (homes, roads, city walls, etc.) and mobile (people, transportation technologies, goods, etc.), towns began to be conceived as delineated spaces within which activity needed to be controlled. This activity involved the circulation, convergence, divergence, etc. of elements. The reduction of uncertainty became the object and goal of state power. 'Indeed, in the eighteenth century what emerged for the town was a need to organize circulation, not to enclose and prohibit spaces as sovereignty had long done through juridical-legal and disciplinary mechanisms, but rather to *let things happen,* to encourage "good" circulation, and discourage "bad".'[54] Whereas sovereign power was externally wielded from above, imminent in the king's blade, and disciplinary power was internalized by self-regulating subjects haunted by the panoptic gaze, we see here with governmentality—and its attended conceptual infrastructure (security, territory, population)—a different kind of power articulation. '[S]*ecurity* began to attempt to install a *milieu* of circulation, in which elements and events (as well as probable elements and events) are regulated "within a multivalent and transformable framework" that raised probabilities and populations as the major problem of government.'[55] Governmentality is about establishing spaces or *milieux* within which things can happen. It is productive power, rather than oppressive. A space is marked out within which uncertain elements can circulate. The space then needs to be administered—observed, policed, and ordered—by ways of seeing and doing that can reduce uncertainty. The fact of 'uncertainty' itself is a function of shifts in the modern period—from determinate to indeterminate, eternal Gods to precarious facts. Thus emerged statistics, induction, and calculation as new conjunctions of taming chance, solutions to the new problems of the governmental state.

Werbin's analysis shows that forms such as lists play a crucial role in delineating and administering *milieux* of circulation that comprise 'apparatuses of security' in governmental societies. It is within such a *milieu* that state power is produced and articulated. State power establishes the borders of the field and the 'rules of the game' before policing those rules vigorously. Lists enact *caesurae* within such *milieux* that delineate 'healthy' vs. 'diseased' elements of the population, which becomes under National Socialism conceived as a biological entity that requires maintenance and surgery.

> The list served a Nazi *milieu* of circulation where the *naming* and *policing* of elements of abnormal populations, Jews and other, was installed as a way of *seeing* and *doing* a 'healthy' cultural body, in which elements circulate freely, but are distributed and regulated by apparatuses of security.[56]

This effect is obvious in the words of Willy Heidinger, founder and major shareholder of *Deutsche Hollerith-Maschinen Gesellschaft mbH* (*Dehomag*), in 1934.

> The physician examines the human body and determines whether all organs are working to the benefit of the entire organism [...] We [*Dehomag*] are very much like the physician, in that we dissect, cell by cell, the German cultural body. We report every individual characteristic on a little card. These are not dead cards, quite the contrary, they prove later on that they come to life when the cards are sorted at a rate of 25,000 per hour according to certain characteristics. These characteristics are grouped like the organs of our cultural body, and they will be calculated and determined with the help of our tabulating machine. We are proud that we may assist in such a task, a task that provides our nation's physician [Hitler] with the material he needs for his examinations.[57]

But *caesurae* between healthy || diseased are not simply about establishing rules of permission or prohibition, such as they might have done in sovereign or disciplinary societies. In a governmental society, they are about optimization and efficiency, those modern virtues discussed at the outset of this chapter. According to Nazi ideology and policy, a healthy population was not simply one that was racially 'purified', but also one that was operating at a maximum productive capacity. Human labour and vitality in undesirable or 'diseased' elements of the *Volk* were not simply discarded, but were *mobilized* until their productive power was used up. This programme worked Jews to death. General Oswald Pohl, head of the SS Economics Office that administered all concentration and work camps, created the 'Extermination by Labour' programme on the basis that 'expeditiously gassing Jews deprived the Reich of an important resource.'[58] 'Only after outliving their usefulness would they be deported to death camps for gassing.'[59] Even the racist, dehumanizing ideology of National Socialism was secondary to productive capacity. The thousand-year Reich could only be conjured through a total mobilization of all resources, human and non-human.

> Studies conducted by the Department of the People's (*Volks*) Health at the *Deutsche Arbeitsfront* deserve special recognition, as the questionnaires they developed serve to ensure the health and productivity of the present generation and the productivity of every individual into old age in working at the highest level of efficiency for the well-being of the ethnic German community (*Volksgemeinschaft*).[60]

Undesirable populations were isolated, observed, policed, and mobilized through cultural techniques such as listing, technologies such as the Hollerith machine, and attendant knowledge structures such as statistics. We therefore see that core values at the heart of Nationalism Socialism included efficiency and productivity, and all national policies of security and governmentality were engineered to facilitate effective and efficient circulation in this *milieu*. As Werbin shows, lists are a crucial constitutive form of this security apparatus.

I have shown so far in Chapters three and four that the Nazi administrative apparatus, historically overlooked by most Holocaust and World War II scholarship, was a hyperbolic extension of an epistemological framework that can be traced back to early modern practices such as double-entry bookkeeping. The Nazi census must be conceived as an essentially modern event. This event embodied the modern tendencies to privilege compression, calculation, and circulation, which find expression in valuing speed, rationality, efficiency, and order above all else. Lists are implicated in each of these practices: they compress language and communication away from ornate rhetoric and towards *brevitas*. Alongside Hollerith punch cards, lists accelerated and made more efficient processes of enumeration. In statistics and other calculative sciences, lists collect and structure the raw data to be calculated. Lists help establish modern *milieux* of circulation wherein probabilities and calculations are developed in order to 'let things happen'. In each case, listing is a cultural technique that processes distinctions and inscribes borders upon which concepts and practices are built.

Logistical orientation

The word 'logistics' has appeared frequently throughout this chapter and it is now worth spending some time clarifying my use of the term. I believe it to be a more accurate descriptor of modern processes that are variously described as 'administrative', 'bureaucratic', or 'informational'. I have used these other terms sporadically above, following other thinkers, but, in truth, find each of them unwieldy and inadequate. 'Information' has become a bloated term that says too many things to too many people.[61] 'Administration' lacks the precision required to describe the way that measurement, institutional demands, and human social activity intersect in modern institutions. 'Bureaucracy', meanwhile, has become a convenient bogeyman invoked to denounce any institutional encounter, particularly those involving public regulation and oversight. Throughout the twentieth century, these terms increasingly folded in on one another to the point that they are now interchangeable. And though each word possesses its own history and descriptive or conceptual strengths, individually each fails to describe the complex relations *between* them. Relations between administration, bureaucracy, and information arise in the name of logistics. What is contemporary administration, whether in institutional bureaucracies or individual offices, other than the facilitation of logistical operations, i.e. the calculation of the most efficient means by which to move people, things, and data through space and time? 'Logistics' also captures the interrelationships between calculation, circulation, and compression. Rationality in calculation + efficiency in compression + speed in circulation are the *modus operandi* of logistical modernity. More operations in less time enhances the extraction of surplus value for the corporation, the entrenchment of the authority to rule for the state, and everything that happens in between these two paradigmatic modern institutions. More operations in less time is about making things happen and getting things done, or, logistics.

Recall that John Durham Peters uses 'logistical' to describe certain media technologies that serve to abstract, order, organize, and compute 'basic coordinates of time and space.'[62] Logistical media 'stand alongside more obvious media that overcome time (recording) and space (transmission) and produce messages and text' and 'establish the zero points of orientation, the convergence of the x and y axes. They often seem neutral and given—something which gives them extraordinary power.'[63] The above case studies—from double-entry ledgers, to lists of the Nazi census, Hollerith punch cards, and modern statistical techniques—are all logistical. They are the forms, formats, and protocols by which people and objects are compressed, calculated, and made to circulate. They establish zero points of orientation. Encoded in each are cultural techniques like listing.

Having cleared out some of the terminological undergrowth, I can now discuss more specifically the modern, logistical orientation to the world that reduces its contents, living and non, to a standing-reserve of material to be ordered, manipulated, and exploited according to human desires, problems, and objectives. My understanding is derived from Martin Heidegger's late work. Though he never uses the term, Heidegger's meditations on technology offer a robust conceptual vocabulary for describing logistical modernity. The following passage, drawn from the minutes of a Nazi party meeting held on 6 September 1939, demonstrates the increasing convergence of calculation, compression, and circulation.

> Both the Reich Ministry of Agriculture and the Ministry of Farm Workers stressed the need to speed up the collecting of data for the residential populations according to sex and ages of children and older youth, as they will need estimates of future food production. Both the Ministry of the Interior and the *Reichsführer-SS* argued that it was extremely important to complete lists of names of foreigners, members with non-German ethnic backgrounds, Jews, and mixed Jews [...] After the completion of these items, the High Command of the German Military and the Reich Ministry of Labor argued that the next step should be the completion of the vocation census (vocations in connection with the social structure).[64]

Future food production depended on census data about population distribution and composition, number and location of foreigners and Jews, and identification of vocational data. These items are marshalled in the service of a desire for the total mobilization of the Reich's resources. The latter comprised not simply natural resources or material wealth but also the Reich population, made up of heterogeneous objects called persons. Nazi statisticians, as we have seen, wished to use statistics to obtain a comprehensive numerical picture with which to visualize and optimize the Reich. Their goal was to calculate maximum productive capacities to feed, house, and arm the war effort; to compress transport times, administrative protocols, and communication backlogs; to circulate things, people and words at the rate required by the project of building a thousand year Reich. This was a project primarily of logistics, of re-calibrating the spaces, times, terrains, populations, networks, and history of Germany.

Stuart Elden shows that the Nazis had a specific concept for this project, *Gleichschaltung*. The concept is usually translated as 'co-ordination' or 'synchronization', but 'has a sense of unification, of bringing into line or the elimination of opposition. Literally the word means 'same wiring' or 'connection', the bringing of things under a common measure, subordination.'[65] *Gleichschaltung*, for instance, was the conceptual grounding of two

1933 laws aimed at reconfiguring German state institutions to become more homogenous. Regional governments (*Länder*) were remade in the image of the *Reichstag*, effectively neutering regional authority and further centralizing power in the capital. Universities were also *gleichgeschaltet*, with rectors being re-branded as 'Führers of the Universities'. Innumerable other organizations were similarly remade, including associations of lawyers and doctors.[66] Hollerith machines and their input-output lists provided the technical and documentary infrastructure by which social, economic, and administrative life in Germany was 'synchronized',

> *Gleichschaltung* [...] demanded that endless accountings be submitted regularly to government bureaus, Nazified trade associations, and statistical agencies. *Kommissars* and government regulations required companies to install Hollerith machines to ensure prompt, uniform, up-to-the-minute reports that could be reprocessed and further tabulated.[67]

In Elden's reading, *Gleichschaltung* emerges not simply from the idea that humans, groups, and organizations can be understood as either same or different, but in the notion that such difference can be rendered the same, i.e. eradicated.[68] *Gleichschaltung* is a concept that implicitly assumes that difference can be re-engineered, re-calibrated, altered and subjugated to sameness. Difference is not to be disciplined, or even policed, but is to be *made same:* the social order as an engineering problem.

Gleichschaltung was mobilized alongside more familiar concepts like *Lebensraum* ('living-space') and *Blut und Boden* ('blood and soil') so as to effect this 'same-wiring' or recalibration of the Reich. Elden characterizes this project as an expression of a 'politics of calculation' underpinning Nazism. Heidegger's late-career meditations on the question concerning technology attempted to respond to this historical and epistemological event. I build on these insights to develop a sketch of Nazism as a radical expression of an orientation that was not simply about calculation but logistics.[69]

Bestand

Heidegger develops several concepts to address the famous 'question concerning technology.' Because this chapter is primarily descriptive and diagnostic, I make use here only of Heidegger's diagnostic concepts (most notably *Bestand, Gestell,* and *Gleichschaltung*). I am bracketing, for now, the more generative discussion of the 'saving power' that comes after Heidegger's diagnosis. This dimension of his nest of concepts concerning technology will be explored at length in Chapter six's exploration of lists in art and poetry.

The most well-known of the diagnostic concepts is *das Gestell* ('the frame'), which describes the transformative encounter between modern 'man' and what Heidegger calls 'global technology'. The philosopher conceives of this encounter as one in which man is held in 'the sway of *Gestell*':

> I see the essence of technology in what I call the frame [*das Ge-stell* ...] The frame holding sway means: the essence of man is framed, claimed and challenged by a power which manifests itself in the essence of technology, a power which man himself does not control.[70]

We are structured and delineated by the 'frame' of technology, which is a kind of ontological grid that stands behind, within, underneath, around, and *as* the world. There is no outside of technology; the modern world, and man's relationship to it, is essentially technical. This is an understanding of technology that moves away from the trite, hubristic notion that technology is a tool that can ever be mastered by human beings. The scandal of modernity and its technical society, according to Heidegger, is that man elevates himself to the role of God. Blind to *das Gestell*, he has sought to conquer the world, to bring forth a world under a common measure that is controllable, manipulable, calculable.

Heidegger describes this orientation with the concept of *Bestand,* usually translated as 'standing-reserve'. *Bestand* describes the reduction of the world to a standing reserve of materials, resources, and energy to be extracted, mobilized, utilized, brought into order, synchronized, coordinated and ultimately annihilated. The world is subordinated to man and his tools. Any connection to the world as dwelling—as rooted in tradition and home—has been severed. 'Everything is functioning. This is exactly what is so uncanny, that everything is functioning and that the functioning drives us more and more to even further functioning, and that technology tears men loose from the earth and uproots them.'[71] Such an understanding of the modern technical world was not unique to Heidegger. Contemporaries such as Ernst Jünger and Oswald Spengler, for instance, characterized technologization as a Faustian phenomenon by which 'man turned nature into a stockpile of raw materials whose only value lay in their usefulness for his titanic purposes.'[72] The world as *Bestand* is brought forth through the progressive subjugation of the world and its beings to systems of order and movement.

Lived, phenomenological experience is abstracted away. To live in the sway of *Gestell* is to misapprehend the world as *Bestand*.

By the mid-1930s, Heidegger had come to conceive of Nazism, a movement that previously received his enthusiastic support, as the limit case of *Machenschaft* ('machination'). This concept predates both *Gestell* and *Bestand*. 'For Heidegger, machination depends upon a particular notion of metaphysics, a particular casting of being, that is, to be is to be calculable.'[73] The shift towards machination is a long one, dating back to the scientific changes of the sixteenth and seventeenth centuries, which Heidegger traces through figures such as Galileo, Descartes, Leibniz, and Newton.[74] Elden reads Heidegger to understand that

> there are three ways in which the question of being—his key concern—has come to be forgotten in the modern age. These are calculation [*die Berechnung*], massiveness [*Massenhaften*] and acceleration [*die Schnelligkeit*]. In all three we see interlinked themes of measure [*Maß*], and calculative thinking, grounded on a particular way of reckoning [*Rechnung*], based on number and the celebrative of quantitative enhancement.[75]

National Socialism is the limit case of modernity's tendency towards calculation, massiveness, and acceleration, because it recasts and attempts to re-engineer the world in such terms. These modern tendencies violently converge in and as the Nazi logistical orientation, which is a way of reckoning that reduces the world to *Bestand*.

Logistics is both solution to, and product of, the massification of spaces and scales by modern technical constructions. One must overcome the challenges of moving people and things through a massive spatial territory by improving logistical operations. At the same time, enhanced logistical operations contribute to and enable us to construct projects of a scale previously impossible. Logistics involves the constant calculation of optimum rates of circulation and transport. These are problems of engineering spaces and times. Optimization tends towards acceleration and compression. Put another way, the Nazi desire for the re-calibration of the world, *Gleichschaltung*, is a logistical problem. Compression, calculation, and circulation are applied as solutions to this problem. Elden's careful reading of Heidegger brings the ontological conditions of Nazism to the surface: calculation, massiveness, acceleration, measure, number, quantification. These resonate strongly with the values and tendencies of modern administration explored above: compression, calculation, circulation, as made manifest in lists, statistics, and technologies like the Hollerith punch card.

Gleichschaltung is an expression of a logistical orientation. I propose this new category precisely because it ties together each of the three above categories, thus moving beyond Aly's and Roth's emphasis on Nazi efficiency (i.e. compression), Elden's focus on the 'politics of calculation', or Werbin's on circulation. Focusing only on efficiency conflates the actual mechanisms by which administrative work was sped up (there is little in *The Nazi Census* on the Hollerith machine, for instance), and glosses over work that argues claims to Nazi efficiency are often exaggerated.[76] The desire for speed and efficiency is different than its actualization. To focus, on the other hand, only on calculation implies the latter to be an end rather than a means. Such a misdiagnosis misses that techniques of calculation were deployed alongside other techniques of order, circulation, and compression to create a vision of the world as something not just to be calculated but re-wired. In this re-wiring, Jews and other undesirables did not circulate. Their mobilization was from point A, a home or ghetto, to point B, a camp, where they were made to produce, labour, and die so as to optimize circulation in the Reich from which they were excluded. They were literally walled off from the *milieu* of circulation—geographically by the fences of the camps, on paper by the borders of deportation or statistical lists. To wall off such external spaces and subject positions became a thinkable proposition in the context of a logistical approach to the world that viewed it as *Bestand*: a standing-reserve of resources, objects, forces, etc. to be ordered and manipulated according to the desires and objectives of 'man'. In this way, the administrative apparatus of National Socialism is the apotheosis of a modern trajectory towards logistics—total mobilization, everything calculable, pure speed, *Bestand* in motion.[77] This trajectory begins with the technique by which fifteenth century Italian merchants compressed their inventories and transactions, calculated their balances, and ensured the circulation of their goods and services: double-entry bookkeeping.

Conclusion

In Chapters three and four, I have sought to show how lists function as a cultural technique of logistical modernity. This technique is encoded in various epistemological frameworks, administrative formats, and media-technological systems that achieve hegemony in the modern period. My argument is not that lists are essentially evil, nor that they are a neutral form made evil by the thoughts and deeds of humans. More simply, listing is a technique by which orientations to the world congeal as practices, systems, and institutions. Lists process distinctions upon which concepts are built. They materialize assumptions and enable categorizations that follow. In this way, lists are constitutive, creating categories and subject positions for people and things, the easier to be calculated and circulated: Jew vs. non-Jew; Citizen of the Reich vs. Undesirable. Lists also facilitate; policy directives are enacted through them. The 'truthful' status of Nazi lists grants them authority as 'proof' of some fact. Their economy of presentation accelerates the rate at which lists can communicate such facts. Once extant, they often acquire a momentum that is difficult to slow down.[78]

By analysing historical events at the level of cultural techniques, we are able to see the systems and vectors that precede the distinctions and categories upon which ideologies, policies, and worldviews are founded. This chapter built on research that addresses a tendency in holocaust and Nazi scholarship to gloss over the administrative dimensions of Nazi governmentality. Going further than Aly and Roth, Black, and Werbin, I have sought also to show that listing is a cultural technique embedded in a much longer trajectory of modernity. Foucault schematizes this trajectory as a series of shifts: from societies of justice and sovereign power, to those of administration and disciplinary power, to those of circulation and governmental power. I have shown how such shifts are enacted at the level of paperwork, wherein the modern compulsions for compression (rationality), calculation (number), and circulation (speed) are articulated in new fields of knowledge, such as statistics, and new technologies like the Hollerith machine, which together establish a *milieu* of circulation. Within and before each of these stands the humble list form. Finally, this chapter has shown the Nazi security apparatus to be a nightmarish expression of what I call a logistical orientation, in which the modern predilections for compression, calculation, and circulation converge. I have proposed logistics as a frame by which to understand modern technics because it encapsulates the dynamic interactions between these three categories.

Looking at the list, and the technologies and fields of knowledge with which it is intimately related, opens up a window through which to view an entire ecology of administration and counting. This ecology tells us not only about how the holocaust was made to happen but also how it rests on techniques, desires, and systems of thought that achieved hegemony from about 1500. Analysing Nazi administration at the level of cultural techniques and formats allows us to see how Horkheimer's and Adorno's 'administered society' actually operated. Rather than a purely ideological or philosophical program, Nazism is a limit case of a particular way of approaching the world that fetishizes data and information. The latter is a function of what Heidegger described with his late works on the 'essence' of modern technology.

But the logistical orientation did not disappear after the Russians took Berlin. It was not wiped away with Hiroshima and Nagasaki. In fact, the strength and influence of this orientation only accelerated and expanded—as logistical operations usually do—in the late twentieth and early twenty-first centuries. This will be the topic of Chapter five.

5. Logistics: Listicles, Algorithms, and Real Time

'Times are more interesting than people.'[1]
– Honoré de Balzac

In 2006, Jonah Peretti, technology director and co-founder of *Huffington Post*, started a modest lab for experimenting with data analytics and content circulation on the web. He was interested in understanding 'viral culture': the nebulous processes by which certain stories would explode online, moving rapidly and unpredictably across then-ascendant social media platforms and blogs. The project was a logical extension of Peretti's earlier experiments with digital networks. From early in his career he had an interest in, and proclivity for, understanding the spread of viral content. A 2001 e-mail exchange between Peretti and Nike over his request to have custom sneakers emblazoned with the word 'sweatshop' was a high-profile early example of something from the web 'going viral'. A few years later, Peretti pioneered the monthly 'Contagious Festival' at *Huffington Post*, an open competition with simple rules for entrants: create a website that garners the most views in a month, win $2500.[2] Of these early days, he says, 'I got really fascinated by the idea of people sharing things with each other and thought it could be a bigger network than a social media network.'[3] Peretti set the project up as a lab in a basement in New York's Chinatown and gave it the name BuzzFeed.

BuzzFeed appears, superficially, to be a cultural phenomenon quite different from the techniques of population administration and measure discussed in Chapters three and four. I will show in this chapter that BuzzFeed listicles, and the algorithms that generate them, are expressions of a similarly logistical orientation to the world, which approaches it as a standing-reserve of material to be marshalled towards human ends. Listicles may get all the headlines (especially those heralding the scorn of cultural critics), but within the BuzzFeed platform are operational lists geared towards data mining and computational processes that employ the same techniques of compression, calculation, and circulation observed in Chapter three and four. The list form is a heuristic that allows us to see the logistical and infrastructural operations of digital culture that are typically hidden from view; it enables comparison between listing activities in contemporary networks and those in the trajectory of the modern 'thinking cap' sketched out above. And yet, tracing the list through digital networks will land us in surprising territory. As we will see, operative, time-based lists in digital computation have a family resemblance to ancient techniques of relaying data about the past, such as annals and chronicles. These poetics, however surprising, are an essential part of the tale. To properly understand them, however, we must first look to lists in computation and the broader cultural trends, like BuzzFeed, they structure.

Lists and computation[4]

The logic of the list is integral to the world of computing in data structures such as arrays, queues, databases, and the stack.[5] Adam defines 'List' in computing as 'a data structure that is an ordered group of entities.'[6] This structure can be either static or dynamic. Static structures allow only observation and enumeration of elements, dynamic allow for manipulation – the insertion, replacement, or deletion of elements. The programming language Lisp (short for List Processor) is the second oldest high-level computing language still in use and is an instructive example. The constitutive data structure of Lisp is, of course, the list, out of which almost all other entities are constructed.[7] Echoing Vismann's description of algorithmic (paper) file-notes, Adam points out a double function of lists in Lisp that both program and store data: a list is sent first as a command, which is processed via the list form. After this, the data sent and processed stands as a listed record of what has occurred: transmission, processing, storage.[8]

Lisp accommodates the mixing of data types (a data type is any type of thing) within the same list. In Lisp, 'a variable can hold values of any type and the values carry type information that can be used to check types at runtime.'[9] That is, you may enumerate within the same list trees, cars, a cat, and bandages without declaring them to be any single type:

(7 TREES 4 CARS 1 CAT 2 BANDAGES)

Lisp does not require a programmer to declare data types in advance according to any guiding principle in order for them to be processed. This runs contra to programming languages such as C++ and Java. The latter require at the outset a declaration regarding what type of object each variable can hold (and if an object does not match the value assigned it cannot be processed). Because they do not require a human programmer to establish their criteria, lists in Lisp are 'self-typing' and thereby inherently more flexible.

Lisp arises from a different a priori than most conventional programming languages. Rory Solomon shows that Lisp was designed around the principles of Alonzo Church's Lambda calculus, rather than those of Alan Turing's famous machine (itself based on Charles Babbage's 'Difference Engine'). Turing's machine and Babbage's engine rest on an IF/THEN logic of conditional branching, which is 'the construct within a computer program that allows it to alter its flow of instructions based on the result of some other calculation.'[10] Solomon quotes Kittler describing conditional branching: 'IF a preprogrammed condition is missing, data processing continues according to the conventions of numbered commands, but IF somewhere an intermediate result fulfils the condition, THEN the program itself determines successive commands, that is, its future.'[11] In contrast, the Lambda calculus 'is based purely on the ability to define functions (subroutines) and for these functions to be able to call each other in an arbitrarily nested or recursive way.'[12] Solomon, a computer programmer, argues that both the Turing machine and the Lambda calculus are equally powerful though they implement conditional branching in different ways. Lisp, using Lambda calculus principles, implements recursively callable functions using a structure called a functional call stack. 'Using this structure, the computer stores the state of the current function being evaluated, and if that function calls another function, it will 'push' everything down and repeat, so that when the latter function returns, it will 'pop' off the top and return back to the prior function.'[13] A functional call stack is a flexible, temporally operational list of functions.[14] The list form provides the required flexibility for the push-pop processes of recursively callable functions; it provides the 'nest' within which functions can call one another. Rather than a series of function checks and processes set out in advance by a programmer (IF x occurs THEN y follows; IF x does not occur THEN z, etc.), functions in Lisp recursively call each other and move up and down the list as required. The flexibility inherent in the list form ensures this freedom of movement.

Furthermore, lists provide a structure that allows Lisp to process symbols rather than simply numbers. Lisp was developed by American computer and cognitive scientist John McCarthy, one of the most influential figures in developing 'artificial intelligence' (AI) research into a coherent discipline and even a policy initiative (he coined the term in 1955). According to McCarthy, developing a programming language capable of moving beyond 'number crunching' and towards reasoning about the world would involve

> representing information about the world by sentences in a suitable formal language and a reasoning program that would decide what to do by making logical inferences. Representing sentences by list structure seemed appropriate—it still is—and a list processing language also seemed appropriate for programming the operations involved in deduction—it still is.[15]

The list has proven attractive to McCarthy and other AI researchers because it provides an elegant data structure, not limited by pre-existing abilities, that can both absorb and potentially reason through (rather than simply process), a significant amount of data. As a 'programmable programming language', Lisp very easily absorbs paradigm shifts in programming and will likely continue to do so.[16] Because its constitutive form is adaptable and can create its own processes, Lisp has survived epistemic shifts in programming better than other languages.

This brief overview of Lisp is meant to show one example in which the list is formally operative in computation. Others can be found, such as ArrayLists in Java or linked lists in C (similarly open-ended data structures). 'List' was one of the thirteen original HTML tags designed by Tim Berners-Lee, and the form has always been important to the Graphic User Interface. Early programmers will no doubt recall 'program listing' printouts that stored pages upon pages of line-by-line code on fan-fold paper.[17] Algorithms, essential operators in digital computation, are finite lists of instructions that enable the calculation of functions. An algorithm without a database to operate on is useless, as is a database without an algorithm to extract and structure its data. 'The possibility of abstracting useful knowledge from the end user of a website, for example, is dependent upon the extent to which data is structured.'[18] Lists give form to such protocols, and in these algorithmic capacities the list is revealed as a building block of computation. As Ernst describes, '[c]omputer programming, the cultural force of today, is non-narrative; its algorithmic forms of writing–alternative forms of minimal, serial time-writing [...] are close to the paradigm of computing itself.'[19] Computational lists are present-based processing forms, lists of 'etcetera' that are inherently open, flexible and able to operate in real time as required by the computational networks of which they are a part. In this way, they perform the operations and calculations of logistical modernity, which has cultural outgrowths to which we will now turn.

Logistics, again

The concept of logistics is rooted in the military imaginary, war being the mother of technical invention—at least, according to thinkers like Kittler, Virilio, and Heraclitus. It is generally accepted that the term logistics comes to us from the French *logistique*, a late nineteenth-century word used to describe the 'art of moving and quartering troops,'[20] though the activities involved have occurred since at least antiquity.[21] But 'logistics' as a concept has spread rapidly over the last sixty years as technical solutions to military problems were imported into such civilian spheres as economics and transportation.[22] The migration of the term logistics from the military to civilian realms runs concomitant to a change in what I have been calling the logistical orientation: from an unspoken logic underpinning certain techniques, practices, and machines to a fully articulated concept and field called 'Logistics'. Business practices and literature have zeroed in on this concept; efficiency and efficacy in logistics have become perhaps the supreme desiderata in twenty-first century capitalism. Unsurprisingly, an entire field of study focused on logistics and supply chain management has sprung up to provide companies with a competitive edge. The Council of Supply Chain Management (née Logistics Management) proposes the following definition:

> Logistics: The process of planning, implementing, and controlling procedures for the efficient and effective transportation and storage of goods including services, and related information, from the point of origin to the point of consumption for the purpose of conforming to customer requirements. This definition includes inbound, outbound, internal, and external movements.[23]

Business owners and operators are encouraged to streamline and compress the flow of goods and information within logistical channels. Such compression involves the calculation of best practices—standard operating procedures (SOP)—that optimize the movement of material, goods, and labour. Such definitions, as used by the Business and Management subfield of Supply Chain and Logistics Studies,[24] specify the extent to which logistical operations involve a complex network of heterogeneous actors and forces that establish parameters within which things can happen.

Logistical procedures and operations establish what Foucault calls a *milieu* of circulation. 'Logistics' describes not circulation itself, but rather the setting of the 'rules of the game' via fields of study, practice, and policy that establish parameters within which circulation can occur. Contemporary logistics is therefore not simply a problem of economy but of governmentality. Logistics is governmental in its logic of circulation, with 'economy' and 'security' as basic categories.[25] This logic is not new, as we have seen. Recall that Foucault sees governmentality beginning in earnest after Machiavelli as

> a completely different problem that is no longer that of fixing and demarcating the territory, but of allowing circulations to take place, of controlling them, sifting the good and the bad, ensuring that things are always in movement, constantly moving around, continually going from one point to another, but in such a way that the inherent dangers of this circulation are cancelled out.[26]

Where once power was about the delineation of territory, now it is about establishing parameters within which people, things, and data can circulate. For what purposes this circulation occurs is irrelevant. What matters is that it occurs; 'security' is the maintenance of the equilibrium required for efficient and effective circulation. With the onset of digital technology, the speed and scale of networks of circulation exceed earlier analog networks by a massive degree. From high-frequency trading to the just-in-time logic of global supply chains, new spaces and times have emerged with corresponding techniques of order and metrics of measure that we are only beginning to understand.[27] Lists give form to protocols and data structures that enable these logistical operations.

Human subjects, once administered by the written formats discussed in Chapters three and four, become users administered by digital algorithms and code. In both cases, lists structure the administration of life. An obvious example is the ubiquity of 'no-fly' and even 'kill' lists in the wake of 9/11 and its subsequent, ongoing 'war on terror'. These lists emerge from data-mining techniques that target certain persons with 'suspicious' patterns of movement and communication. Such patterns are triangulated using locative data from mobile media and other signals intelligence, e.g. IP addresses. Algorithms, designed to identify and track informational behaviour deemed suspicious or unlawful by the state, parse troves of metadata collected by surveillance operations such as National Security Agency's (NSA) top-secret PRISM program (famously leaked by Edward Snowden in 2013).[28] Information about the criteria used to define 'suspicious' behaviour and patterns has been so far almost impossible to acquire. Instead, the public receives clichés such as US State Department legal advisor Harold Koh's claim that '[o]ur procedures and practices for identifying lawful targets are extremely robust, and advanced technologies have helped to make our targeting even more precise.'[29] It is clear that specific users emerge as 'targets' when they have made one too many 'suspicious' moves in the course of their online and mobile behaviour. A coherent 'pattern-of-life' analysis emerges.[30] According to NSA whistleblower Russell Tice,

> This is garnered from algorithms that have been put together to try to just dream up scenarios that might be [...] associated with how a terrorist could operate. If someone just talked about the daily news and mentioned something about the Middle East, they could easily be brought to the forefront of having that little flag put by their name that says potential terrorist [...] Then all the sudden [*sic*] it marries up with something else 10 years from now, and they get put on a no-fly list [without having] a clue why.[31]

These techniques have only ramped up in recent years, as shown in recent studies on drone warfare by Chamayou, and by journalists at *The Intercept_* on an intelligence leak regarding the United States drone program ('The Drone Papers').[32]

As with Nazi census lists outlined in Chapter three, algorithmic pattern analysis produces lists that inscribe categories on people: 'go' or 'no go' to fly; 'citizen' or 'terrorist'; 'civilian' or 'target'. These facilitate 'healthy' logistical circulation by identifying and targeting those segments of the population deemed 'unhealthy' or 'diseased' with the goal of immobilizing and removing them from circulation. Such techniques, according to Werbin, operationalize 'us' versus 'them' dichotomies that underpin and authorize the war on terror.[33] The list appears as both the surface expression of this logic, i.e. no-fly lists that are distributed to security personnel as protocols for policing, and also in the software infrastructure that enables this activity to proceed: algorithms (finite sets of instructions) and databases (listed units of collected metadata). It falls beyond the scope of this chapter, but my hope is that readers will see that cultural-technical analysis of the kind pursued here may facilitate more precise and forceful policy arguments about how to curtail watch-listing and other invasive state surveillance practices.

Such practices occur not only in state governance but also in cultural and corporate commercial sectors.[34] The year 2013 showed just how indiscernible the two realms actually are. Edward Snowden's leak of details regarding NSA's PRISM program brought to light the collusion of Silicon Valley giants like Facebook, Microsoft, Google, Apple, AOL, Yahoo! and others with the intelligence arm of the American state.[35] The program involved Silicon Valley's acquiescence to NSA requests that these companies build in secret 'back doors' by which the NSA could mine user data without knowledge or consent of users. The scale of this and other projects is still very much an open question and the political and philosophical stakes of Big Data surveillance are only beginning to emerge.[36]

The cultural story of Big Data is now familiar. With social media and so-called Web 2.0, a staggering amount of user data is created, tracked, mined, analysed, bought, sold, and hoarded. IBM estimates that users create 2.5 quintillion bytes of data per day.[37] According to Facebook in 2013,

> [e]very day, there are more than 4.75 billion content items shared on Facebook (including status updates, wall posts, photos, videos and comments), more than 4.5 billion 'Likes', and more than 10 billion messages sent. More than 250 billion photos have been uploaded to Facebook, and more than 350 million photos are uploaded every day on average.[38]

These figures have only increased. While systems that observe, measure, identify, track, and archive persons are not new—they have been an essential part of modernity, as demonstrated in Chapter three—the sheer *amount* of data generated about the modern subject, and the range of tools available to amalgamate and analyse it, are unprecedented in history. A new cadre of intermediaries has developed software and programming that can harvest, analyse, and distribute such data for profit: Big Data as Big Business. Data generated by users in their engagements with various digital devices, our 'digital footprints', pass after collection through a series of algorithms and databases that output statistics and metrics around which commercial producers reconfigure their operations. Not only are public relations and marketing efforts shaped in response to Big Data analytics, but also cycles of production and circulation (recall the famous example of a Minnesota teenager whose purchasing behaviour led Target's marketing algorithm to guess, correctly, that she was pregnant—much to her parents' surprise and her dismay). Our behaviour as consumers is continuously marshalled by computational processes that we cannot see and often do not understand. Lists of Amazon or Netflix recommendations arise out of one's browsing, viewing, or purchasing history; each search, click, and order is tracked. Proprietary, black-boxed algorithms usher us towards certain products but not others. Consumers, meanwhile, seem only too happy to sacrifice their anonymity, privacy, and choice in the name of convenience.

> Users embrace the world and start making lists. We are honored to be invited by the Machine to submit our opinions and preferences. How do you categorize yourself? There must at least be some 'good-value' content out there as a reward, after we feed the databases [...] What is fascinating is not so much the flux of opinions, as Jean Baudrillard once described democracy in the media age, but the ability to indulge in similarity with others. We are invited to create reading lists, rank music, and evaluate the products we consumed. User bees working for queen Google.[39]

These remarks from Geert Lovink testify to the connection between the list mania of online environments and big data mining techniques. Nowhere is this relationship more evident than with the web media corporation BuzzFeed.

BuzzFeed, listicles, and data

BuzzFeed describes itself as 'a cross-platform, global network for news and entertainment that generates seven billion views each month' and that 'creates and distributes content for a global audience and utilizes proprietary technology to continuously test, learn and optimize.'[40] The company's corporate structure and platform differs significantly from social media giants like Facebook and Twitter. For all the hype about how it has 'disrupted' the web, BuzzFeed has a very traditional organizational structure. It is vertically integrated in the same way studios were in the classical Hollywood system of the early-mid twentieth century. There, each studio owned and controlled virtually every aspect of the culture supply chain: studio space, props and equipment, rigidly-contracted labour, distribution networks, exhibition houses, marketing and legal departments, and so on. BuzzFeed has adopted and updated this organizational model. It keeps everything from software development and data analysis to content creation, video production, and advertising in-house. The company employs over 1200 developers, editors, data scientists, and content creators across 12 international offices: journalists, cartoonists, graphic designers, writers, and list-makers. The explicit goal of the creative team is to create pieces of branded 'sharable content' that will spread quickly and measurably through social networks: everything from images, memes, animated gifs, and video, to serious journalistic investigations and, yes, listicles (articles delivered in list form, e.g. '25 things every grown-ass adult should have', '13 totally convincing pieces of evidence that Jews invented the listicle').

Whereas Facebook is in the business of aggregating content created elsewhere, BuzzFeed dis-aggregates. It sends small content morsels out into social networks to generate clicks, shares, and views. Originally, these morsels served as hooks to draw eyeballs back to BuzzFeed's homepage and advertisers (like most of the tech world, BuzzFeed remains a glorified ad company), but, in late 2014, Peretti shifted the company's approach. Understanding that users did not want to leave the social media ecosystem of newsfeeds and apps, BuzzFeed begin publishing 'original text, images, and video directly to where its audience already spent its time, some 30 different global platforms, from Facebook to the Russian social networks VK and Telegram.'[41] This shift opened up new revenue streams, given the eagerness of social media companies to 'prove they can funnel money directly to partners [like BuzzFeed] that publish directly to their platforms.'[42] BuzzFeed's model of dis-aggregation is a novel way of leveraging the nature of search aggregators like Google and also shows a canny understanding of the way users engage with social media platforms like Facebook. In fact, from early on Peretti prioritized 'social' over search, focusing on sharing as a 'priority metric'.[43]

At its core, BuzzFeed is about harvesting, analysing, and monetizing data about the circulation of online cultural content. The software behind this model is developed in-house at BuzzFeed and is the primary source of the company's billion dollar-plus valuation. Information about this proprietary system is closely guarded. What we do know is that BuzzFeed tracks how users navigate their site and what they think of its stories and videos (by 'up' and 'down-voting' as on Reddit). These techniques of measure and analysis are, by now, standard operating procedure for social networking sites, online newspapers, and blogs. What sets BuzzFeed apart are projects like 'Pound' and 'Hive', which provide the company with data and analysis about how viral content circulates across *other* platforms and apps. The Pound team has developed various metrics and 'propagation graphs' to move beyond the walled garden of BuzzFeed's own site and network. Journalist Noah Robischon explains:

> Let's say I find an interesting article on Twitter and then copy the link and post it to Facebook, where one of my friends reshares it to his network, and then one of those people puts it back on Twitter. Pound connects the dots to show how I'm connected to that friend-of-a-friend who put it back on Twitter, even when that social chain—the "propagation graph"—is several links deep and includes multiple platforms.[44]

The Pound program generates data that BuzzFeed also uses to understand the durations involved in multi-platform content circulation.

The goal of such programs is to isolate patterns and identify content that is particularly 'shareable'. BuzzFeed's creative team then designs content to emulate these widely-shared forms. The company has developed a proprietary metric called 'viral lift' that quantifies how widely and how quickly a piece of content is shared. According to BuzzFeed senior editor Matt Stopera, interviewed by Robischon, '[i]f something has a 1.5 viral lift and 100,000 views and above, that was worth doing. It's a failure if you have 400,000 views and a 1.1 or 1.2 lift. That's a flop. It wasn't shared. It was all seed. The fun in the game is getting people to share something.'[45] Significantly, BuzzFeed's content creation also involves advertising design. The company creates ads for clients based on its data metrics and tracks how those ads perform across platforms. From the company's website:

> BuzzFeed's in-house creative team works with brands and agencies to craft custom social posts that are designed for sharing. Content ranges from humor to inspirational, and comes in various formats, lists to premium content like quizzes, infographics, and cinemagraphs. Custom social posts are crafted in an authentic voice that communicates a brand's aspirations and themes, and inspires consumers to share. BuzzFeed clients see an average lift of 48.8% in brand affinity and 42% in purchase intent from our custom social content![46]

BuzzFeed ads are 'native'. They appear in the same templates and with the same design features as BuzzFeed's editorial content on its website and on every platform where it publishes directly. The goal is to blur the line between advertisement and editorial; it is all just 'content'. BuzzFeed's algorithms manage this content on the site in real time, moving the most-linked, most-liked, and most-clicked content—editorial or advertisement—into privileged feeds that appear in high-trafficked spaces on its home and other pages (e.g. the colour-coded badges at the top of the homepage: red for 'trending, yellow for 'LOL', 'win', 'omg', 'cute', 'wtf' and, in Canada, 'sorry').[47] This movement of content up and down its feeds is similar to crowd-sourced content management sites like Reddit, but far less transparent (guided not only by up-votes on the BuzzFeed site, but also clicks and user navigation data collected from other platforms).

The key point is that the various components of the BuzzFeed system are vertically integrated. The company's organizational model is as closed and hierarchical as its software. BuzzFeed owns and controls its own platform,

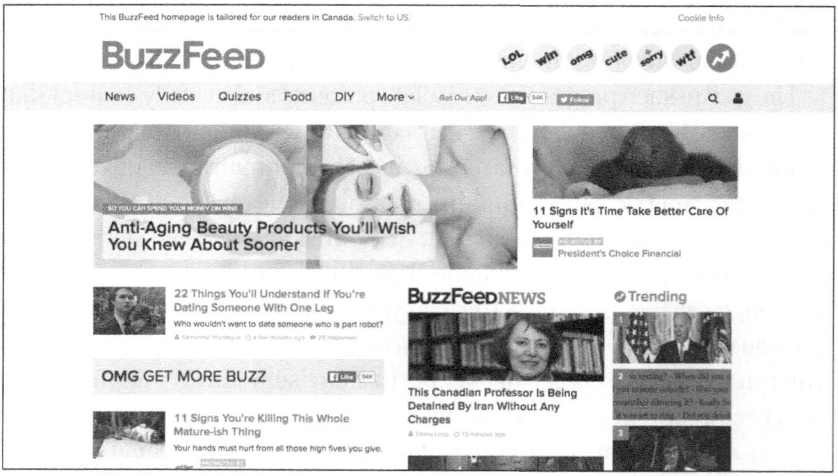

BuzzFeed Canada homepage (9 June 2016).

network infrastructure, content, and ads; its proprietary technology integrates these and other component parts. It has labour under contract to build, refine, and maintain the system of content creation and distribution. Robischon describes BuzzFeed as 'a continuous feedback loop where all of its articles and videos are the input for its sophisticated data operation, which then informs how BuzzFeed creates and distributes the advertising it produces.'[48] No one outside the company has access to the nature of these software and data ecologies. The artificial scarcity of the system and its potentially-lucrative uses in other cultural and economic contexts have been tantalizing to investors, driving the company's valuation as high, according to some, as 1.5 billion USD.

As I wrote in the opening lines of this book, in many ways it feels like the zeitgeist of contemporary web culture is the BuzzFeed listicle. Though online culture was inundated with lists long before Peretti's company, it has done the most to exploit our proclivity for the list form and to encourage its spread. But if we think about the relationship between BuzzFeed and the list less in terms of content or meaning, a different picture of the company and its cultural resonance emerges. We see the list as a guiding structural principle, the algorithm at the heart of BuzzFeed, at each layer: interface, software, corporate structure. The company is organized as a top-down hierarchy. Employees fall in line beneath the board of directors and CEO. Ranked listicles populate its surface, shaping the way users navigate the site, from entry 1 down to the final entry (usually an arbitrary number like 34). Listicles are closed systems—34 things are included but many others are excluded—mirroring the 'everything-included' proprietary nature of BuzzFeed as a company. Listicles are themselves ranked by algorithms that measure user clicks, likes, and shares, constantly updating and reconfiguring the layout of the homepage in real time. BuzzFeed is interesting not for questions about whether or not it is 'serious journalism', but because it shows us how listed protocols are baked into the circulation of cultural content, the data and software infrastructure that enables and maps such circulation, and the corporate organizational schemes that build, maintain, and monetize these networked systems. The list structure is a heuristic that allows us to see a shared logic behind listicles, algorithms and databases, and companies. This logic is logistical; it is about calculation, compression, and circulation of people (i.e. users), things (i.e. content), and data.

Alongside the tremendous success of data-driven entertainment platforms like BuzzFeed has been a spike in 'data journalism'. Nate Silver's 'FiveThirtyEight' is indicative of a new genre of reportage that uses statistical analysis and big data to observe patterns in everything from election cycles to professional sports (which, in 2016, aren't looking so different). Silver's high-profile success in modelling the 2012 US election enhanced his profile and that of data journalism (he correctly predicted the winner in 49 of 50 states). The success of BuzzFeed and FiveThirtyEight are symptomatic of data emerging as an orienting principle in everything from city planning ('smart cities') and political campaigning ('data consultants') to counterterrorism ('predictive policing'). Not everyone sees value in these contributions to public discourse and debate. That Big Data can provide certain efficiencies and solve certain problems is beyond question. What should be open to question, critics argue, are the *kind* of problems we use it to solve, though these are typically glossed over by advocates of the Big Data 'revolution'. Evgeny Morozov, one of the sharpest critics of Silicon Valley's 'solutionist' ideology, argues that the problems addressed by Big Data are typically trivial indulgences of consumption ('smart' garbage cans), or gross simplifications of complex issues ('solving' world hunger through Big Data), rather than systemic social problems of collective society.[49] Morozov may romanticize a vague public sphere of 'informed debate', but his point is well taken: right now Big Data analytics has currency in policy circles, where it crowds out voices that propose less tech-savvy solutions to social problems, or which argue the need to address an entirely different set of problems in the first place.

BuzzFeed and data journalism as part of a broader cultural shift towards Big Data and visualization. This shift is often framed as essentially *new* but it is, in fact, the latest iteration of ways of looking at the world that are essentially modern. Big Data is logistical. It is about compression, calculation, and circulation. It reduces people and things to a standing reserve of data to be collected, compiled, and analysed. Big Data proposes technological solutions to systemic problems that create more problems for it to solve, echoing Ellul's *la technique*.[50] 'Big Data' as a marketing term masks the convergence of the military and economic spheres with Silicon Valley's peculiar brand of libertarianism—the attempt to enclose the 'hacktivist' spirit so that it might be marshalled towards the surveillance needs of the state and the corporation. The keynote address and recruitment efforts of former head of the NSA, General Keith Alexander, at the popular hacker conference Defcon 2012, testify to this convergence. These sectors converge around the problem of logistics: the efficient and effective movement of people, things, and data through space and time. Logistical operations pose problems that technological devices seek to fix, while the new spaces and times opened up by those devices and processes encourage the extension and acceleration of logistics as a field of study, practice, and theory. This situation is often described from the human perspective as 'information overload' (though recall, again, that we have complained that there is 'too much to know' since the early modern period). Crary makes a key point about the latest iteration of this existential malaise.

> The only consistent factor connecting the otherwise desultory succession of consumer products and services is the intensifying integration of one's time and activity into the parameters of electronic exchange. Billions of dollars are spent every year researching how to reduce decision-making time, how to eliminate the useless time of reflection and contemplation.[51]

What Crary understands is that this malaise has to do with time. Specifically, the clash between experiential human time and new times 'invented', or at least conjured, by modern computation. BuzzFeed is also essentially about time. The company is at all times harvesting, analysing, and adapting to patterns that emerge from user behaviour and content circulation data. BuzzFeed, state surveillance, and the computational and logistical networks that support them are cultural-technical problems that demand time-critical methods.

The return of time

It is a cliché to say that technological development and digital culture are endlessly accelerating. Moore's Law has been an observable phenomenon for 50 years, even if the breathless pronouncements of Singularians are overwrought. There is much at stake, philosophically and politically, in the rise of what media theory calls 'time-criticality'. Time is critical for a worker in an Amazon-like distribution centre, as a recent plethora of stories documenting working conditions inside such centres teach us. These conditions stretch the principles of Taylor and Gilbreth's time-motion studies to almost human breaking point. One of the more memorable stories, by journalist Mac McClelland, is worth quoting at length.

> The place is immense. Cold, cavernous. Silent, despite thousands of people quietly doing their picking, or standing along the conveyors quietly packing or box-taping, nothing noisy but the occasional whir of a passing forklift. My scanner tells me in what exact section—there are nine merchandise sections, so sprawling that there's a map attached to my ID badge—of vast shelving systems the item I'm supposed to find resides. It also tells me how many seconds it thinks I should take to get there. Dallas sector, section yellow, row H34, bin 22, level D: wearable blanket. Battery-operated flour sifter. Twenty seconds. I count how many steps it takes me to speed-walk to my destination: 20. At 5-foot-9, I've got a decently long stride, and I only cover the 20 steps *and* locate the exact shelving unit in the allotted time if I don't hesitate for one second or get lost or take a drink of water before heading in the right direction as fast as I can walk or even occasionally jog [...] Often as not, I miss my time target [...] Plenty of things can hurt my goals. The programs for our scanners are designed with the assumption that we disposable employees don't know what we're doing. Find a Rob Zombie Voodoo Doll in the blue section of the Rockies sector in the third bin of the A-level in row Z42, my scanner tells me. But if I punch into my scanner that it's not there, I have to prove it by scanning every single other item in the bin, though I swear on my life there's no Rob Zombie Voodoo Doll in this pile of 30 individually wrapped and bar-coded batteries that take me quite a while to beep one by one. It could be five minutes before I can move on to, and make it to, and find, my next item. That lapse is supposed to be mere seconds.[52]

Her report is littered with references to time beyond the algorithmically-generated time targets coded into her scanner. It supports Rossiter's claim that '[l]ogistics robs living labour of time'[53] and in so doing subjects life to robust forms of technical- and self-regulation. Amazon-like distribution centres are petri dishes of time-criticality. They are standing-reserves of material, human and non, whirring around constantly: *Bestand* in motion, 24/7.

Jonathan Crary takes 24/7 seriously, crafting from a cliché a critical concept to describe a society re-calibrated around nonhuman, machinic time.

> 24/7 is a static redundancy that disavows its relation to the rhythmic and periodic textures of human life [...] It is only recently that the elaboration, the modeling of one's personal and social identity, has been reorganized to conform to the uninterrupted operation of markets, information networks, and other systems.[54]

Lists abound in the logistical world of 24/7, giving form to everything from instructions, schedules, and standard operating procedures to warehouse pickers' daily lists of targets and the algorithms that produce them. Such computational protocols, processes, and mechanisms enframe life and logistics everywhere, not just in Amazon-like distribution centres. Rossiter, quoting Kanngieser, shows how the movement of workers in warehouse and transport industries is 'increasingly regulated by global positioning system (GPS) vehicle tracking, radio-frequency identification tags that profile workers within database time and voice-directed order picking technologies "that manage the passage and pace of workers through the workplace with the aim of maximising efficiencies".'[55] And, as should be evident, the effects of these changes are not exclusive to production or labour. 'The rhythms of technological consumption are inseparable from the requirement of continual self-administration.'[56]

For Rossiter, in logistical modernity 'code is King,' and 'whoever sets the standard rules the world.'[57] This does not delve deeply enough; code and standards are only effective tools of logistical governmentality because they have the capacity to capture, manipulate, and program time. Database 'contents' (for lack of a better term) materialize on our screens dozens of times each day, re-presenting digital data sets and code in a format recognizable to human senses, such as a Google search results list. What is on the screen is a product of data that has been run through an algorithm and rendered for display on an interface. In such a format, data appear as spatial 'things' organized on a screen as we might organize written material on a page. Historically, such formats have structured experiential and conceptual space, as we saw in Chapter three. However, when we focus solely on screens—a tendency Kirschenbaum, following Montfort, describes as 'screen essentialism'[58]—we mistake as spatial abstractions the operations of computational databases that are actually about time. The popular press has often cast Google or Wikipedia as actualizations of

Borges' library of Babel, emergent archives of 'all the world's knowledge'. These comparisons conjure images of vast archives where contents are stored as extant individual items (or coherent sets of 1s and 0s) to be accessed as we might a book on a shelf in a library. Such understandings cast databases as a digital equivalent of a physical archive and miss the fact that any data 'contained' by a database are summoned, materialized, and made to function in an essentially temporal operation.[59] Data points in a database are categorically different from physical objects such as files in an archive or a name written on paper. They do not sit on shelves waiting to be pulled out and opened. Their physical reality is detectable only at the micro-level of inscriptions made on silicon chips. Our language to describe computational databases is infused with metaphors that reference the world of analogue technology, but these metaphors paper over the fact that the 'data' of databases are sequences of code that materialize and de-materialize in real time as required by a programmer or, increasingly, an algorithm.

The mining, measure, and analysis of Big Data is different from earlier administrative contexts in that Big Data is essentially about real time, the creation of databases—archives—that do not simply exist in space (on server racks), but are constantly made and remade according to the ever-accelerating feedback loop of input/output. The form that structures this feedback loop is very often the list—not only as input/output format, but also as code. The difference from earlier administrative and logistical *milieux* is that control of the archive is no longer only about physical space but now, increasingly, operational time. Put rather crudely, the database that programs time has replaced the register that inventories space. With such new problematics and objects of analysis—algorithms, databases, digital footprints, infopersons, and so on—we need new tools that can parse the temporality of digital culture.

Time-critical media studies

Time-criticality gained a foothold in media studies through the work of Friedrich Kittler, whose unique discovery was the capacity for time-axis manipulation of modern technical media like gramophone, film, or typewriter.[60] Technical media produce time as a storable and manipulable unit, one among many, shattering the previous inseparability of time from human experience and finitude. What writing and representation had done to space, ideas, and objects (abstract them onto surfaces and thus into manipulable data units), technical media do for time. When a gramophone records sound, or a cinematograph a series of images, these media are not simply recording content but are capturing data that unfold through time. Such data streams can be sped up, slowed down, reversed, or otherwise manipulated to produce new times previously unknown and incomprehensible to human beings.[61]

Kittler's insights about the relation between media and time have flowered in the German tradition of media analysis, where he occupies an architectonic yet controversial role. More recently, Wolfgang Ernst has forged ahead with a Kittlerian emphasis on time. Ernst is most interested in the way categories and practices of memory and history emerge as a corollary of the ways that media-technics process and store time. He follows Kittler in pushing Foucauldian discourse analysis beyond its space bias. He takes Foucault out the archive and into the realm of technical media, pushing the archive concept beyond language and the written word. Ernst writes, '[i]t is worth remembering that the archive as the condition for our knowledge of history becomes dependent on the media of its transmission [...] The mechanisms that regulate entry into the discourse of history or exclusion from cultural memory are therefore part of the media archaeological investigation.'[62] Foucault grasped this in part, but an inability to see beyond the Gutenberg galaxy prevented his archaeologies of knowledge from moving outside the spaces of the written word (e.g. formal state archives and libraries, the paper surfaces of documents, observation charts and tables, concepts, etc.). After technical media, the mechanisms that transmit, store, and process archival information are not reducible to their spatial functions (as with writing) but instead inaugurate whole new regimes of time. They do so precisely because they are themselves new modalities of measuring and recording time.[63]

Digitization offers a similar rupture: '[i]t is only with the digital computer that the symbolic regime *dia*lectically returns, this time in a genuinely dynamic mode (which differentiates implementation of software from the traditional Gutenberg galaxy): algorithmic time and operative diagrams.'[64] Technical media inaugurate time-critical media studies by illuminating how media record the 'flow' of human and machine time. It is not until digital media that we understand this flow is comprised of discrete units and processes operating beyond human perception. Digital times are processual and discrete rather than static and continuous, operational rather than narrative. They re-inscribe the symbolic as binary 1s and 0s in place of alphanumeric letters. The digital archive is an entity always in flux and continuously in-formation.

Observing the list form as a constitutive processual operator, as in the earlier analysis of Lisp, enables a time-critical understanding of logistical networks. As algorithmic forms of writing, such lists are non-narrative. Ernst forges surprising but suggestive connections between the algorithmic lists of network society and earlier non-narrative modes of relaying data.

> In digital computing, the sequence of operations required to perform a specific task is known as an *algorithm*. Medieval annalism also stands for a writing aesthetics of organizing a sequence of events in serial, sequential order [...] Here diachronical *clustering* serves as a memory operation beyond the narrative unification of data.[65]

Digital computation has more in common with the way data is processed in ancient modes of relaying the past than with the monopoly of narrative in modern historiography; pre-modern modes engender sorting and counting, enumeration rather than causation, and in so doing constitute a sense of time rooted in calculation rather than narrative: counting rather than recounting. The relevant connection McLuhan first glimpsed between oral culture and the 'electric' age is not about orality but time. Modern historiography excised 'calculative' time, but this was not always so:

> The old English *tellan* derives from a prehistoric Germanic word meaning 'to put in order' (both in narration and counting). We find this kind of non-explanatory and paratactic mode in the epic discourse. Homer, in his *Iliad,* already used the form of listing in the appropriately called 'Catalogue of Ships' [...] Here telling is counting— a practice well known from ancient oriental lists of rulers.[66]

Epic discourse mobilizes the list form to relay the past non-narratively, to tell via counting. Goody shows this with written lists from even earlier periods (c. 3000 BCE), which visualize words and things into data that can be re-ordered and manipulated in new, non-narrative ways.[67] Later, Leibniz 'actually mused on the option to calculate a virtual protocol of the world by counting, not narrating: combining and recombining every letter that has ever been written in world history. Once registered in discrete symbols, events could be literally processed [...] The form can match every object, every referent.'[68] The algorithmic logic of protocols, stacks, and compilers in digital computation are the distant echoes of such operations. Digital aesthetics and computation enact a situation in which telling has become counting once again, '[n]arrative on the emphatic literary level (*raconter*) is being replaced by literally counting microevents on the media archaeological level.'[69] Languages such as Lisp show that computer programming, which does not tell stories but calculates units, takes shape and unfolds formally via certain understudied but vitally important entities such as the list, or as emphasized by Solomon and Bratton, the stack.[70] Tracing such list functions allows for McLuhan-esque 'pattern recognition' that connects computational a priori that exist within the very different media environments of logistical modernity, ancient administrative writing, and early modern philosophical speculation.

Eco's constitutive tension between etcetera and everything-included resonates in each context: the unfolding of non- or pre-narrative historical time becomes thinkable through the listing of events, actors, and things from the past in the annals. These *enumerate* data as a bulkhead against the entropy of infinity. They reach towards the future by compiling as much information as possible. Meanwhile, algorithms streamline processing mechanisms and protocols as a means by which to *tellan* (give order to) the numerical ontology of computation (while also maintaining a flexibility that enables modes of self-generating, indefinite processing). In both instances, operative forms like lists constitute and facilitate the required networks of actors, signs, processes, events, mechanisms, etc. Such a Benjaminian folding of time, in which different epochs resonate, arises through time-critical analysis.

Conclusion

This chapter offered an analysis of certain infrastructural elements of contemporary logistics and demonstrated that they are essentially about time. Logistical modernity is about the efficient and effective movement of people and things, but these are only moveable via the collection and management of data. The result is a culture increasingly oriented around Big Data and certain logistical media forms (protocols, SOPs, formats, algorithms, etc.) that allow for its mobilization. Logistical media have displaced previously hegemonic media, whether technical (gramophone, film, typewriter), transmission-based (telegraph, telephone), or ritual-based (oral speech).[71] I argue Big Data analytics to be a less extreme expression of the logistical orientation that we observed around the Nazi dream of *Bestand in motion*. The latter should be understood as an extension of certain modern ways of looking at the world that precede World War II by centuries. The logistical orientation was not eradicated with Nagasaki and Hiroshima, but accelerated. Logistics have become the animating problematic and supposedly perfect solution to similar problems in digital culture. The tasks towards which computation is deployed in twenty-first century capitalism are logistical: more operations in less time to produce perfect, frictionless circulation. Forms such as the list are logistical, operating in physical spaces (Amazon-like distribution centres), on user interfaces, and in computational infrastructure. Lists do so primarily because they are flexible structures that operate in real time to facilitate what is required in physical and computational realms: compression, calculation, and circulation.

But this chapter has also drawn out a peculiar aspect of logistical media forms like lists. Alongside their ability to conjure nonhuman machinic times comes a capacity to conjure ancient, non-narrative modes of relaying the past, which are perhaps not so different. This offers an entry point into understanding mnemonic and poetic functions of listing that will be the focus of the final chapter of this book.

6. Poetics: Uncanny Modernity in Heidegger, Borges, and Marker[1]

> 'Let no thought pass incognito, and keep your notebook as strictly as the authorities keep their register of aliens.'
> – Walter Benjamin[2]

Heidegger's Poiesis

Martin Heidegger's late-period work on the question concerning technology, introduced in Chapter four, has been influential in shaping the critique of modernity over the last 50 years.[3] Of particular note are parallels Heidegger draws between seemingly unrelated aspects of modern society and culture, which cast technics, politics, and ethics in the same light.

> Agriculture is now a motorized food industry—in essence, the same as the manufacturing of corpses in gas chambers and the extermination camps, the same as the blockading and starving of nations, the same as the manufacture of atom bombs.[4]

Heidegger's controversial list forges connections between the banal and horrific so as to reveal what he sees as a common orientation to the world that unpins each technology, technique, or activity. He captures these connections with the concept *das Gestell* ('enframing' or 'the frame'), which at a broad level describes the 'transformative encounter' between modern 'man' and what he calls 'global technology'.

Heidegger's analysis engendered a sharp critique of the post-war industrial world. As previous chapters show, this analysis loses none of its diagnostic power as the world is re-calibrated around digital computation. What the analysis grasps is the logistical character of modernity common to its emergent, industrial, and digital periods. I characterized these connections earlier with the idea of a 'logistical orientation'. But, however effective and cathartic Heidegger's concepts are in revealing, describing, or lamenting the dark side of the logistical orientation, the analysis was never intended to be solely diagnostic. In the last several pages of the famous essay on the question concerning technology, Heidegger comes to understand that concealed within the 'constellation' of *Gestell* we find the very force that can free humankind from its sway: the 'saving power' that he links to poetry and art with the concept *poiesis*. '[P]recisely the essence of technology must harbor in itself the growth of the saving power.'[5] The 'saving power' is related to Heidegger's later remark that 'only a God can save us.'[6] He does not have in mind a salvation-granting deity; to break free from the sway of *Gestell* is to recognize and displace *Bestand*, to cultivate in its place an orientation to the world in which humans do not enjoy a privileged position—or at least, do not view the world solely as a standing reserve of material to be ordered and manipulated. Put another way, the 'God' Heidegger has in mind describes humility before the earth and its inhabitants—deference to the world as humankind once deferred to the Gods. These related acts of recognition and cultivation constitute humankind's highest calling, the saving power.

Outside of Heidegger scholarship, this flip side of the question concerning technology has received less attention than the diagnostic critique.[7] This may be because, in addition to the ever-present problem of Heideggerian language (it feels trite and pretentious in 2016 to write of 'saving powers' and 'destinies'), both *poiesis* and the 'saving power' are frustratingly opaque in Heidegger's work. But frustration is at the same time opportunity; the concepts are tantalizingly open-ended. And ostentatious prose should not prevent us from more fully exploring the late-period technology texts. There is much they can teach us about contemporary media-technical realities. The goal of this chapter is thus to explore the flip side of *Gestell*: the 'saving power' of *poiesis*. My argument is that listing is a cultural technique that channels spaces, times, and modes of thinking that can displace the processes and logic of logistical modernity that lists elsewhere facilitate. It does this by interrupting linear writing and the pre-digested stories and histories linear forms like narrative tend to produce. The monopoly of modern narrative, described by White[8] and Ernst,[9] engenders a relationship to history and memory that marginalizes spaces and times that do not abide by the logic of logistical modernity, which is one of total efficiency and rationality in the extraction of value and labour, 24/7. As intruders, lists open a window on alternate logics, spaces, and times; they are a tool with which to think differently about history, technology, and modernity.

Lists are embedded within the constellation of *Gestell*, operative in the seemingly unrelated realms of administration and art, *Bestand* and *poiesis*. As such, they reveal the nearness of these realms and open a window onto what Heidegger saw as the ambiguous 'essence' of technology.

> The irresistibility of ordering and the restraint of the saving power draw past each other like the paths of two stars in the course of the heavens. But precisely this, their passing by, is the hidden side of their nearness.
>
> When we look into the ambiguous essence of technology, we behold the constellation, the stellar course of the mystery.
>
> The question concerning technology is the question concerning the constellation in which revealing and concealing, in which the essential unfolding of truth propriates.
>
> But what help is it to us to look into the constellation of truth? We look into the danger and see the growth of the saving power.[10]

Heidegger grasps for language to describe the existence of humankind's saving power in precisely the place that we are most endangered, *Gestell*. There is no space outside technology from which to overthrow it. Only by developing the proper orientation to the world within *Gestell* might something like a saving power grow. The latter is a process of revealing, an 'unconcealment' of the essence of technology that Heidegger argues shows humankind's highest dignity as the guardian and safe keeper of all revealing, i.e. of truth. 'For the saving power lets man see and enter into the highest dignity of his essence. This dignity lies in keeping watch over the unconcealment—and with it, from the first, the concealment—of all essential unfolding on this earth.'[11]

The stakes could not be higher, but precisely how humankind is to cultivate this space, which he elsewhere calls *die Lichtung des Seins* ('the clearing of Being'),[12] remains unclear. It is not enough to look into the constellation and recognize the double-function of concealment and revealing at the heart of *Gestell*, though we might take this as a start (*Gestell* and *Bestand* originated, after all, as diagnostic concepts). We must also 'hol[d] always before our eyes the extreme danger.'[13] This danger is a situation in which all revealing, i.e. truth, is reduced to the truth of order, of logistics—calculation, compression, and circulation—resulting in an orientation that understands all things as *Bestand*. Processes of revealing that break free from the logic of order, though they cannot cultivate the saving power entirely, can at least clear a space or *Lichtung* for its cultivation and growth.

Clearing or preserving such a space is the task of thought and art. But these realms do not 'escape' *Gestell*. For Heidegger, the way forward is to re-connect the seemingly divergent realms of art and technology, which would engender a more profound and meaningful relationship between humans, 'technology' (taken not just as devices, but also as orientation or ways of thinking), and the world. He points, as usual, to Greek antiquity for inspiration. In that brief historical moment, art and technology were known simply as *technē*, and the essential relation between them was obvious and imminent. 'There was a time when it was not technology alone that bore the name *technē*. Once the revealing that brings forth truth into the splendor of radiant appearance was also called *technē* [...] The *poiesis* of the fine arts was also called *technē*.'[14] This was art of a disparate kind from that of the modern world. 'The arts were not derived from the artistic. Artworks were not enjoyed aesthetically. Art was not a sector of cultural activity.'[15] Art was, instead, the craft of 'bringing forth' that is connected to Heidegger's understanding of revealing—that which does not declare itself to be telling truth, but which in its essence dwells in the realm of truth. *Technē*-as-*poiesis* is a kind of crafting by which the orientation *of* the world (as *Gestell*) and an orientation *towards* the world are brought into contact. If this crafting is limited to concealment (if it lacks the power of revealing), the resulting orientation towards the world is that of order, *Bestand*. But when the 'two stars' are brought together, something like a 'saving power' can emerge.

In what follows, I show lists as a form that both conceals and reveals. As such, it offers a heuristic by which to explore *technē*-as-*poiesis*. I follow Heidegger here not to claim, once and for all, the fixed meaning of his text or his concepts. This is not a work of Heidegger scholarship. My intent is to use literary lists as case studies of *poiesis* that help explain their presence in human writing and imagination for thousands of years. Lists persist because at the same time that they conceal the 'sway of *Gestell*', operating within its administrative and technical apparatuses, they can also reveal the essence of those apparatuses. Poetic ruptures are provoked by a form that typically inscribes the borders of logistical modernity. Lists of the kind described below intrude on modern structures and processes described in earlier chapters, revealing a poetry at the heart of *Gestell* wherein a 'saving power' can grow. I understand 'saving power' to be a concept that describes an openness to new and other kinds of thinking, a clearing of the way for alternate knowledges, affects, and engagements to emerge. Certain kinds of lists clear such a space. They exist at the fulcrum of *Bestand* and the saving power.

This chapter serves another, more local, purpose, which is to emphasize the literary character of media theory. Foundational texts and figures from McLuhan and Foucault to Kittler and Vismann have always used art and literature to shake loose our thinking about technology and processes of mediation. Recent debates around materiality have tended to gloss over the degree to which media-technology, knowledge, and art are indissociable in these theorizations. McLuhan, who in later years always claimed modernist poetry inspired his media studies,[16] understood art as an 'early alarm system, [...] enabling us to discover social and psychic targets in lots of time to prepare to cope with them.'[17] Literary lists have served such a function many times. Three instances in particular expand the language at our disposal to describe the function of art and *poiesis* in the modern technical world: (1) Borges' use of lists and other 'informational' forms to render uncanny the epistemological undergrowth of modern thought, i.e. the frame of *Gestell*; (2) a temporal dimension of lists that conjures a relation to the past that resists the monopoly of modern historiography. Here, I turn to Walter Benjamin to guide a discussion of the Chronicler; (3) the use of list-like techniques in literature and film to create affects and modes of engagement rooted in wonder. These clear a space for thinking other, as evidenced in Chris Marker's films *La Jetée* (1962) and *Sans Soleil* (1983).

Borges' uncanny modernity

What does it mean to call lists 'poetic'? There is no better guide to this question than Borges. In a series of lectures delivered at Harvard in 1967,[18] he wrestles with the problem of how to describe poetry without sapping it of its power and beauty.

> Whenever I have dipped into books of aesthetics, I have had an uncomfortable feeling that I was reading the works of astronomers who never looked at the stars. I mean that they were writing about poetry as if poetry were a task, and not what it really is: a passion and a joy. For example, I have read with great respect Benedetto Croce's book on aesthetics, and I have been handed the definition that poetry and language are an 'expression'. Now, if we think of an expression of something, then we land back at the old problem of form and matter; and if we think about the expression of nothing in particular, that gives us really nothing. So we respectfully receive that definition, and then we go on to something else. We go on to poetry; we go on to life. And life is, I am sure, made of poetry. Poetry is not alien—poetry is, as we shall see, lurking round the corner. It may spring on us at any moment.[19]

Later, in the same lecture, Borges quips, '[i]f we are in a Chestertonian mood [...] we might say that we can define something only when we know nothing about it.' His open-ended understanding of poetry as the stuff of life rather than a specific literary genre or formula suits our purpose here because it allows for seeing poetry beyond sentences or even words. The claim that 'life is made of poetry' runs perilously close to cliché (clichés are located at the fulcrum of banality and profundity), but, when received in the context of Borges' larger body of work, it illuminates his interest in the materiality of language and knowledge. It is easy to see poetry in the fluttering wings of a butterfly or the babbling of a brook only because we have been trained to understand these realms as uniquely poetic. It is more difficult to see the poetic quality of banal realms like administration, where forms like lists dwell. This is not simply poetry of 'everyday life' or individual lived experience. Borges instead explores the poetic in institutions, structures, and practices borne from the modern mind and shared in collective experience of the modern world. These appear in his myriad stories about libraries, archives, maps, forgotten or lost encyclopedias, lists, editorial projects, etymologies, and systems of classification. Borges created a rich imaginative laboratory from the objects of modernity often degraded by its critics. One is tempted to say he infused the bars of the iron cage with magic. But Borges is no magician or escapist; he is closer to a mathematician in his rigour and commitment to sketching the contours of empirical reality.[20] He explores the gap between physical reality and mental life—ontics, ontology, and epistemology—by making the familiar strange. Systems and numbers are the stuff of poetry because they reveal the world in its contradictory wonder. In refusing to define poetry as some particular thing—a literary form, an expression, etc.—Borges bristles against the kind of epistemological structure that he elsewhere revels in: the modern proclivity to define, classify, and categorize. In so doing, he throws a mirror up to the modern gaze (the proliferation of mirrors throughout his fiction is no coincidence).

Borges' understanding of poetry aligns with the ancient Greek verb *ποιέω*, also the source of Heidegger's understanding, which describes making, producing, creating, bringing into existence, composing. Borges understands that these actions are not the exclusive purview of poets that work with language; they are also occurrences that arise in quotidian spaces and practices. Borges teaches that the everyday structures that delimit thought and action are rich with poetry because they reveal, among other things, the essential contingency of thought. The epistemological operators that Borges foregrounds belong to the modern world. They are the conceptual and imaginative undergrowth of Heidegger's *Gestell*, the systems of measure and order that perform and organize ontic operations. They engender modern technological apparatuses and concepts such as knowledge, fact, history, category, and so on. In rendering this undergrowth uncanny, Borges crafts moments of *poiesis*. The role such structures play in concealing the essence of the technical world is itself *revealed* by these same structures when Borges helps us peer at them through the looking glass. Such a revealing preserves a space for thinking differently about knowledge, time, history, and memory that resonates with Heidegger's saving power.

Foucault's famous encounter with the strange and ingenious Borgesian taxonomy cited earlier is a powerful example of such *poiesis*:

> In its remote pages it is written that the animals are divided into: (a) belonging to the emperor, (b) embalmed, (c) tame, (d) sucking pigs, (e) sirens, (f) fabulous, (g) stray dogs, (h) included in the present classification, (i) frenzied, (j) innumerable, (k) drawn with a very fine camelhair brush, (l) et cetera, (m) having just broken the water pitcher, (n) that from a long way off look like flies.[21]

This encounter compelled Foucault to consider the nature of his own thought. What is it that makes this list so confounding? How to understand its impossibility? What does it say about knowledge and history? Borges' beguiling list causes a rupture for Foucault. By drawing together a heap of things that does not simply resist, but radically negates any conventional classification system, this list materializes for Foucault the inability of a historical subject to think outside the conditions that delimit his or her thought, or, in Foucault's terms, to think outside the archive. The French philosopher understands himself to be a modern subject 'stamped' by the thought of his age. These borders of thought (what he elsewhere calls 'conditions of possibility') are made immanent by the list's content (its random series of items), and form (the placement of things beside one another in writing, the confounding nature of its classification). Its affective power is derived from the very fact that this is a closed list. There is a system to the finite collection of things, but it is unthinkable. In this encounter, we can see the material role played by lists in collecting, organizing, and structuring information—in creating 'knowledge' as networks of known and knowable things. This role is revealed by negation that is achieved via form. We can here see the poetry of quotidian forms that Borges told us was 'lurking around the corner.'

Foucault claims this moment as the birth of the 'archaeological' approach that would define his *oeuvre:*

> [*The Order of Things*] first arose out of a passage in Borges, out of the laughter that shattered [...] all the familiar landmarks of my thought—*our* thought, the thought that bears the stamp of our age and our geography

> [...] In the wonderment of his taxonomy, the thing we apprehend in one great leap [...] is the limitation of our own, the stark impossibility of thinking *that.*[22]

The contours of modern thought present themselves for study as historically specific and contingent. These contours are revealed because their logic has been exploded by Borges' use of the list, a form that elsewhere enforces the logic of modernity (such as we have seen in earlier chapters). Classificatory lists such as this taxonomy are expected to be agents of efficient, rational thought. But this list is radically other, occasioning a poetic rupture of the kind Heidegger describes. Foucault is provoked to think about alternative, seemingly 'illogical' classification schemes that do not abide by standard rules of his contemporary historical *milieu.* This led him, eventually, to discover and explore the 'Lives of Infamous Men' hidden in dark and forgotten corners of archives.[23] Borges' taxonomy reveals the list as a form that is at the same time (1) embedded within the epistemological undergrowth of modernity, and thus implicated in the 'danger' of *Gestell,* but also (2) the site by which a space is cleared for thinking *other.* Lists can be dangerous, yet here they are shown to hold within them the capacity to negate the totalizing logic of modern thought.

The list leaps off the page at Foucault, seemingly from nowhere, occasioning a laughter that 'shatters' the contours of a previously unseen system of thought. Shattering laugher arises because this is not just any list, but a heterotopian list. Heterotopia is a term Foucault develops elsewhere to describe 'other-spaces' ('*des espaces autres*') in which layers of meaning, contradiction, function and history are grafted onto one another in surprising and confounding ways. In contrast to utopias ('fundamentally unreal places'), heterotopias are

> places that do exist and that are formed in the very founding of society—which are something like counter-sites, a kind of effectively enacted utopia in which the real sites, all the other real sites that can be found within the culture, are simultaneously represented, contested, and inverted.[24]

In heterotopian spaces, the relations (or lack thereof) between items and histories bubble to the surface and stimulate contemplation. When taken individually, the items in Borges' taxonomy are unproblematic. They are not purely imaginary, nor do they deny communicability in language. Foucault knows them. Their spatial juxtaposition provokes his shattering laughter because this juxtaposition can take place only in the space of writing. His laughter is produced by the realization that this heterotopian list draws things together that cannot be so drawn anywhere else. It is a space that generates *thinking-other.* The sparks from this explosion caught fire as Foucault's radically new approach to understanding knowledge and history. This legacy is a powerful example of the generative capacities of poetic lists.

Poiesis for Heidegger is the ability of art to reveal the essence of technology. This essence is an ambiguity at the heart of *Gestell,* wherein both the danger and the saving power grow. To be clear, Foucault speaks nowhere in this passage about technology, nor of Heidegger. However, we should understand by 'technology' and *Gestell* not simply devices and systems, but also the modern ways of thinking and doing, rooted in order, that produce them. We can then understand how Borges' heterotopian list reveals to Foucault the essence of a particularly modern *way of thinking* that is intimately related to Heidegger's *Gestell.* Foucault sees Borges' list as a form that conceals and reveals. Its affective power propels him towards a new line of thought. Developing such new modes of thought and facilitating moments of rupture are for Heidegger the task of thought and art because they can harbour the saving power. We should understand Foucault's ability to generate a radically other approach to studying knowledge and history as an example of what Heidegger had in mind as the task of thought. Foucault's project reconfigured conventional approaches to knowledge and history, throwing into relief some of the ways truth is produced in any given historical moment and mobilized as power. It is an example of Heideggerian other-thinking. In facilitating the rupture that generated this project, the list is shown to be a poetic form through which such 'saving power' can be found and harboured.

With his taxonomy, Borges throws a mirror up to Foucault's modern gaze.[25] But Borges did not craft such mirrors simply to 'critique' modern thought and institutions. We find in his stories not polemic but ambivalence. Affection for order and its satisfactions is accompanied, always, by understanding of the relationship between order and tyranny. This ambivalence resembles that at the heart of *Gestell.* Such tensions and contradictions are for Borges, as for Heidegger, the site of poetry. His most famous story, 'The Library of Babel', captures this ambivalence. The confounding paradoxes that Borges explores in the story are essentially modern. They arise out of modernity's jarring recalibration of space and time. Modern people are simultaneously in awe of the plethora of knowledge at our fingertips and burdened by its weight. Thinking about the infinity of 'all the world's knowledge' as contained in a Library of Babel produces both exhilaration and anxiety: awe at the possibilities and power of such a collection, anxiety at its dizzying, incomprehensible scales and speeds. Order is the impossible goal, entropy the dizzying reality. This tension is at work throughout Borges' story. We hear it in the melancholy tone of the narrator who, though exhausted by a lifetime of speculating about the nature of the library and its texts, continues to revere the library as sacred. She is unable to give up hope that someday her efforts will find meaning, '[l]et me be tortured and battered and annihilated, but let there be one instant, one creature, wherein thy enormous Library may find its justification.'[26] She also tells of fanatical bursts of excitement from groups of librarians regarding new theories about the library. Such theories at first promise a metaphysical master key to unlock its mysteries; when inevitably proven incorrect they provoke despair and violence.

The tension between order and entropy is also evident to readers unable to grasp the dimensions and scale of the library. Borges' descriptions induce an unnerving vertigo. The library is an infinite loop. Infinite in space means infinite in time: '*The Library is unlimited but periodic.* If an eternal traveler should journey in any direction, he would find after untold centuries that the same volumes are repeated in the same disorder—which, repeated, becomes order: the Order. My solitude is cheered by that elegant hope.'[27] Such passages capture the unthinkable scales and circulation speeds of knowledge and data in the modern world. We are invited to marvel at the possibilities, maybe even to be hopeful, as the librarian is. Yet, darkness is never far from the scene. We read of librarians driven to insanity or violence against each other and themselves—the madness of infinity.

> When it was announced that the Library contained all books, the first reaction was unbounded joy [...] thousands of greedy individuals abandoned their sweet native hexagons [...] spurred by their vain desire to find their Vindication. These pilgrims squabbled in the narrow corridors, muttered dark imprecations, strangled one another on the divine staircases, threw deceiving volumes down ventilation shafts, were themselves hurled to their deaths by men of distant regions. Others went insane.[28]

Solutions developed to reconcile the tension between awe and anxiety bring both pleasure and violence. The story is a litany of such solutions: theories and concepts proposed in books, letters, catalogues, systems of classification, sections and shelves. 'Someone proposed searching by regression: To locate book A, first consult book B, which tells where book A can be found; to locate book B, first consult book C, and so on, to infinity [...] It is in ventures such as these that I have squandered and spent my years.'[29]

Through form and content in 'The Library of Babel', Borges explores various means humans develop to resolve the tensions and paradoxes of the modern world. Such work recalls what Eco describes as an operative tension at the heart of listing between 'everything included' and 'etcetera.'[30] This tension, he shows, crops up not just in the modern world but continuously throughout the history of human representation. Some of the most famous literary lists are those of etcetera, e.g. Homer's catalogue of ships in *The Odyssey*. These are inevitably futile attempts of achieving *All*: a total registry of things, the number of which exceeds the possibilities of the human mind. Recall Borges' embattled librarian:

> *All*—the detailed history of the future, the autobiographies of the archangels, the faithful catalog of the Library, thousands and thousands of false catalogs, the proof of the falsity of those false catalogs, a proof of the falsity of the *true* catalog, the Gnostic gospel of Basilides, the commentary upon that gospel, the commentary on the commentary on that gospel, the true story of your death, the translation of every book into every language, the interpolations of every book into all books, the treatise Bede could have written (but did not) on the mythology of the Saxon people, the lost books of Tacitus.[31]

Umberto Eco sees in such lists a unique capacity to materialize what he calls the '*topos* of ineffability,' an aesthetic gesture towards the infinite and unknown that is repeated, again and again, throughout the ages.[32] Borges and Homer channel this *topos* through the poetics of 'etcetera'.

Georges Perec did the reverse, exploring it through 'everything included'.' Lists litter Perec's work, from fully formed projects like *Things: A Story of the Sixties* ('*Les Choses*', 1965) and *Je me souviens* ('*I Remember*', 1978), to more experimental pieces like 'Attempt at an Inventory of the Liquid and Solid Foodstuffs Ingurgitated by Me in the Course of the Year Nineteen Hundred and Seventy-Four' (1974). Listing enabled Perec to explore what he called the 'infra-ordinary' or 'endotic' (as opposed to extraordinary and exotic). Wilken and McCosker argue that lists in Perec's writing are 'an effective lever with which to pry open for inspection the seemingly inscrutable inner workings of everyday spaces, things, memories, in order that they might [quoting Perec] "speak of what is and of what we are".'[33] The impossibility of any attempt to see or catch everything is inherent in Perec's work; his inventories continuously touch an ecstatic madness of infinity. Perec also used lists to explore the melancholy passage of time. Marc Lowenthal suggests that with *An Attempt at Exhausting a Place in Paris*, Perec worked through the notion that 'everything that happens and that does not happen ultimately serves no other function than that of so many chronometers, so many signals, methods and clues for marking time, for eroding permanence.'[34]

The chronicler

Literary lists of the kind created by Perec and Borges and described by Eco confront us with time, history, and, memory in a way that does not reduce them to historical narrative. Homer's famous chronicle is a representation of events from the past in a form that does not inscribe a causal chain or explanatory framework upon them. Chronicles are, according to White, 'open-ended. In principle, they have no *inaugurations;* they simply 'begin' when the chronicler starts recording events. And they have no culminations or resolutions; they can go on indefinitely.'[35] The chronicler's relation to the past is holistic and rooted in lived experience; he or she declares no moment too large or small to be part of a tale. Narrative and conventional history hierarchize the past and omit certain voices, events, histories, and objects. Such omissions are revealed when modern time is disrupted by non-narrative times and stories. Walter Benjamin, lover of list and aphorism, captures this point in his reading of a passage from Johann Peter Hebel's story 'Unexpected Reunion'. Benjamin suggests Hebel is akin to the ancient chronicler (rather than the modern historian) and marvels at Hebel's ability to embed his story in 'the great inscrutable course of the world.'[36] To infuse it with such weight—the weight of eternity—Hebel conjures death using the non-narrative, premodern time of the chronicler.

> When Hebel, in the course of this story, was confronted with the necessity of making this long period of years graphic, he did so in the following sentences: "In the meantime the city of Lisbon was destroyed by an earthquake, and the Seven Years' War came and went, and Emperor Francis I died, and the Jesuit Order was abolished, and Poland was partitioned, and Empress Maria Theresa died, and Struensee was

> executed. America became independent, and the united French and Spanish forces were unable to capture Gibraltar. The Turks locked up General Stein in the Veteraner Cave in Hungary, and Emperor Joseph died also. King Gustavus of Sweden conquered Russian Finland, and the French Revolution and the long war began, and Emperor Leopold II went to his grave too. Napoleon captured Prussia, and the English bombarded Copenhagen, and the peasants sowed and harvested. The millers ground, the smiths hammered, and the miners dug for veins of ore in their underground workshops. But when in 1806 the miners at Falun [...]".[37]

The story is severed from modern time not only because the list form conjures pre-modern modes of relaying the past, but because death pervades the passage in a way that treats it as co-present to life. Rather than pathologizing or romanticizing death, as do modern forms such as the novel, this story reveals death as an organic component of being. As Benjamin says, '[n]ever has a storyteller embedded his report deeper in natural history than Hebel manages to do in this chronology. Read it carefully. Death appears in it with the same regularity as the Reaper does in the processions that pass around the cathedral clock at noon.'[38]

Such lists conjure non-historical time in a poetic revealing of the kind Heidegger describes. The list, which elsewhere enforces the logic and logistics of modernity, brings forth alternate modes of engagement with the past. This double function, the capacity to both conceal and reveal, lies at the heart of Heidegger's *Gestell* and at the heart of lists. To find and harbour the saving power, art must hold within its grasp this simultaneous concealing and revealing. Literary lists of the kind crafted by Borges and Perec, or described by Eco and Benjamin, do this. They reveal the strictures of modern time and historiography by interrupting them. These lists tell stories—they are not unintelligible—but they do so in a way that is strange and uncanny to the modern ear and eye. They confront us with the fact that as long as we have contemplated the cosmos we have sought to capture it *and* to revel in its infinity—often with the same formal gesture. Lists like Hebel's, or Homer's catalogue of ships, or Ancient Sumerian king-lists, call forth the past in a way that narrative and prose do not. They conjure the *topos* of ineffability, an affect of etcetera.

As Benjamin and Perec understood, and as I noted in the Preface of this volume, lists are a melancholy form that swirls around death. They are ruins of possibility never realized (no wonder Benjamin was so fond of the form). They provoke thought, grief, and wonder.

Wonder

I explore, in this final section, the relationship between wonder and Heideggerian *poiesis*. Wonder is a concept that accurately describes modes of affect and engagement that resonate with Heidegger's discussions of the saving power at the heart of the modern technical world.

Ian Bogost writes of re-inscribing wonder, in the sense of awe, back into the Western philosophical and theoretical tradition. He argues another sense of wonder, as in wondering about a specific question, has enjoyed a monopoly for too long.[39] For Bogost, wonder is provoked when we are confronted by the strangeness of things in the world, the 'objects' of object-oriented ontology (OOO) that are always withdrawing from our ability to comprehend them. Bogost is interested in lists because they are an 'ontographic' form uniquely positioned to disclose the alien weirdness of things. To the narrative ear the 'off-pitch sound' of lists 'only emphasizes their real purpose: disjunction instead of flow. Lists remind us that no matter how fluidly a system may operate, its members nevertheless remain utterly isolated, mutual aliens.[40]

Lists in literature parachute heaps of words onto the page in a way that the reader does not expect. They render words and language uncanny, revealing the conventional structures of syntactic prose by interrupting and negating them. Such lists run counter to the linear modes of reading we usually bring to literature that seek out character arcs, thematic motifs, and compelling plot twists that together can teach us the 'meaning of a life' (which, according to Benjamin, is 'really the center about which the novel moves[41]). Lists break the fourth wall of a text. Even those that drive a narrative take us momentarily out of the story by inviting us to marvel at the uncanniness of text, writing, language, history, and time. We think not just about the items listed, but also the tissue that ties them together, the 'gentle knot of the comma' in Bogost's lovely phrase,[42] or the lack thereof, as Foucault learned. We do not read such lists as we read narrative or even sentences. We instead survey them, scanning, skipping ahead, or going back. We flip to the end to see how long Melville's cetological classifications in *Moby Dick* run, or how many pages Saramago's litany of Christian violence and death in *The Gospel According to Jesus Christ* will last (15 pages!). We are taken momentarily out of the story to observe the strange qualities of words and language, or of the book as sheets of paper bound between two covers. Such lists reveal the textuality or tactility of whatever medium contains them. Lists here invoke the plenitude of the world in all of its minutiae, imaginatively and on the page. In so doing, they perform real philosophical work. Recall Emerson's quip: 'bare lists of words are found suggestive, to an imaginative and excited mind.'[43] Lists perform such work, writes Bogost, not just by naming objects, but also by 'disrupt[ing] being, spilling a heap of unwelcome and incoherent crap at the foot of the reader [...][so that] a tiny part of the expanding universe is revealed through cataloguing.'[44] He continues: '[l]ists of objects without explication can do the philosophical work of drawing our attention toward them with greater attentiveness.'[45] Belknap concurs, arguing that the function of literary lists is to do more than record, 'it is to display, to lay out, to arrange—to create reality—whether that be to represent a moment of complete awareness of the world or just to experiment, to conjure by naming.'[46] Or, recall Sontag on creating lists: 'I *perceive* value, I *confer* value, I *create* value, I even create—or guarantee—*existence*.'

The power of lists to render uncanny, to reveal, in Heidegger's language, is not confined to the realm of objects or language. Non-narrative lists of the kind described above resonate with cinema that does not grant narrative a monopoly over its unfolding. Many filmmakers experiment with such techniques–Terence Malick, Peter Mettler, Peter Greenaway, Luis Buñuel–but none more clearly demonstrates the relationship between lists, wonder, and *poiesis* than Chris Marker. We can use the list as an interpretive tool to understand how Marker experiments with the poetics of etcetera so as to free his films from the strictures of everything-included narrative. He produces lists of sounds, images, music and words—sound-images—that perform affective and memory work. These require very little interpretation in terms of plot or theme, though they inspire much thinking. His films meander and do not abide by conventional cinematic time; they are much closer to poetry than genre cinema. Marker does not place the demands of narrative on the audience, which we follow along with a story or that we decode hidden content and themes. He invites us, simply, to wonder. The films do not escape narrative entirely, but this does not seem to be Marker's goal. He is interested in contrasting the cohesion of the narrative (the stories we tell of ourselves) against the disjunction of the list (life as it actually unfolds through time). Moments of intrusion break up narrative time so as to provoke a different kind of affect than that of mainstream cinema. Such moments clear a space for *poiesis*.

La Jetée (1962) is a series of sequential still photographs, a photomontage rather than a motion picture. Its unfolding establishes a tempo and rhythm akin to poetic verse. The voice-over is aphoristic and often only tangentially related to the images. There is a story, a narrative unfolds, but it is no more essential to the filmic experience of *La Jetée* than imagery or sound. This runs contra Hollywood cinema (particularly during *La Jetée*'s period), in which formal and stylistic elements are typically subservient to narrative.[47] The film shows us a post-apocalyptic future in which surviving humans are forced to live underground, beneath the destroyed surface of Earth. How and when the cities were destroyed is left unclear. What is clear is that without daylight, and with no connection to the past, human memory is fading. To preserve memory in the hope it will facilitate time-travel, or even hold the key for human survival, certain humans are subjected to experiments. The protagonist of the film is chosen because of his ability to hold an image of the past. For Jonathan Crary, the film negotiates modern anxieties about technology and information, which had galvanized public attention in 1950s and 1960s France,[48] and remain with us still.[49] The film asks, '[h]ow does one remain human in the bleakness of this world when the ties that connect us have been shattered and when malevolent forms of rationality are powerfully at work?'[50] Marker offers no prescriptive or even descriptive answer, but Crary argues *La Jetée* 'affirms the indispensability of the imagination for collective survival.'[51] This affirmation is articulated formally, rather than rhetorically or thematically. For Crary, '[m]uch of the richness of Marker's film stems from its distancing of photography from empirical notions of reality or indexical models of this medium. An image is 'real' affectively, in how it feels, in how it verifies the intensity of a lived or remembered moment.'[52] The 'reality' of the images in the protagonist's memory is not what Marker seeks to question. He is interested in the power of such images to preserve a realm of otherness, of imagination, in which alternate times, spaces and futures can be revealed or invented. The logic of *La Jetée* appears to be enumeration and accumulation, which are list-like features. Yet, the final images reveal the secret and scandal at the heart of the film: it is, in fact, a Möbius strip. As with Borges' Library of Babel, *La Jetée* is infinite but periodic. Etcetera is transformed into everything-included.

The collection of still images and aphoristic voice-over interrupts conventional cinematic time and space, bending the logic of cinema so as to 'pos[e] the extreme difficulty and exhilaration of [the film's] central vocation: 'to imagine or dream another time.''[53] *La Jetée* is an attempt to displace the forces of modernity that have destroyed the planet and replace them with imagination, to overrun 'history' with memory, to find *poiesis* in *Gestell*. These effects become formally available to Marker in his development of a kind of filmic list. Rather than presenting sound-images shot through with explanation, he presents a seemingly disjointed series so the audience can explore the spaces between them, the connective tissue that does or does not hold them together. The film is an experiment, a precarious text that may fall apart at any moment. We are never sure what will come next in the series or even if another item will emerge. The spectre of blankness haunts the unfolding of the series. The film's power arises from the oscillation between exhilaration and anxiety it provokes, tensions similar to those explored by Borges.

Marker's *Sans Soleil* (1983) is even less connected to narrative, and, even more than *La Jetée*, can be viewed as a list transported into film. Transcriptions of the film's voice-over read as a litany of philosophical observations and quotations, similar in form to Benjamin's *Arcades Project*. To take one example:

> He wrote: I'm just back from Hokkaido, the Northern Island. Rich and hurried Japanese take the plane, others take the ferry: waiting, immobility, snatches of sleep. Curiously all of that makes me think of a past or future war: night trains, air raids, fallout shelters, small fragments of war enshrined in everyday life. He liked the fragility of those moments suspended in time. Those memories whose only function had been to leave behind nothing but memories. He wrote: I've been round the world several times and now only banality still interests me. On this trip I've tracked it with the relentlessness of a bounty hunter. At dawn we'll be in Tokyo.[54]

An interest in banality echoes Borges and Perec, as do Marker's formal techniques. The fabric of *Sans Soleil* is non-narrative. It is held together by the rhythm and borders of a list. Marker himself tells us this:

> Sei Shonagon [a lady in waiting to Princess Sadako at the beginning of the eleventh century] had a passion for lists: the list of 'elegant things,' 'distressing things,' or even of 'things not worth doing.' One day she got the idea of drawing up a list of 'things that quicken the heart.' Not a bad criterion I realize when I'm filming; I bow to the economic miracle, but what I want to show you are the neighbourhood celebrations.[55]

The passage is accompanied by the following shots: a space shuttle shedding its jets above earth; an explosion and falling projectile (possibly from the shuttle); the undersea launch of a missile, which penetrates the surface before disappearing into the atmosphere; three shots of a bomber from below; the screen of a radar. We hear implacable, otherworldly sounds throughout. These are later revealed to be made by a 'pal' of the narrator's, Hayao Yamaneko, who uses them as a solution to the following problem:

'if the images of the present don't change, then change the images of the past.'[56] This sequence is placed between shots of two Japanese street festivals. These have no voice-over, but are accompanied by Yamaneko's synthesizer mixed with the soundscape of the festivals. Marker refuses to impose a logic of classification upon this list of sound-images; there is no criterion or even theme that unites the items. Visual images of war are accompanied by talk of a list of things that quicken the heart and book-ended by exuberant images of everyday life. In an echo of Borges' taxonomy that so confounded Foucault, *Sans Soleil* confronts us as an open-ended list that at any moment may switch directions, become something new, something other. And it does. The list continuously denies the order we assume it will provide. It instead invites breaks, ruptures, disjunctions, interruptions, diversions, digressions, contradictions, revisions, recursions, and reversals. There is an exhilarating contingency in lists like Borges' and Marker's, a danger that the next item might undo all that has preceded it.[57] This is precisely how entries such as Borges' '(h) included in the present classification' and '(l) etcetera'[58] function, as do Marker's haunting final lines of *Sans Soleil*:

> Then I went down into the basement where my friend—the maniac [Yamaneko]—busies himself with his electronic graffiti. Finally, his language touches me, because he talks to that part of us which insists on drawing profiles on prison walls. A piece of chalk to follow the contours of what is not, or is no longer, or is not yet; the handwriting each one of us will use to compose his own list of 'things that quicken the heart,' to offer, or to erase. In that moment poetry will be made by everyone, and there will be emus in the 'zone.'
>
> He writes me from Japan. He writes me from Africa. He writes that he can now summon up the look on the face of the market lady of Praia that had lasted only the length of a film frame. Will there be a last letter?[59]

There is sense to these words, but it is unfamiliar, affective rather than narrative. The film draws together this and other moments as a series of passages, images, and sounds so that we can explore and wonder at the Benjaminian 'world of secret affinities'[60] Marker has excavated.

As in *La Jetée*, Marker explores in *Sans Soleil* modes of engagement with alternate worlds, spaces, and times, though *Sans Soleil* is more explicitly concerned with time. Marker uses the *poiesis* of lists to intrude on and break up the continuous and homogeneous temporality of narrative, prose, history, and other modern representational forms.

> He used to write me from Africa. He contrasted African time to European time, and also to Asian time. He said that in the 19th century mankind had come to terms with space, and that the great question of the 20th was the coexistence of different concepts of time. By the way, did you know that there are emus in the Île de France?[61]

The film is not shot through with explanation, but invites reflection. We are given time to think. The cumulative effect of *Sans Soleil* gestures towards etcetera. The fixed duration of the film (103 minutes) compels it towards everything included. Marker deploys the former to explode the latter. His film channels a non-narrative time of plenitude such as Benjamin describes in chronicles. *Sans Soleil* shows that the non-narrative time of lists is an effective way to produce affect in film, as it is in literature, poetry, and music—recall Ravel's Bolero (the constant repetition and re-orchestration of a single theme[62]) and Wagner's *vorspiel* to *Das Rheingold* (a four-minute drone piece that continuously sounds the note E-flat major).[63] Such strategies can be read as attempts to gesture towards the infinity of the world, to avoid reducing it to a neat package imposed by the limitations of any medium: a film or novel must have an end; photographic frames and sheets of paper are only so many square inches; the human ear can only hear so many frequencies; human lives end in death. The list form is attractive because it channels plenitude, a sense of time that can break free from these strictures. It positions items within Benjamin's 'great inscrutable course of the world.' Marker's sound-image litanies go on. They grapple with the fact that we cannot reach out and touch, read, hear, smell, feel, or write everything. They provoke an affect that reveals and revels in the paradox of this impossibility—the inability to catch the cosmos, but the compulsion to try.

Marker's films are in conversation with Borges' uncanny poetry of the quotidian, Benjamin's time of the chronicler, and Eco's *topos* of ineffability. Each thinker provokes moments of Heideggerian *poiesis* through modern tensions and paradoxes, and by creating modes of engagement and affect based in wonder. The painter Jack Chambers of London, Ontario, offered us a useful way to conceive of wonder:

> Interviewer: You are doing with time what you have already done with space. There's a central preoccupation here. What do you think it is?
> Chambers: Wonder I guess. Something can be so familiar that I see it for the first time. Or maybe it is not being able to see especially what is most familiar so you reach out and shape it again and again in the hope of

> revealing it. So in that sense I am working with the life within the object and not just the object's appearance.[64]

Benjamin describes memory work in a similar fashion, as an 'excavation': 'He who seeks to approach his own buried past must conduct himself like a man digging. Above all, he must not be afraid to return again and again to the same matter; to scatter it as one scatters earth, to turn it over as one turns over soil.'[65] Chambers' and Benjamin's descriptions encapsulate the filmmaking techniques of Marker, who created works that shape the familiar 'again and again in the hope of revealing it,' with 'it' being something like the ineffability of time, space, and the experience of the modern world, *Gestell*. Marker reveals the contours of *Gestell* using a form, the list, which elsewhere conceals these contours. This is Heideggerian *poiesis*, the clearing of a space for other-thinking wherein the saving power might grow, for 'protect[ing] the interplay of unconcealment and concealment in the *Lichtung des Seins* ['clearing of being']. Such protection Socrates called "wonder," whose daughter is iridescent speech.'[66]

Conclusion

Excavating these kinds of articulations in literature and art (wonder at the ineffable, tensions between entropy and negentropy)—and importantly, understanding their medial dimensions (the forms and devices through which they are articulated)—is the kind of project that Erkki Huhtamo suggests media archaeology can help develop, through 'identifying *topoi*, analysing their trajectories and transformations, and explaining the cultural logics that condition their 'wanderings' across time and space.'[67] I have tried to use the list in order to think through some of these trajectories, to turn them over as one turns over soil so that we might understand with a bit more precision the 'deep time' of poetics encoded in this humble form.

This chapter has shown that the list is not simply an administrative or logistical format. The complicated series of operations traced above (and throughout this book) preclude any easy judgment, whether positive or negative. They show how lists illuminate contours of modern epistemologies that are typically unnoticed and unquestioned, rendering them uncanny. We have also seen how lists intrude on modern historical and narrative time by channelling other, non-narrative times and affects. Ernst suggests that the non-narrative time conjured by chronicles might more accurately account for the calculative-bias inherent in digital computation and its corresponding logistical networks and cultural expressions.[68] Such a capacity shows that listing can clear a space for other-thinking that is productively thought in relation to Heidegger's understanding of *poiesis*. In that understanding, the power of revealing, i.e. truth, is dislodged from order where it typically resides. A form that, as earlier chapters show, facilitates the operations and enforces the logic of *Gestell* here reveals the latter as the essence of the modern technical world. Lists dialectically conceal and reveal the contours of logistical modernity's 'frame'. This operation is akin to what Heidegger described as the 'saving power'. In my interpretation this power describes the clearing and preserving of a space wherein alternate logics, systems, and futures might be conceived and explored. The lists described above craft such heterotopian spaces.

Conclusion: Etcetera...

Lists are important because they travel across media networks and historical ways of knowing. They operate at a layer that is not often studied: formats, paperwork, and cultural techniques. Listing activities inscribe distinctions that have material effects on the composition of populations, knowledge formations, and temporal operations. Lists show us how media networks function and change. They even offer a space for imagining alternate possibilities—not just for media and technological development, but for social and political life. Modern listing activities trend towards oppression and control. A deeper history of the form shows that there are other kinds of lists. These offer a glimmer of ways we might make our administrative and calculative techniques more just. The point is not to escape or ignore bad political trajectories by retreating into aesthetics. It is to demonstrate poetic techniques and traditions that clear a space for thinking about alternative political realities.

Because listing is a cultural technique that processes distinctions foundational to social and imaginative life, it cannot be easily dismissed or endorsed. It is not enough to say lists are good or bad. They endure in our thoughts, texts, and programs because they negotiate tensions and paradoxes that have confounded us for centuries: fear and desire, wonder and horror, entropy and order. What other quotidian forms can teach us such lessons? What other ontical operations silently enframe our thoughts and activities? I hope my collection of case studies may generate further research into such questions.

But this book is not only about lists. In using approaches from media materialism to capture a protean form, I sought to show how these approaches can enrich not only media and communication studies, but the humanities more broadly. Media archaeology, associated theories of cultural techniques, actor-network theory, and logistical media studies complement well-established analytic approaches because they take into account more than the institutions, texts, and audiences that have historically been the focus of the humanities. A demonstration of the importance of listing techniques to the history of human thought and action is a concrete example of what media materialism brings to the table. Such approaches help to fill gaps in methodologies and debates that are better-established, such as the ongoing clash between 'political economy' and 'cultural studies'. Though conceptually and historically important, such debates often produce entrenched positions that are inhospitable to the development of more experimental research questions that can push our fields in new directions (which, as media archaeology shows, are sometimes old directions). Media Studies' traditional 'interpretive triangle' of text-audience-institution,[1] for instance, often misses or glosses over the material layers—technical, historical, formal, etc.—that together enable the operation of media devices and networks. This book addresses that gap, and engages a tradition that focuses on objects and techniques such as buttons, doors, maps, undersea cables, and files.[2] These projects provide a window on the way broader spatio-temporal infrastructures are assembled in any given society or historical moment.

Such projects have roots in the 'civilizational' approach to media and communication research pioneered in the 1950s and 1960s by the Toronto school of communication, particularly by Harold Innis and Marshall McLuhan.[3] This tradition has been lately out of fashion, but it is proving ever more relevant as questions of time and space emerge as essential to understanding logistical modernity and digital culture. It provides tools to illuminate the emergence of new spaces and, especially, times that clash with extant regimes in ways that can be productive or potentially destructive for democratic and ethical life. High Frequency Trading, e-waste, server farms and mass cooling systems, supply chain management, just-in-time delivery, and massive logistical projects such as China's New Silk Road Economic Belt[4] are not about representation, identity, ideology, or even political economy as traditionally understood. They demand different approaches.

My desire to foreground this tradition stems from my sense of a general hesitancy to engage with 'civilizational' ideas or to take chances with research by stepping outside the conventional canons of media-cultural-communication studies. The pattern is familiar: we find a specific 'media' text or institution and take a deep dive into its meaning, use, or history. We often spend so much time qualifying the specificity of the chosen object (and the limitations of its analysis) that by the time the object itself appears both reader and writer are exhausted. There is a reluctance to extrapolate from specific objects or texts or make risky historical comparisons. This is a new development for a field that was invented so as to engage, head on, civilizational questions. Innis, McLuhan, Mumford, et al. were unafraid to borrow from disciplines like philosophy, classics, mathematics, and art history, which had historically been 'hands off' to non-experts. Thinkers from the German tradition of media analysis have been doing the same for the last 30 years. I appreciate their fearlessness, and think we in Anglo-America need more of it. We tend not to touch figures like Aristotle, Jesus, or Pythagoras (with some notable exceptions[5]), but the German tradition understands that these figures usually have as much or more to say than Marconi, Edison, Hearst, or Zuckerberg. Despite much discussion in Anglo-America about interdisciplinarity, the German media studies climate has proven more hospitable to the generative weaving together of disciplines and traditions. Counter-intuitively, by going more granular this tradition has become more far-reaching in the scope of its conclusions. Specificity in devices and techniques leads to questions of ontology and being, of data and *Dasein*. These return us to the civilizational questions of the Toronto school. Such questions have largely receded over the same time period in Anglo-America, replaced by those of identity, representation, subversion, critique, and agency. How and why this happened is an interesting question, though not one I can answer here (pejorative dismissals of 'technological determinism' and 'grand narratives' are at least part of the tale). With this book, I have tried to emulate a bit of the German fearlessness without getting too far off course. The nature of such risks is that you sometimes miss the mark. I hope these pages have had more hits than misses.

This book offers one more brick in a transatlantic bridge being built between German and Anglo-American media studies *milieux*. It borrows from both traditions to develop concepts and methods that account for forms, formats, and techniques that have not yet received enough attention. Each chapter could be developed into a book on its own. More case studies might be added, their topics debated. This book is necessarily haunted by the spectre of entropy. All one can do is collect, drawing seemingly incongruous examples together to see what their comparison might teach us—about lists, yes, but also about our disciplines, and even, perhaps, our position in Benjamin's 'great inscrutable course of the world.'

Notes

Preface

1. Eco in Beyer and Gorris, 2009
2. Emerson, 2009, p. 294. See Belknap, 2004, p. 36-72, for an extended discussion of Emerson's lists.
3. Ardam and Schmidt, 2014.
4. Sontag in *Ibid.*
5. Martin Heidegger proposed 'ontical' to describe the things and practices of physical reality as they occur outside of any categorization or classification as 'knowledge'. *Dasein* is a being capable of self-awareness and reflexivity, i.e. of understanding the world in ontological terms. Ontics, for Heidegger, are the concrete instantiations of ontology as the deep structure or conditions of possibility for being in the world. Recent German media-theoretical debates around *Kulturtechniken* ('cultural techniques') zero in on the realm of ontics but invert Heidegger's conception: ontics are not instantiations of ontology as deep structure but are in fact constitutive of ontology. (See Siegert, 2015). Much more will be said about ontics and cultural techniques in chapter one.

Introduction

1. Aspects of this chapter are published in Young, 2013a.
2. McLuhan, 2003, p. 14.
3. Carney, 2014.
4. The Supreme Court of Canada argued, for instance, that the Act is 'aimed directly at biophysical environmental concerns that affect navigation' and that 'the NWPA has [an] expansive environmental dimension, given the common law context in which it was enacted.' Supreme Court of Canada, 1992, paras. 88–89.
5. Ecojustice, 2012, p. 7.
6. Johnson, 2015.
7. Scahill, 2015.
8. Usher, 2014b.
9. Werbin, 2008, p. 1. See also Werbin, 2009.
10. To take two examples: in *The Rules of Art* and *On Television*, Pierre Bourdieu goes after the 'new masters of thoughtless thought' that wrestle public debate away from political professionals and intellectuals by producing '*specific power plays* such as surveys aiming to produce manipulated classifications, or the "top ten" lists which newspapers publish on anniversary occasions.' Bourdieu, 1996, p. 346. See also Bourdieu, 1998. More recently,

Guillory describes how the displacement of 'literary' and 'scholarly/scientific' by 'informational' writing in the modern period shifted conventions of argumentation and even truth. Lists are a species of informational writing that privileges spatial organization over logic or rhetoric, brevity and concision over rhetorical performance. 'Conclusions [are] supposed to be implicit in the order in which information is presented,' and, 'the effect of such brevity can be a kind of poverty, an over reliance on mere enumeration as a result of which logical relations fail to manifest themselves at all [...] argument is reduced to mere list' (Guillory, 2004, p. 128).

11. Good examples of the ubiquity of the concept of 'information overload' can be found on its Wikipedia page (http://en.wikipedia.org/wiki/Information_overload). The popularization of the term is there attributed to Alvin Toffler's 1970 book *Future Shock*, in which the bulk of contemporary social problems are attributed to the psychological effects of information overload.
12. Shannon and Weaver, 1949.
13. Baudrillard, 1993, pp. 50–87. See also Terranova, 2004, pp. 6–38.
14. See Blair, 2011.
15. Doni in Krajewski, 2011, p.9.
16. See Engels, 1968. Thanks to John Durham Peters for this suggestion.
17. See Gelb, 1952.
18. Blair, 2011, pp. 16–17.
19. Krajewski, 2011, p. 4.
20. Borges, 2000, p. 103.
21. Belknap, 2004, p. 2.
22. *Ibid.*, p. 7.
23. I am here taking up Bernd Frohmann's call for generative, experimental approaches to documents and documentation, 'which have as their aims not so much the precision and accuracy of a scientific representation of what documents and documentation might be, but forging concepts in a Deleuzian spirit, seeking to enhance their power and force, with more concern for what they do than for what they mean or represent. The benefits of extending the concepts of document and documentation are located here, and with a closely associated aim, that of multiplying these concepts and seeking ways of also extending an encouraging hospitality to many different areas of their application.' Frohmann, 2009, p. 301. Adopting this approach necessarily implies that the category of 'list' is inclusive of a broad range of formats.
24. See Innis, 2002.
25. Eco, 2009, p. 7.
26. Latour, 1987, p. 21.
27. Hacking, 1986.
28. Bratton in Virilio, 2006.
29. Ernst, 2013, p. 251.

30. Benjamin, 1999, p. 67. Howard Eiland and Kevin McLaughlin discuss Benjamin's use of quotation in their foreword to *The Arcades Project:* 'The transcendence of the conventional book form would go together, in this case, with the blasting apart of pragmatic historicism [...] Citation and commentary might then be perceived as intersecting at a thousand different angles, setting up vibrations across the epochs of recent history [...] all this would unfold through the medium of hints or 'blinks'—a discontinuous presentation deliberately opposed to traditional modes of argument.' Eiland and McLaughlin in Benjamin, 1999, p. xi.

1. History: Lists and Media Materialism

1. 'list', *OED* Online, 2015.
2. quoted in 'list, n.3', *OED* Online, 2015. See original: Keating Clay, 1851, p. 90.
3. Shakespeare, 2002, V.ii.270–273.
4. The only other usage of 'list' that is recognizable to modern eyes is that describing the 'careening or inclination of a ship to one side' (c. seventeenth century), probably related to an earlier minor usage that denoted pleasure, joy, or a desire, i.e. inclination towards something. The origin of this meaning is obscure but may be Icelandic. Is there a connection between the leaning of the listing ship and the earliest known use of 'list' (from the Old English *hlyst*) to describe sound and hearing? To give 'a list' was to offer one's attention, to lend one's ear, or *lean towards* in attention. See 'list n. 5' and 'list n. 4', *OED* Online, 2015.
5. Werbin, 2008, p. 1. See also Le Goff, 1992; Bourdieu, 1998; Sharkey, 1997.
6. Berube, 2000; Poletti, 2008.
7. Goody, 1977, p. 76.
8. *Ibid.*, p. 80.
9. *Ibid.*, p. 76.
10. *Ibid.*, p. 81.
11. *Ibid.*, p. 76
12. *Ibid.*, p. 81.
13. Velhuis, 1997, p. 140.
14. '21 ewes, 6 female lambs, 8 full grown rams, 4 male lambs, 6 she-goats that have given birth, 1 he-goat, 2 female kids.' See Schmand-Besserat, 1982, p. 2. See also Schmand-Besserat, 1996, for an elaboration of her thesis regarding 'how writing came about'.
15. *Ibid.*, p. 2.
16. *Ibid.*, p. 4.
17. *Ibid.*, p. 5. For more on the media-theoretical implications of Schmand-Besserat's findings, see Peters, 2013b, pp. 212-13 and Forbes, 2016.
18. Raible in Krämer, 2003, p. 521.
19. Krämer, 2003, pp. 518–519.

20. Vismann, 2008, pp. 81–82.
21. See Ong, 1983 but also Goody and Watt, 1963; Havelock, 1963; McLuhan, 1962; Parry, 1971.
22. Vismann, 2008, pp. 6–7.
23. Velhuis, 1997, p. 137.
24. *Ibid.*, p. 137.
25. In addition to Swartz, 2006, see Neusner, 1990; Hughes, 2003; Tzoref, 2011.
26. Swartz, 2006, pp. 190–191.
27. *Ibid.*, pp. 193–194, originally published in Schäfer and Shaked, 1994, pp. 199–205.
28. Guillory, 2004, p. 111 ff.
29. See also Latour, 1987; Krämer, 2003; Rotman, 2008.
30. Condorcet quoted in Kafka, 2012, p. 56.
31. Lejeune quoted in *Ibid.*, p. 67.
32. Kafka, 2012, p. 65.
33. Weber, 2001, pp. 76–77.
34. Vaughn, quoted in 'list v. 4', *OED* Online, 2015.
35. Franklin, 1996, pp. 64–65. Also quoted in Belknap, 2004, pp. 37–38.
36. Hacking, 1982, p. 279.
37. Foucault, 1990, p. 143.
38. Foucault, 1980, p. 99.
39. Aly and Roth, p. 1.
40. Werbin, 2008, p. 17.
41. *Ibid.*, p. 44
42. Carnot, quoted in Kafka, 2012, p. 63.
43. See Agamben, 1998; Aly and Roth, 2004; Black, 2001; Werbin, 2008.
44. Weber, 1958.
45. Horkheimer and Adorno, 2002.
46. Innis, 1995, pp. 350-355
47. Vismann, 2008, p. 6.
48. *Ibid.*, p. 7.
49. Krajewski, 2011, pp. 9–13.
50. *Ibid.*, p. 31.
51. *Ibid.*, p. 32.
52. *Ibid.*, pp. 27–35.
53. Goody, 1977, p. 81.
54. See Belknap, 2004; Eco, 2009; Doležalová *et al.*, 2009.
55. Eco, 2009, p. 49.
56. Peters, 2012, p. 45.
57. Kerwin, 2011.
58. Huhtamo and Parikka, 2011, p. 2.
59. Huhtamo, 1997, p. 223.
60. Ernst, 2013, p. 25.
61. *Ibid.*, p. 59.

62. See Kittler, 1990, 1999, 2010.
63. As Geoffrey Winthrop-Young quips: 'Kittler is controversial. That, probably, is the only uncontroversial thing that can be said about him' (Winthrop-Young, 2013, p. 120).
64. Parikka in Ernst, 2013, p. 11.
65. As exemplars, see Sterne's two major works, *The Audible Past* (2003) and *MP3* (2012).
66. Gitelman, 2006, pp. 3–5.
67. Parikka, 2014, p. 39 ff.
68. Monea and Packer, 2016. See also Manzerolle and Kjøsen, 2012.
69. Young, 2017.
70. See Winthrop-Young, 2013, pp. 120–146 for a thorough overview of debates and controversies around Kittler, from 'technodeterminism' and gender to war and anti-humanism.
71. See Matthew Kirschenbaum's wide-ranging discussion of processing and computational mechanisms involved in digital computation (Kirschenbaum, 2008).
72. Sterne uses the term mediality 'to evoke a quality of or pertaining to media and the complex ways in which communication technologies refer to one another in form or content [...] the mediality of the medium lies not simply in the hardware, but in its articulation with particular practices, ways of doing things, institutions, and even in some cases belief systems' (Sterne, 2012, pp. 9–10).
73. *Ibid.*, p. 7.
74. *Ibid.*, p. 6.
75. *Ibid.*, p. 5.
76. *Ibid.*, p. 11.
77. Aspects of this discussion appear in Young, 2015.
78. Kittler, 1999, p. 5.
79. Siegert, 2013, p. 49.
80. Winthrop-Young, 2013, p. 45.
81. As described by Williams, 1983, pp. 87–93.
82. Siegert, 2013, p. 58.
83. Siegert, 2011, p. 14.
84. Siegert, 2008, 2013. For a related approach from the Anglosphere, see Rotman, 2008, pp. 33–54 and Rotman, 1987.
85. Vismann, 2013, p. 83.
86. Don Norman famously used doors that do not signal clearly or intuitively whether they are push or pull as an example of bad design in his seminal *The Design of Everyday Things.* See Norman, 2013.
87. Vismann, 2013, p. 84.
88. The word 'list' carries this sense of boundary given its early usage to denote border, edging, or strip. Incidentally, a peculiar American usage of 'list' as a verb described precisely the activity of drawing a furrow to prepare the

land for the crop: 'Some of it [...] had been twice ploughed, then listed, then twice harrowed before sowing,' Washington, quoted in 'list v. 3', *OED* Online, 2015.

89. Vismann, 2013, p. 84. Another discussion of the furrow example is found in Siegert, 2013, pp. 53–54.
90. Siegert, 2015, pp. 20–23.
91. Mumford, 1963, p. 12.
92. *Ibid.*, p. 13.
93. See Williams, 1983, pp. 87–88.
94. Most famously, Innis explored the histories of the fur trade and cod fisheries in Canada by starting with the physiological and habitational characteristics of the animals themselves in Innis, 1973, 1978.
95. See Innis, 2002, 2007.
96. John Durham Peters, for instance, identifies a number of 'logistical media' like calendars, clocks, and towers, which 'arrange people and property into time and space.' These are 'prior to and form the grid in which messages are sent [...] Logistical media establish the zero points of orientation, the convergence of the *x* and *y* axes.' Even though he uses the term 'media', Peters actually identifies a moment prior to media in which certain devices and techniques process logistical distinctions that establish concepts like time, space, and being. See Peters, 2013a, p. 40. See also Case, 2013 and Rossiter, 2014 on logistical media; Starosielski, 2015 and Bowker and Star, 1999 on critical infrastructure studies.
97. Peters, 2009, p. 4.
98. *Ibid.*, pp. 4–5.
99. See Innis, 2002, 2007. Innis is the great political superego of this tradition, with his insistence that the key to peace and prosperity is balance among the biases of communication (as opposed to religiously dogmatic societies that overemphasize time, or militaristic ones that overemphasize space). There are strong political stakes here, though they are not the familiar ones of identity or class we in the Anglo-American tradition are used to working with.
100. Un-black boxing concepts and knowledge is a hallmark of Latour's work from the early Science Studies through Actor-Network Theory and into his latest inquiries into 'Modes of Existence'. See Latour, 1987, 2005, 2013.

2. Epistemology: Pop Music Charts and the Making of a Cultural Field

1. Aspects of this chapter are published in Young, 2013a.
2. I use the term 'operator' as a substitute for what 'in a more subject-centered vocabulary are called agents' (Bennett, 2010, p. 9). I rely here on connections drawn by Jane Bennett between Deleuze's 'quasi-causal operator'—'that which, by virtue of its particular location in an assemblage and the fortuity

of being in the right place at the right time, makes the difference, makes things happen, becomes the decisive force catalyzing an event'—and Latour's 'actant', which is 'neither an object nor a subject but an 'intervener'.' See Bennett, 2010, p. 9 ff.

3. Latour, 1999, p. 65.
4. Serres with Latour, 1995, pp. 105–106.
5. Goody, 1977, pp. 136–138; also pp. 90–93.
6. See Goody and Watt, 1963.
7. Latour, 1987, pp. 215–224.
8. See, as touchstones, Latour 1987, 1990, 1999, 2005.
9. Blair, 2011, pp. 34–35.
10. Frohmann, 2004a, p. 400.
11. *Ibid.*, p. 402.
12. Aside from Frohmann, 2004a, see Latour, 1987; 1999; Hacking, 2006. Science studies is the scholarly field that examines, in meticulous detail, this process of slow sedimentation. A direct engagement with the myriad debates of science studies falls beyond the purview of this book. My purpose here is to explore what certain tools from science studies can bring to a work of media theory.
13. See Quiñones, 2007; Henderson, 2008; Morris, 2015, pp. 62–64.
14. Straw, 2015, p. 130.
15. In a recent essay, Will Straw highlights the capacity of popular music charts to perform each of the media functions in Kittler's famous typology: processing, storage, and transmission. For Straw this demonstrates the pop music chart's 'mediality', which he defines as 'a distributed and intermittent property, the occasional (but not definitive) state of an object depending on its particular use at a given time or the prism through which it is viewed' (2015, p. 128). Using the language of intermediality theory, Straw mounts an argument similar to mine: that media and cultural studies need to focus less on media objects and content and more on 'intermedial' functions and relationships, of which he sees pop music charts as a privileged example.
16. Williams, 1991, pp. 66–76.
17. This section relies on extensive archival work done by Russell Sanjek, 1988, and on the extension and elaboration of his work done by Parker, 1991 and Hakanen, 1998.
18. quoted in Anand and Peterson, 2000, p. 273.
19. See Anand and Peterson, 2000, pp. 272–274.
20. Schlager, 2006.
21. Parker, 1991, p. 206.
22. Hakanen, 1998, pp. 102–103.
23. Sanjek, 1988, p. 202.
24. Parker, 1991, p. 207.
25. Hakanen, 1998, p. 102.
26. *Ibid.*, pp. 102–103. See also Ennis, 1994.

27. Ennis, 1994.
28. Hakanen, 1998, p. 104
29. *Ibid.*, p. 106.
30. See Shumway, 2007.
31. Hakanen, 1998, p. 105.
32. Anand and Peterson, 2000, p. 274. See Also Sanjek, 1988.
33. Sanjek, 1988, p. 273.
34. Parker, 1991, p. 208. *Billboard* has consistently adapted to changes in the nature of the popular music commodity and its distribution—its first charts reported on songs heard in Vaudeville theatres in three cities before shifting to sheet music sales, then to a mix of radio airplay, jukebox plays, and recorded sales, before adopting a singular focus on single 45-rpm records (see Anand and Peterson, 2000, pp. 273–274). When emphasis shifted from singles to albums in the 1960 and 1970s, the magazine developed the '*Billboard* 200' chart. With mobile media came ringtone sales, which for a time had their own *Billboard* chart. With the digital music commodity and MP3 came an entirely new chart ecology (see fns 41-42 below) aimed at adapting to the collapse of physical sales. The 'Hot 100' is now based on 'radio airplay audience impressions as measured by Nielsen Music, sales data as compiled by Nielsen Music and streaming activity data provided by online music sources' (Straw, 2015, p. 130).
35. Hakanen, 1998, pp. 102–103.
36. *Ibid.*, p. 103.
37. *Ibid.*, 107.
38. *Ibid.*, p. 103.
39. Parker, 1991, p. 211.
40. Hakanen, 1998, p. 107.
41. 'Overall Popularity' charts (as of Spring 2016) are: The Hot 100, Billboard 200, Artist 100, Billboard Twitter Real-Time, Radio Songs, Digital Songs, Streaming Songs, Billboard Twitter Top Tracks, Billboard Twitter Emerging Artists, On-Demand Songs, Top Album Sales, Digital Albums, Independent Albums, Social 50, Catalogue Albums, Tastemaker Albums, Heatseekers Albums. 'Genre' charts are: R&B/Hip Hop, Adult/Pop, Country, Rock, Dance/Electronic, Latin, Christian/Gospel, Holiday, and Jazz. 'Additional Genre' charts are: Blues Albums, Classical Albums, Comedy Albums, Kid Albums, Jazz Albums, Smooth Jazz Songs, New Age Albums, Reggae Albums, Soundtracks, World Albums.
42. International charts are: Japan Hot 100, China V, UK singles, UK albums, Canadian Hot 100, Canadian Digital Songs, Canadian Albums, Germany Songs, Germany Albums, France Songs. Web charts are: Next Big Sound, LyricFind US, LyricFind Global, YouTube.
43. See Hakanen, 1998, p. 105.
44. Parker, 1991, p. 208.
45. Siegert, 2011.

46. Parker, 1991, p. 208.
47. Straw, 2015, p. 129.
48. Hakanen, 1998, p. 106.
49. Straw, 2015, p. 132.
50. Hakanen, 1998, p. 106.
51. Wendy Chun uses this term to describe the cycles of data processing, storage, and transmission that render the supposedly permanent into an 'enduring ephemeral' that constantly circulates: old e-mails, YouTube videos, comment threads, erased files and the like are here today, gone tomorrow, back next week. This 'permanence' is of a different order and is what sustains the 'newness' of new media. It is not fixed in place, such as in an analogue archive, or linearly degenerative, such as in human memory, but rather a peculiar mix of the two. Pop music charts remind us that perhaps the enduring ephemeral is not so new. See Chun, 2008.
52. Peters (1988, p. 19) is here close to Walter Benjamin's understanding of the term: 'Information [...] lays claim to prompt verifiability. The prime requirement is that it appear 'understandable in itself' [...] it is indispensable for information to sound plausible,' and later in the same essay: 'The value of information does not survive the moment in which it was new. It lives only at that moment; it has to surrender to it completely and explain itself to it without losing any time.' Benjamin, 1968, pp. 89–90. Much more is said about Benjamin in Chapter four.
53. Parker, 1991, p. 213. There is a strong temporal orientation to these charts, challenging what I have described as their space bias; it is important to recall that 'bias' is a heuristic term that demonstrates tendencies, rather than hard and fast boundaries.
54. Huber, 2010, p. 149.
55. Attali, 1989, p. 109.
56. Straw, 2015, p. 134.
57. Parker, 1991, pp. 214–215.
58. *Ibid.*, pp. 215–216.
59. Berube, 2000, p. B7.
60. See Poletti, 2008.
61. Straw, 2015, pp. 132–134.
62. Examples of such include *Rolling Stone's* 'Icons: The Greatest 100 Artists', or their 'Greatest 500 Songs of All Time' and 'Greatest 500 Albums of All Time'—collections that offer a palatable survey of popular music history. They establish canons of artists, songs, and albums deemed important to the unfolding of popular music history according to *Rolling Stone*. *Pitchfork* online magazine also has an extensive list section (which has best album and song collections for each decade since 1960 and each year since 2000). Alan Cross's now-defunct radio show *The Ongoing History of New Music* broadcast numerous countdown shows, among them the 'Top 100 Moments in Alt Rock', a list that compares and ranks actual historical moments.

63. Huyssen, 2003, p. 18.
64. Brooks, 1982, p. 14.
65. Hakanen, 1998, p. 107.
66. Frow, 1997, p. 244.
67. *Ibid.*, p. 246.
68. Hesmondhalgh in Scott, 2013, p. 68.
69. Parker, 1991, p. 215.
70. Lovink, 2011, p. 58.
71. Notes on the book's material composition: it is presented in coffee-table book format with dimensions of 23.9 x 23.1 x 2.5 cm. It has 216 glossy pages with colour photographs throughout. There is an introduction by Mersereau of about 2000 words, after which are listed the top 100 singles (starting with #1). Each entry has an accompanying section of text that describes the song and attempts to contextualize it historically. Each of the first ten entries has 3–4 pages devoted to them: 2–3 pages of text (of 800–900 words) and one full-page photo of the artist or group. Entries 11–50 are two pages each: one full-page picture, one page of text (400–500 words). Entries 51–100 are one page each: the top half of the page devoted to small photo and song title/rank, the bottom half to text (300–400 words). Interviews were conducted for the song write-ups with artists 'or someone who was close to them at the time' in order to 'present clear and fresh perspectives on the works' (Mersereau, 2010, p. 9). Full-page or sidebar lists of celebrity jurors (such as John Roberts, Paul Quarrington, Denise Donlan, Rich Terfry, etc.) are dispersed throughout the text, breaking up the progression of the list occasionally. All of the jurors are listed in the back of the book, along with their occupation, institutional affiliation, and location. The book also contains an autonomous, unannotated list of the 'Top-100 French-Canadian singles' (pp. 78–79). Finally, the book contains a standard alphabetized index section.
72. Mersereau, 2010, pp. 8–9.
73. *Ibid.*, p. 10.
74. See Dunphy, 2010.
75. Quill, 2010.
76. See Latour, 1987, pp. 34–42.
77. *Ibid.*
78. Mersereau quoted in Quill, 2010.
79. To qualify as Canadian content a musical selection has meet two of four 'MAPL' criteria: 1) Music: the music is composed entirely by a Canadian; 2) Artist: the music is, or the lyrics are, performed principally by a Canadian; 3) Performance: the musical selection consists of a performance that is recorded wholly in Canada, or performed wholly in Canada and broadcast live in Canada; 4) Lyrics: the lyrics are written entirely by a Canadian. See CRTC, 2015.
80. quoted in Meany and Barber, 2010.

81. Mersereau, 2010, p. 7.
82. Mersereau quoted in Quill, 2010.
83. Latour, 1987, p. 53.
84. *Ibid.*, p. 57.
85. *Ibid.*, p. 227.
86. Mersereau, 2007.
87. Straw, 2015, p. 136.
88. Latour, 1990, p. 34.

3. Administration I: The State, the Fact, and Double-Entry Bookkeeping

1. Hacking, 1986.
2. A term Bratton uses to describe Virilio in Virilio, 2006.
3. See Ellul, 1964; Mumford, 1963; Berman, 1982; Harvey, 1989.
4. Harvey, 1989, pp. 240–242.
5. Foucault, 2007.
6. Mumford, 1963, pp. 112–118.
7. See Horkheimer and Adorno, 2002; Marcuse, 1991; Fromm, 1994
8. Baumann, 2001.
9. Herf, 1984.
10. See Heidegger, 1991a.
11. Poovey, 1997, offers a meticulous tracing of the origins of the fact as an epistemological category. 'Essential facticity' is not her term, but one Hacking uses (2002, p. 12) to describe her work.
12. See 'administer, v.', *OED* Online, 2015.
13. *Ibid.*
14. 'Bureaucracy, to be sure, is as old as civilization. Any large scale polity requires some kind of monitoring [...] But the scale and intensity of bureaucratic growth over the last two hundred years is quite unprecedented in human history.' Peters, 1988, p. 14.
15. See Vismann, 2008, pp. 5–10.
16. Poovey, 1997, p. xix.
17. See Mumford, 1963; McLuhan 1962, 2003; Berman, 1982; Peters, 1988, 2013a.
18. Mumford, 1963, pp. 12–17. Peters, 2013a, also discusses the organization of time by calendars, clocks, and towers.
19. McLuhan, 2003, pp. 6–7.
20. Peters, 1988, pp. 14–16.
21. On writing's dissociation of communication from speech, see Ong, 1982; Goody, 1977; and Peters, 2013b.
22. Harvey, 1989, p. 240.
23. Butterfield, 1965, p. 1.
24. Hacking, 2006, p. xx.

25. See Guillory, 2004; Kafka, 2012; Gitelman, 2014.
26. Guillory describes this writing as a genre. I have, at times, added 'mode', so as to preserve a sense of the processual aspect of writing as a technique, in which inscription surface, tool, hand, eye, mind, etc. converge to produce a document. Genre describes the latter perfectly well, but I wish to add an emphasis on the way techniques structure documentation, after which come documentary genres.
27. Guillory, 2004, p. 126.
28. *Ibid.*, p. 126.
29. *Ibid.*, p. 127.
30. See Innis, 2002; Harvey, 1989; Lefebve, 1992; de Certeau, 1988.
31. See Murphy, 1996; Spruyt, 1994.
32. Kafka, 2012, p. 32.
33. Clanchy's seminal work on medieval writing and bureaucracy argues further that lay literacy as a cultural convention 'grew out of bureaucracy, rather than from any abstract desire for education or literature' (Clanchy, 1993, p. 19). Vismann, 2008, also offers a wide-ranging discussion of the importance of writing to power that moves from the history of writing to modern literature; from Roman chanceries (and their study in the Renaissance), through the travelling archives and registries of monarchical power in middle ages, to the proto-bureaucracy of Maximilian I's imperial court chancery; from the bizarre world of baroque secretaries to the self-administration of the Prussian proto-state; from Goethe's personal archive to Nazi governmentality; from vertical files and binder technology to the Stasi surveillance state.
34. Poovey, 1997, p. 4.
35. *Ibid.*, p. 33.
36. Vismann, 2008, pp. 57–58.
37. Hacking, 1982.
38. Hacking, 1991, p. 184.
39. *Ibid.*, p. 181.
40. *Ibid.*, p. 189.
41. *Ibid.*, p. 186.
42. *Ibid.*, p. 189.
43. *Ibid.*, p. 190.
44. Peters, 1988, p. 14.
45. *Ibid.*
46. *Ibid.*
47. Kafka, 2012, p. 21.
48. *Ibid.*, p. 32.
49. In addition to Poovey, 1997, see Fleck, 1979 and Mumford, 1963.
50. Poovey, 1997, p. 5.
51. Frohmann, 2004a, pp. 398–404.
52. *Ibid.*, 403.

53. See also Dear, 1991 and 1995; Shapin, 1984; Schaffer and Shapin, 1985.
54. Poovey, 1997, p. 3, emphasis in original.
55. See, for instance, Vismann's discussion of how conventions of rhetoric were imported into administrative practices and formats. Baroque secretaries, she shows, did this in order to preserve their monopoly of knowledge as the media environment shifted from the oral tradition of rhetoric to paper. See Vismann, 2008, pp. 102–108. John Guillory also discusses the withering of rhetoric as 'informational' genres replaced the *art* of persuasion with simple persuasion. See Guillory, 2004, pp. 114–122.
56. Poovey, 1997, p. 38.
57. *Ibid.*, p. 30.
58. *Ibid.*
59. See Guillory, 2004, p. 23.
60. Poovey, 1997, pp. 61–62.
61. The relationship between accounting practices and godliness is further pursued in Quattrone's analysis of the sixteenth- and seventeenth-century accounting practices of the Society of Jesus. See Quattrone, 2004.
62. Hacking, 2002, p. 12. See also Schaffer and Shapin, 1985.
63. See Poovey, 1997, pp. 175–197.
64. Hacking, 2006, p. xxi.
65. See *Ibid.*
66. Peters, 1988, pp. 14–16.
67. 'Imagined community' is a concept Peters borrows from Benedict Anderson. See Peters 1988, p. 14 and Anderson, 1983.
68. Kafka, 2012, p. 9.
69. Peters, 1988, p. 15.
70. Poovey, 1997, p. 15.

4. Administration II: The Nazi Census and Making Up People

1. quoted in Aly and Roth, 2004, p. 66.
2. This chapter is heavily indebted to the extensive archival research of Götz Aly and Karl Heinz Roth, 2004; Edwin Black, 2001; and Kenneth C. Werbin, 2008.
3. Aly and Roth, 2004, p. 1.
4. On the literary and rhetorical basis of what they call the 'Nazi myth' see Lacoue-Labarthe and Nancy, 1990.
5. Black in Aly and Roth, 2004, p. ix.
6. See Softsky, 1999; Gonen, 2000; Kogon, 1950.
7. Aly and Roth, 2004, p. 40.
8. *Ibid.*, p. 21.
9. *Ibid.*, p. 80.
10. *Ibid.*, pp. 15–16.

11. See *Ibid.*, pp. 16–17.
12. Burgdörfer quoted in *Ibid.*, p. 17.
13. See Aly and Roth, 2004, p. 19.
14. *Ibid.*, p. 20.
15. *Ibid.*, p. 22.
16. Göring quoted in *Ibid.*, p. 44.
17. Korherr quoted in *Ibid.*, p. 31.
18. Peters, 1988, p. 15.
19. Liebermann and Kääb quoted in Aly and Roth, 2004, pp. 45–46.
20. *General Archive of Statistics* quoted in *Ibid.*, p. 51.
21. Liebermann and Kääb quoted in *Ibid.*, pp. 41–42.
22. *Ibid.*
23. Elden, 2006b, p. 755.
24. Black, 2001, p. 47.
25. Zahn quoted in Aly and Roth, 2004, p. 2.
26. Zahn quoted in *Ibid.*, p. 9.
27. *Ibid.*
28. Heydrich quoted in Aly and Roth, 2004, p. 54.
29. Aly and Roth, 2004, p. 61.
30. *Ibid.*
31. *Ibid.*, p. 74.
32. *Ibid.*, p. 63.
33. *Ibid.*, p. 71.
34. Hacking, 1991, pp. 182–183.
35. Peters, 1988, p. 14.
36. See Kafka, 2012.
37. Schwarz quoted in Aly and Roth, 2004, p. 54.
38. Keller quoted in Black, 2001, p. 49.
39. Black, 2001, p. 25.
40. *Ibid.*, p. 25.
41. Aly and Roth, 2004, p. 11.
42. Black, 2001, p. 30.
43. *Ibid.*, p. 31.
44. See Peters, 2013a and 2015.
45. See Black, 2001, pp. 43–51.
46. *Ibid.*, p. 26.
47. *Ibid.*, p. 58.
48. See Hacking, 1991.
49. See Hacking, 2006.
50. Werbin, 2008, pp. 2 and 43.
51. *Ibid.*, p. 3.
52. *Ibid., p. 45.*
53. Importantly, Foucault does not see this shift as a clean break—disciplinary societies have aspects of governmentality, and vice versa. It is rather a ques-

tion of emphasis within the historical arrangement. 'There is not the legal age, the disciplinary age, and then the age of security. Mechanisms of security do not replace disciplinary mechanisms, which would have replaced juridico-legal mechanisms. In reality, you have a series of complex edifices in which, of course, the techniques themselves change and are perfected, or anyway become more complicated, but in which what above all changes is the dominant characteristic, or more exactly, the system of correlation between juridico-legal mechanisms, disciplinary mechanisms, and mechanisms of security' (Foucault, 2007, p. 8).

54. Werbin, 2008, p. 20.
55. *Ibid.*, quoting Foucault, 2007.
56. *Ibid.*, p. 45, emphasis in original.
57. Heidinger quoted in Black, 2001, pp. 50–51.
58. Black, 2001, p. 21.
59. *Ibid.*
60. Zahn in Aly and Roth, 2004, p. 10.
61. On the limits of the information concept see Frohmann, 2004b and Nunberg, 1996.
62. Peters, 2013a, p. 41.
63. *Ibid.*
64. quoted in Aly and Roth, 2004, p. 21.
65. Elden, 2006b, p. 755.
66. *Ibid.*
67. Black, 2001, p. 88.
68. Elden, 2006b, pp. 755–756.
69. I should note, briefly, that the problematic relationship between Heidegger and Nazism has been debated extensively for well over 60 years. This book is not a work of Heidegger scholarship, and can therefore add little to these debates. The question of Heidegger's fascism is not one I have set out to answer. My interest is solely in his post-war diagnoses of modern technology. I hope the reader will allow me this distance.
70. Heidegger, 1993, p. 107.
71. *Ibid.*, pp. 105–106.
72. Spengler quoted in Ihde, 2010, p. 10.
73. Elden, 2006b, p. 756.
74. See Heidegger, 1999.
75. Elden, 2006b, p. 756.
76. See Brozat, 1981; Kershaw, 2000.
77. My thanks to Atle Mikkola Kjøsen for his brilliant formulation of logistics as '*Bestand* in motion'. This formulation was inspired by the penetrating analysis of modern technology delivered by Warren Steele in a series of lectures at The University of Western Ontario between 2011–2014.
78. Take Dr. Fritz Arlt's report on the ethno-biology of Leipzig, for instance, which included on its final page a list of places in Poland where 'Jews pres-

ently living in Leipzig were born.' Because the report offered insight not just into the concentration of Jewish populations in Poland, but also into the meaning of space and place for Jewish communities, '[t]he listing of such places can [...] be of interest to demographic researchers in the future.' Isolated for particular emphasis on Dr. Arlt's list were future centres for 're-settlement': Warsaw, Lodz, and Auschwitz (Arlt in Aly and Roth, 2004, p. 77).

5. Logistics: Listicles, Algorithms, and Real Time

1. Quoted in Benjamin, 1999, p. 456.
2. For a discussion of the Nike incident and how it informed Peretti's career trajectory, see Wasik, 2009, pp. 84–86.
3. Peretti in Suleiman, 2016.
4. Parts of this discussion are taken from Young, 2013b.
5. See Vismann, 2008; Manovich, 2001; Adam, 2008.
6. Adam, 2008, p. 174.
7. While this is true for the original Lisp language designed by John McCarthy, contemporary iterations such as 'Common Lisp' incorporate other data types such as vectors and hash tables. See Robinson, 2008, p. 104.
8. Adam, 2008, p. 177.
9. Siebel, 2005, p. 265.
10. Solomon, 2013.
11. Kittler, 1999, p. 258.
12. Solomon, 2013.
13. *Ibid.*
14. On the stack, also see Bratton, 2016.
15. McCarthy, 1996.
16. See Siebel, 2005.
17. Program listings stand as an interesting bridge between digital computation and Vismann's analogue world of files. Program listings testify to a moment in which the storage and transmission capacities of computation had not yet caught up to processing capacity.
18. Fuller and Goffey, 2009.
19. Ernst, 2011, p. 252.
20. Quotation from 1898 issue of *The Athenaeum* cited in *OED*, 'logistics, n.2', 2015.
21. Bratton in Virilio, 2006, p. 11.
22. A Google Ngram search shows a precipitous rise in the appearance of the term 'logistics' starting in 1938, the first year of World War II.
23. See Council of Supply Chain Management, 2013.
24. See Martin, 2013.
25. See Foucault, 2007, pp. 95–96.
26. *Ibid.*, p. 65.

27. The burgeoning field of critical infrastructure studies is doing much of the early heavy lifting. See Bowker and Star's now classic *Sorting Things Out* (1999) as well as more recent work by Starosielski, 2015; Mattern, 2015; and Peters, 2015. Michael Lewis's 2014 *Flash Boys: A Wall Street Revolt* is to my knowledge the most lucid and comprehensive treatment of the infrastructural dimensions—both computational and physical—of high frequency trading.
28. See Werbin, 2009, pp. 619–622.
29. Koh quoted in Chamayou, 2013, p. 46.
30. See Chamayou, 2013, pp. 46–51.
31. Tice quoted in Werbin, 2009, p. 620.
32. See Chamayou, 2013 and Scahill, 2015.
33. Werbin, 2009, pp. 615–617.
34. See Andrejevic, 2013, for indispensable work on the connections between state and corporate data analytics, in particular pp. 19–41.
35. See Miller, 2013.
36. Some of the shrewdest analysis of PRISM, NSA, and the surveillance state in general has been provided by journalist Glenn Greenwald, writing first for *The Guardian,* and later for *The Intercept_*.
37. IBM, n.d.
38. Facebook, 2013, p. 6.
39. Lovink, 2011, p. 25.
40. BuzzFeed, 'About', n.d.
41. Robischon, 2016.
42. *Ibid.*
43. Peretti in Suleimann, 2016.
44. Robischon, 2016.
45. Stopera, in Robischon, 2016.
46. BuzzFeed, 'Advertise', n.d.
47. This process was described on the BuzzFeed blog in June 2010. The original post no longer appears, but it was transcribed and posted by Frommer to *BusinessInsider*'s 'Tech' blog. See Frommer, 2010.
48. Robischon, 2016.
49. See Morozov, 2013.
50. Ellul, 1964.
51. Crary, 2013., p. 40.
52. McClelland, 2012.
53. Rossiter, 2014, p. 67.
54. Crary, 2013, p. 9.
55. Rossiter, 2014, p. 68, quoting Kanngieser, 2013, p. 601.
56. Crary, 2013, p. 46.
57. Rossiter, 2014, pp. 65 and 68.
58. Kirschenbaum, 2008; See also Montfort, 2004.

59. For more on the temporality of the digital archive, see Ernst, 2013; Parikka, 2011; and Kirschenbaum, 2008.
60. See especially Kittler, 2010, but also 1990 and 1999.
61. See also Krämer, 2006, and Winkler, 2010 on time-axis manipulation.
62. Ernst, 2013, p. 42.
63. Ernst's most recent work in English pushes this temporal emphasis further, developing the concept of 'sonicity' to describe the relationship between sonic frequencies beyond human perception, time, and being. See Ernst, 2016.
64. Ernst, 2013, p. 30.
65. *Ibid.*, p. 150.
66. *Ibid.*, p. 148. Peters also emphasizes the ancient connection between telling and counting to challenge the modern suspicion of number and quantification (2001, p. 440). McLuhan, meanwhile, refers to the wisdom of Homer and Heisod as 'operational' in the 'Introduction to the Second Edition' of *Understanding Media* (2003, p. 12).
67. See Goody, 1977.
68. Ernst, 2013, p. 151.
69. *Ibid.*, p. 155.
70. See Solomon, 2013, and Bratton, 2016.
71. For more on the distinction between ritual- and transmission-based media, see Carey, 1989, especially pp. 11–28.

6. Poetics: Uncanny Modernity in Heidegger, Borges, and Marker

1. This chapter is indebted to insights developed by Warren Steele in a series of unpublished lectures on 'The Meaning of Technology' at The University of Western Ontario. (see Steele, 2011–2014).
2. Benjamin, 1996, p. 458.
3. Jacques Ellul's *la technique,* for instance, is a concept developed to describe an orientation that privileges rationalism and efficiency above all else in every aspect of human endeavour. See Ellul, 1964. The influence of Heidegger's deconstruction of metaphysics on French theory is well documented, especially on Derrida and Foucault; while lately there has been a 'return' to Heideggerian themes in strands of 'new' materialism like Object-Oriented Ontology. See Srnicek, Bryant, and Harmon, 2011.
4. These remarks were offered in a 1949 lecture series regarding *das Gestell,* on which the famous 'Question Concerning Technology' essay was based. The quotation used can be found in Caputo, 1993, p. 132.
5. Heidegger, 1991a, p. 334.
6. Heidegger, 1993, p. 105.
7. Bruno Latour, for instance, focuses almost entirely on Heidegger's diagnosis and badly misreads the *poiesis* concept to be not more than a defense of canonical poetry. In the process, Latour confuses Heidegger's wither-

ing critique for lazy fatalism. He lampoons the German philosopher as a conservative 'modern' that retreated to his cabin in the Black Forest to fret pessimistically about humankind's fall (see Latour, 1993, pp. 65-67 and 1999, pp. 211-12). Jeff Kochan argues that Latour's misreading of Heidegger is a rhetorical tactic of dissimulation aimed at deflecting criticism away from Latour's own problematic concepts. Kochan suggests that when subjected to Heidegger's critique of modernity, Latour's self-proclaimed 'non-modern' approach is revealed as instead the apotheosis of modern technoscience. Kochan sees Heidegger as 'open[ing] a conceptual space in which an alternative to modernity might yet be formulated' (Kochan, 2010, p. 587). *Poiesis* is Heidegger's proposal—inadequate but preliminary—for the kind of alternative that Latour claims to be (but for Kochan fails in) creating. Glenn McCulloch discusses St. Augustine's moral psychology as an example of Heideggerian *poiesis* that offers a means of 'renewing the technological mind,' i.e. reorienting our understanding of the world and nature as gifts from the Christian God rather than as *Bestand* (see McCulloch, 2002). John W.M. Krummel traces a shift in Heidegger's thought from an early concept of 'imagination' associated closely with representation to a much more open conception captured by the concept of *poiesis*. The latter is 'ontologically more primal than any representing act [...] prior to any function of subjectivity' (Krummel, 2007, p. 262).

8. See White, 1973.
9. See Ernst, 2013.
10. Heidegger, 1991a, p. 338.
11. *Ibid.*, p. 337.
12. Heidegger, 1991b, pp. 441–448.
13. Heidegger, 1991a, p. 338.
14. *Ibid.*, p. 339.
15. *Ibid.*
16. Marchand, 1998, p. 41
17. McLuhan, 2003, p. 16.
18. Published as Borges, 2002.
19. Borges, 2002, pp. 2–3.
20. Balderston debunks the myth of Borges the magician in Balderston, 1993. My thanks to John Durham Peters for suggesting, in personal correspondence, the characterization of Borges as a mathematician.
21. Borges, 2000, p. 103.
22. Foucault, 2009, p. xvi.
23. The title of one of Foucault's clearest meditations on forgotten histories and their importance to his method. Gilles Deleuze famously called the essay, written in 1977, Foucault's 'masterpiece'. See Foucault, 2001.
24. Foucault, 1986, p. 24.
25. Mirrors are, incidentally, a paradigmatic heterotopia for Foucault (see Ibid., pp. 24–25).

26. Borges, 1998, p. 113.
27. *Ibid.*, p. 118 (emphasis in original).
28. *Ibid.*, p. 115.
29. *Ibid.*, p. 117.
30. Eco, 2009, p. 9.
31. Borges, 1998, p. 115.
32. Eco, 2009, pp. 49–50.
33. Wilken and McCosker, 2012, p. 5.
34. Lowenthal in Perec, 2010, pp. 49–50.
35. White, 1973, p. 6.
36. Benjamin, 1968, p. 97.
37. *Ibid.*, pp. 94–95.
38. *Ibid.*, p. 95.
39. Bogost, 2012, pp. 120–125.
40. *Ibid.*, p. 40.
41. Benjamin, 1968, p. 99.
42. Bogost, 2012, p. 38.
43. Emerson, 2009, p. 294.
44. Bogost, 2012, p. 41.
45. *Ibid.*, p. 45. Several practitioners of the Object-Oriented Ontology movement, of which Bogost is a part, have adopted listing and enumeration as rhetorical techniques in lectures and public talks. See, for instance, Timothy Morton's keynote address, 'They Are Here', from 2012's *The Nonhuman Turn* conference at the 21st Century Institute, University of Wisconsin-Madison (in print as Morton, 2015).
46. Belknap, 2004, pp. 19–20.
47. See Bordwell, 1985, pp. 1–84.
48. See Ellul, 1964.
49. See Turkle, 2011.
50. Crary, 2013, p. 92.
51. *Ibid.*
52. *Ibid.*, p. 93.
53. *Ibid.*
54. Marker, 1983.
55. *Ibid.*
56. *Ibid.*
57. Thanks to Warren Steele for this observation and its corresponding list.
58. Borges, 2000, p. 103.
59. Marker, 1983.
60. Eiland and McLaughlin in Benjamin, 1999, p. x.
61. Marker, 1983.
62. See Eco, 2009, p. 47.
63. Interestingly, Terrence Malick, another filmmaker who explores non-narrative cinema, uses Wagner's *vorspiel* to build the final sequence of *The New*

World (2005) into a crescendo of sound-images that moves fluidly through a number of spaces and times.

64. Woodman, 1967, p. 21.
65. Benjamin, 2005, p. 576.
66. Krell in Heidegger, 1991, p. 430.
67. Huhtamo, 2011, p. 28.
68. Ernst, 2013, pp. 158–160.

Conclusion: Etcetera...

1. Peters, 2009.
2. On buttons, see Heilmann, 2014; on doors see Siegert, 2012; on maps see Siegert, 2011 and Peters, 2008; on undersea cables see Starosielski, 2015; on files see Vismann, 2008.
3. Peters characterizes this tradition as 'civilizational' in 2009.
4. The 'New Silk Road' is a massive infrastructure project aimed at connecting Central and West Asia with the Middle East and Europe. The project involves creating or upgrading existing transportation and computational networks so as to link new logistical and industrial zones, pipelines, power plants, seaports, administrative centres, and cities. This network is being inscribed into the earth. To build the Lanzhou New Area (LNA), the Chinese government commissioned the removal of hundreds of mountaintops, clearing space for a brand new urban development and transportation system. See Shepard, 2016; Lulu, 2014.
5. For instance, John Durham Peters' by now classic staging of a primal communication debate between Socrates the dialogist and Jesus the disseminator, 1999, pp. 33–62. From another direction, Brian Rotman's background as a mathematician informs his media-theoretical work on counting and mathematical systems (see 1987), and later on what he calls 'distributed human being' (see 2008).

Bibliography

(All internet documents accessed 7-8 May 2016)

Adam, Alison. 2008. 'Lists'. *Software Studies: A Lexicon*. Matthew Fuller (Ed.). Cambridge, MA: The MIT Press. 174-178.

'Administer, v.' 2015. *Oxford English Dictionary Online*. Oxford: Oxford University Press. December. http://www.oed.com/view/Entry/2531isAdvanced=false&result=2&rskey=jThHLC&.

Agamben, Giorgio. 1998. *Homo Sacer: Sovereign Power and Bare Life*. Daniel Heller-Roazen (Trans.). Stanford, CA: Stanford University Press.

Aly, Götz and Karl Heinz Roth. 2004. *The Nazi Census: Identification and Control in the Third Reich*. Edwin Black (Trans.). Philadelphia, PA: Temple University Press.

Anand, N. and Richard A. Peterson. 2000. 'When Market Information Constitutes Fields: Sensemaking of Markets in the Commercial Music Industry'. *Organization Science* 11, no. 3. 270-284.

Anderson, Benedict. 1983. *Imagined Communities: Reflections on the Origin and Spread of Nationalism*. London: Verso.

Andrejevic, Mark. 2013. *Infoglut: How Too Much Information is Changing the Way We Think and Know*. New York and London: Routledge.

Attali, Jacques. 1989. *Noise: The Political Economy of Music*. Brian Massumi (Trans.). Minneapolis, MN: University of Minnesota Press.

Balderston, Daniel. 1993. *Out of Context: Historical Reference and the Representation of Reality in Borges*. Durham, NC: Duke University Press.

Baudrillard, Jean. 1993. *Symbolic Exchange and Death*. Ian Hamilton Grant (Trans.). London: Sage Publications.

Bauman, Zygmunt. 2001. *Modernity and the Holocaust*. Ithaca, NY: Cornell University Press.

Belknap, Robert E. 2004. *The List: The Uses and Pleasures of Cataloguing*. New Haven, CT: Yale University Press.

Benjamin, Walter. 1968. *Illuminations*. Hannah Arendt (Ed.). New York: Harcourt, Brace and World.

—. 1996. *Selected Writings vol. 1: 1913-1926*. Marcus Paul Bullock, Michael William Jennings, Howard Eiland, and Garry Smith (Eds.). Cambridge, MA: Harvard University Press.

—. 1999. 'N [On the Theory of Knowledge, Theory of Progress]'. *The Arcades Project*. Howard Eiland and Kevin McLaughlan (Trans.). Cambridge, MA: Harvard University Press. 456-488.

—. 2005. 'Excavation and Memory'. *Selected Writings vol. 2 part 2: 1931-1934*. Marcus Paul Bullock, Michael William Jennings, Howard Eiland, and Garry Smith (Eds.). Cambridge, MA: Harvard University Press. 576.

Bennett, Jane. 2010. *Vibrant Matter: A Political Ecology of Things*. Durham, NC: Duke University Press.

Berman, Marshall. 1982. *All That is Solid Melts into Air: The Experience of Modernity*. New York: Simon and Schuster.

Berube, Michael. 2000. 'Pop Culture's Lists, Rankings, and Critics'. *Chronicle of Higher Education* 47, no. 12.

Beyer, Susanne and Lothar Gorris. 2009. 'Spiegel Interview with Umberto Eco: 'We Like Lists Because We Do Not Want to Die''. *Der Spiegel International Online*. 11 November.

Black, Edwin. 2001. *IBM and the Holocaust: The Strategic Alliance Between Nazi Germany and America's Most Powerful Corporation*. New York: Crown Publishers.

Blair, Ann. 2011. *Too Much to Know: Managing Scholarly Information Before the Modern Age*. New Haven, CT: Yale University Press.

Bogost, Ian. 2012. *Alien Phenomenology, or, What it's Like to Be a Thing*. Minneapolis, MN: University of Minnesota Press.

Bordwell, David. 1985. 'The Classical Hollywood Style, 1917-1960'. *The Classical Hollywood Cinema: Film Style and Mode of Production to 1960*. David Bordwell, Janet Staiger and Kristin Thompson (Eds.). New York: Columbia University Press. 1-84.

Borges, Jorge Luis. 1998. 'The Library of Babel'. *Collected Fictions*. Andrew Hurley (Trans.). New York: Penguin. 112-118.

—. 2000. 'The Analytical Language of John Wilkins'. *Selected Non-Fictions*. Eliot Weinburger (Ed.). Esther Allen, Suzanne Jill Levine and Eliot Weinberger (Trans.). New York: Penguin. 229-233.

—. 2002. *This Craft of Verse*. Calin-Andre Mihailescu (Trans.). Cambridge, MA: Harvard University Press.

Bourdieu, Pierre. 1996. *The Rules of Art: Genesis and Structure of the Literary Field*. Susan Emanuel (Trans.). Stanford, CA: Stanford University Press.

—. 1998. *On Television*. New York: New Press.

Bowker, Geoffrey and Susan Leigh Star. 1999. *Sorting Things Out: Classification and its Consequences*. Cambridge, MA: The MIT Press.

Bratton, Benjamin. 2006. 'Logistics of Habitable Circulation'. Paul Virilio. *Speed and Politics*. Los Angeles: Semiotext(e).

—. 2016. *The Stack: On Software and Sovereignty*. Cambridge, MA: The MIT Press.

Brooks, William. 1982. 'On Being Tasteless'. *Popular Music* 2. 9-18.

Broszat, M. 1981. *The Hitler State: Foundation and Development of the Internal Structure of the Third Reich*. J.W. Hiden (Trans.). London: Longman.

Butterfield, Herbert. 1965. *The Origins of Modern Science 1300-1800*. London: G. Bell and Sons.

BuzzFeed. n.d. 'About'. https://www.buzzfeed.com/about.

—. n.d. 'Advertise'. https://www.buzzfeed.com/advertise.

Canadian Radio-Television and Telecommunications Commission (CRTC). 2015. 'The MAPL System—Defining a Canadian Song'. http://www.crtc.gc.ca/eng/info_sht/r1.htm.

Caputo, Jack. 1993. *Demythologizing Heidegger*. Bloomington, IN: Indiana University Press.

Carey, James W. 1989. *Communication as Culture: Essays on Media and Society*. Boston, MA: Unwin Hyman.

Carney, Jay. 2014. 'Fact Sheet: Ukraine-related Sanctions'. *Office of the Press Secretary of the White House*. 17 March. http://www.whitehouse.gov/the-press-office/2014/03/17/fact-sheet-ukraine-related-sanctions.

Case, Judd A. 2013. 'Logistical Media: Fragments From Radar's Prehistory'. *Canadian Journal of Communication* 38, no. 3. 379-395.

Chamayou, Grégoire. 2013. *A Theory of the Drone*. Janet Lloyd (Trans.). New York: The New Press.

Chun, Wendy Hui Kyong. 2008. 'The Enduring Ephemeral, or the Future is a Memory'. *Critical Inquiry* 35, no. 1. 148-171.

Clanchy, Michael. 1993. *From Memory to Written Record: England 1066-1307*. London: Wiley.

Council of Supply Chain Management. 2013. 'Supply Chain Management Terms and Glossary'. https://cscmp.org/sites/default/files/user_uploads/resources/downloads/glossary-2013.pdf

Crary, Jonathan. 2013. *24/7: Late Capitalism and the Ends of Sleep*. London: Verso.

Dafforne, Richard. 1651. *The Merchants Mirrour; or, Directions for the Perfect Ordering and Keeping of His Accounts...* London: Printed by J.L. for Nicolas Bourn, at the South-entrance of the Royal Exchange.

Dear, Peter. 1991. 'Narratives, Anecdotes, and Experiments: Turning Experience into Science in the Seventeenth Century'. *The Literary Structure of Scientific Argument: Historical Studies*. Peter Dear (Ed.). 135-163.

—. 1995. *Discipline and Experience: The Mathematical Way in the Scientific Revolution*. Chicago, IL: University of Chicago Press.

De Certeau, Michel. 1988. *The Practice of Everyday Life*. Steven Rendall (Trans.). Berkeley, Los Angeles, London: University of California Press.

Doležalová, Lucie (Ed.) 2009. *The Charm of a List: From the Sumerians to Computerized Data Processing*. Newcastle upon Tyne: Cambridge Scholars Publishing.

Dunphy, Martin. 2010. 'Bob Mersereau's List of Top-100 Canadian songs will please some, infuriate others'. *The Georgia Strait online*. Oct. 1. http://www.straight.com/article-351070/vancouver/bob-mersereau-list-top-100-canadian-songs-will-please-some-infuriate-others.

Eco, Umberto. 2009. *The Infinity of Lists*. Alastair McEwen (Trans.). New York: Rizzoli.

Ecojustice. 2012. 'Legal Backgrounder: Bill C-45 and the *Navigable Waters Protection Act* (RSC 1985, C N-22)'. 20 November. http://www.ecojustice.ca/wp-content/uploads/2015/03/NWPA_legal_backgrounder_November-20-2012.pdf.

Eiland, Howard and Kevin McLaughlan. 'Foreword'. Walter Benjamin. *The Arcades Project*. Howard Eiland and Kevin McLaughlan (Trans.). Cambridge, MA: Harvard University Press.

Elden, Stuart. 2006a. *Speaking Against Number: Heidegger, Language, and the Politics of Calculation*. Edinburgh: Edinburgh University Press.

—. 2006b. 'National Socialism and the Politics of Calculation'. *Social & Cultural Geography* 7, no. 5. 753-767.

Ellul, Jacques. 1964. *The Technological Society*. John Wilkenson (Trans.). New York: Vintage.

Emerson, Ralph Waldo. 2009. *The Essential Writings of Ralph Waldo Emerson*. New York: Random House.

Engels, Frederick. 1968. *The Condition of the Working Class in England* [1845]. W.O. Henderson and W.H. Chalendor (Trans. and Eds.). Stanford, CA: Stanford University Press.

Ennis, P.H. 1994. *The Seventh Stream: The Emergence of Rock 'n' Roll in American Popular Music*. Hanover, NH: Wesleyan University Press.

Ernst, Wolfgang. 2011. 'Media Archaeography: Method & Machine versus History & Narrative of Media'. *Media Archaeology: Approaches, Applications, Implications*. Erkki Huhtamo and Jussi Parikka (Eds.). Berkeley, CA: University of California Press. 239-55.

—. 2013. *Digital Memory and the Archive*. Jussi Parikka (Ed.). Minneapolis, MN: University of Minnesota Press.

—. 2016. *Sonic Times Machines: Explicit Sound, Sirenic Voices and Implicit Sonicitiy*. Amsterdam: Amsterdam University Press.

Facebook. 2013. 'A Focus on Efficiency: A Whitepaper from Facebook, Ericsson and Qualcomm'. 16 September. http://www.slideshare.net/FiratDemirel/facebook-ericsson-rapor

Fleck, Ludwig. 1979. *Genesis and Development of a Scientific Fact*. Fred Bradley and Thaddeus J. Trenn (Trans.). Chicago, IL: University of Chicago Press.

Forbes, J.A. 2016. 'Material and Technique: On the Origins of Writing in the Ancient Near-East'. Presentation at the Canadian Communication Association annual conference. Calgary, AB. 31 May.

Foucault, Michel. 1980. *Power/Knowledge: Selected Interviews and Other Writings, 1972-1977*. Colin Gordon (Ed.). Hassocks, UK: Harvester Press.

—. 1986. 'Of Other Spaces'. Jay Miskoviec (Trans.). *Diacritics* 16.1. 22-27.

—. 1990. *The History of Sexuality Vol. I: An Introduction*. Robert Hurley (Trans.). New York: Vintage.

—. 2001. 'Lives of Infamous Men'. *Power: Essential Works of Foucault 1954-1984*. Robert Hurley (Trans.). James D. Faubion (Ed.). New York: The New Press. 157-175.

—. 2007. *Security, Territory, Population: Lectures at the College de France 1977-78*. Graham Burchell (Trans.). New York: Palgrave MacMillan.

—. 2009. *The Order of Things: An Archaeology of the Human Sciences* [1966]. London: Routledge.

Franklin, Benjamin. 1996. *The Autobiography of Benjamin Franklin* [1868]. Philip Smith (Ed.). Mineola, NY: Dover Publications.

Frohmann, Bernd. 2004a. 'Documentation Redux: Prolegomenon to (Another) Philosophy of Information'. *Library Trends* 54. 387-407.

—. 2004b. *Deflating Information: From Science Studies to Documentation*. Toronto: University of Toronto Press.

—. 2009. 'Revisiting 'What is a Document?'' *Journal of Documentation* 65, no. 2. 291-303.

Fromm, Eric. 1994. *Escape From Freedom* [1941]. New York: Holt Paperbacks.

Frommer, Dan. 2010. 'Here's How BuzzFeed Works'. *Business Insider* Tech Blog. 11 June. http://www.businessinsider.com/heres-how-buzzfeed-works-2010-6.

Frow, John. 1997. *Time and Commodity Culture: Essays in Cultural Theory and Postmodernity*. Oxford: Oxford University Press.

Fuller, Matthew and Andrew Goffey. 2009. 'Towards an Evil Media Studies'. *The Spam Book*. Jussi Parikka and Tony Sampson (Eds.). New Jersey: Hampton Press.

Gelb, I.J. 1952. *A Study of Writing: The Foundations of Grammatology*. Champaign: University of Illinois Press.

Gitelman, Lisa. 2006. *Always Already New: Media, History and the Data of Culture*. Cambridge, MA: The MIT Press.

—. 2014. *Paper Knowledge: Toward a Media History of Documents*. Durham, NC: Duke University Press.

Gonen, Jay. 2000. *The Roots of Nazi Psychology: Hitler's Utopian Barbarism*. Lexington, KY: University Press of Kentucky.

Goody, Jack and Ian Watt. 1963. 'The Consequences of Literacy'. *Comparative Studies in Society and History* 5, no. 3. 304-345.

Goody, Jack. 1977. *The Domestication of the Savage Mind*. Cambridge: Cambridge University Press.

Guillory, John. 2004. 'The Memo and Modernity'. *Critical Inquiry* 31, no. 1. 108-132.

Hacking, Ian. 1982. 'Bio-power and the Avalanche of Printed Numbers'. *Humanities in Society* 5. 279-295.

—. 1986. 'Making up People'. *Reconstructing Individualism: Autonomy, Individuality, and the Self in Western Thought*. Thomas C. Heller, Morton Sosna, David E. Wellbery (Eds.). Stanford, CA: Stanford University Press. 222-236.

—. 1991. 'How Should We Do the History of Statistics?' *The Foucault Effect: Studies in Governmentality*. Graham Burchell, Colin Gordon and Peter Miller (Eds.). New York: Harvester Wheatsheaf. 181-195.

—. 2002. *Historical Ontology*. Cambridge, MA: Harvard University Press.

—. 2006. *The Emergence of Probability: A Philosophic Study of Early Ideas About Probability, Induction, and Statistical Inference*. Second edition. Cambridge: Cambridge University Press.

Hakanen, Ernest A. 1998. 'Counting Down to Number One: The Evolution of the Meaning of the Popular Charts'. *Popular Music* 17, no. 1. 95-111.

Harvey, David. 1989. *The Condition of Postmodernity: An Enquiry into the Origins of Cultural Change*. New York: Blackwell.

Havelock, Eric. 1963. *Preface to Plato*. Cambridge, MA: Harvard University Press.

Heidegger, Martin. 1991a. 'The Question Concerning Technology'. *Basic Writings*. Joan Stambaugh (Trans.). David Farrell Krell (Ed.). San Francisco: Harper Collins. 307-341.

—. 1991b. 'The End of Philosophy and the Task of Thinking'. *Basic Writings*. Joan Stambaugh (Trans.). David Farrell Krell (Ed.). San Francisco: Harper Collins. 431-449.

—. 1993. "'Only a God Can Save Us': *Der Spiegel's* interview with Martin Heidegger'. *The Heidegger Controversy: A Reader*. Richard Wolin (Ed.). Cambridge, MA: The MIT Press. 91-117.

—. 1999. *Contributions to Philosophy: From Enowning*. Parvis Emad and Kenneth Martin. (Trans.). Bloomington, IN: Indiana University Press.

Heilmann, Till. 2014. "'Tap, Tap, Flap, Flap.' Ludic Seriality, Digitality, and the Finger'. *Eludamos: Journal for Computer Game Culture* 8, no. 1. 33-46.

Henderson, Scott. 2008. 'Canadian Content Regulations and the Formation of a National Scene'. *Popular Music* 27, no. 2. 307-315.

Herf, Jeffrey. 1984. *Reactionary Modernism: Technology, Culture and Politics in Weimar and the Third Reich*. Cambridge: Cambridge University Press.

Hesmondhalgh, David. 2006. 'Bourdieu, the Media, and Cultural Production'. *Media, Culture and Society* 28, no. 2. 211-231.

Horkheimer, Max and Theodor W. Adorno. 2002. *Dialectic of Enlightenment: Philosophical Fragments* [1944]. Gunzelin Schmid Noerr (Trans.). Stanford, CA: Stanford University Press.

Huber, Alison. 2010. 'Making Time Stand Still: How to "fix" the transient Top 40'. *International Journal of Cultural Studies* 13, no. 2. 147-162.

Hughes, Aaron. 2003. 'Presenting the Past: The Genre of Commentary in Theoretical Perspective'. *Method & Theory in the Study of Religion* 15. 148-168.

Huhtamo, Erkki. 1997. 'From Kaleidoscomaniac to Cybernerd: Notes Toward an Archaeology of the Media'. *Leonardo* 30, no. 3. 221-224.

—. 2011. 'Dismantling the Fairy Engine: Media Archaeology as *Topos* study' in *Media Archaeology: Approaches, Applications, and Implications*. Erkki Huhtamo and Jussi Parikka (Eds.). Berkeley, CA: University of California Press. 27-47.

— and Jussi Parikka. 2011. 'Introduction: An Archaeology of Media Archaeology'. *Media Archaeology: Approaches, Applications, and Implications*. Berkeley, CA: University of California Press.

Huyssen, Andreas. 2003. *Present Pasts: Urban Palimpsests and the Politics of Memory*. Stanford, CA: Stanford University Press.

IBM. n.d. 'Bringing Big Data to the Enterprise'. https://www-01.ibm.com/software/data/bigdata/what-is-big-data.html.

Ihde, Don. 2010. *Heidegger's Technologies: Postphenomenological Perspectives*. New York: Fordham University Press.

'Information Overload'. *Wikipedia*. http://en.wikipedia.org/wiki/Information_overload.

Innis, Harold. A. 1973. *The Fur Trade in Canada* [1930]. Toronto: University of Toronto Press.

—. 1978. *The Cod Fisheries: The History of an International Economy* [1940]. Toronto: University of Toronto Press.

—. 1995. *Staples, Markets, and Cultural Change: Selected Essays of Harold A. Innis*. Daniel Drache (Ed.). Montreal: McGill-Queen's University Press.

—. 2002. *The Bias of Communication* [1951]. Second Edition. Toronto: University of Toronto Press.

—. 2007. *Empire and Communications* [1950]. Toronto: Dundurn Press.

Johnson, Jenna. 2015. 'Donald Trump Would 'Certainly' and 'Absolutely' Create a Database of Muslims'. *Washington Post*. 20 November. https://www.washingtonpost.com/news/post-politics/wp/2015/11/20/donald-trump-would-certainly-and-absolutely-create-a-database-of-muslims/.

Kafka, Ben. 2012. *The Demon of Writing: Powers and Failures of Paperwork*. New York: Zone Books.

Kanngieser, Anja. 2013. 'Tracking and Tracing: Geographies of Logistical Governance and Labouring Bodies'. *Environment and Planning D: Society and Space* 31, no. 4. 594-610.

Keating Clay, William (Ed.). 1851. *Private Prayers of the Reign of Queen Elizabeth.* Cambridge: Cambridge University Press.

Kershaw, Ian. 2000. *The Nazi Dictatorship: Problems and Perspectives of Interpretation.* London: Arnold.

Kerwin, Lisa (Cur.). 2011. *Lists: To-dos, Illustrated Inventories, Collected Thoughts, and Other Artists' Enumerations from the Smithsonian's Archives of American Art.* New York: The Morgan Library and Museum.

Kirschenbaum, Matthew G. 2008. *Mechanisms: New Media and the Forensic Imagination.* Cambridge, MA: The MIT Press.

Kittler, Friedrich A. 1990. *Discourse Networks 1800/1900.* Michael Metteer and Chris Cullins (Trans.). Stanford, CA: Stanford University Press.

—. 1999. *Gramophone, Film, Typewriter.* Geoffrey Winthrop-Young and Michael Wutz (Trans.). Stanford, CA: Stanford University Press.

—. 2010. *Optical Media: Berlin Lectures 1999.* Anthony Enns. (Trans.). Cambridge: Polity Press.

Kochan, Jeff. 2010. 'Latour's Heidegger'. *Social Studies of Science* 40, no. 4. 579-598.

Kogon, Eugen. 1950. *The Theory and Practice of Hell: The German Concentration Camps and the System Behind Them.* London: Secker & Warburg.

Krämer, Sybille. 2003. 'Writing, Notational Iconicity, Calculus: On Writing as a Cultural Technique'. Anita McChesney (Trans.). *MLN* 118. 518-537.

—. 2006. 'The Cultural Techniques of Time-Axis Manipulation: On Friedrich Kittler's Conception of Media'. *Theory, Culture and Society* 23, vol. 7. 93-109.

Krajewski, Markus. 2011. *Paper Machines: About Cards and Catalogs, 1548-1929.* Peter Krapp (Trans.). Cambridge, MA: The MIT Press.

Krummel, John W.M. 2007. 'Representation and *Poiesis:* The Imagination in the Later Heidegger'. *Philosophy Today* 51, no. 3. 261-277.

La Jetée. 1962. Directed by Chris Marker. Paris: Argos Films.

Latour, Bruno. 1987. *Science in Action: How to Follow Scientists and Engineers Through Society.* Cambridge, MA: Harvard University Press.

—. 1990. 'Drawing Things Together'. *Representation in Scientific Practice.* M. Lynch and S. Woolgar (Eds.). Cambridge, MA: The MIT Press. 19-68.

—. 1993. *We Have Never Been Modern.* Catherine Porter (Trans.). New York: Harvester Wheatsheaf.

—. 1999. *Pandora's Hope: Essays on the Reality of Science Studies.* Cambridge, MA: Harvard University Press.

—. 2005. *Reassembling the Social: An Introduction to Actor-Network Theory.* Oxford: Oxford University Press.

—. 2013. *An Inquiry into Modes of Existence: An Anthropology of the Moderns.* Catherine Porter (Trans.). Cambridge, MA: Harvard University Press.

Lefebvre, Henri. 1992. *The Production of Space.* Donald Nicholson-Smith (Trans.). New York: Blackwell.

Le Goff, Jacques. 1992. *History and Memory.* Steven Rendall and Elizabeth Claman (Trans.). New York: Columbia University Press.

Lewis, Michael. 2014. *Flash Boys: A Wall St. Revolt.* New York: W. W. Nortan & Company.

'List, n.6'. 2015. *Oxford English Dictionary Online.* Oxford: Oxford University Press. December. http://www.oed.com/view/Entry/108991.

'Logistics n.2'. 2015. *Oxford English Dictionary Online.* Oxford: Oxford University Press. December. http://www.oed.com/view/Entry/109817rskey=wrFOZa&result=2&isAdvanced=fals.

Lovink, Geert. 2011. *Networks Without a Cause: A Critique of Social Media.* Cambridge: Polity Press.

Lowenthal, Marc. 2010. 'Translator's Introduction'. Georges Perec. *An Attempt at Exhausting a Place in Paris* [1975]. Marc Lowenthal (Trans.). Cambridge, MA: Wakefield Press.

Lulu, Zhang. 2014. 'Silk Road Economic Belt Differs From Eurasian Union'. *China.org.cn.* 30 June. http://www.china.org.cn/business/2014-06/30/content_32813835.htm.

Manovich, Lev. 2001. *The Language of New Media.* Cambridge, MA: The MIT Press.

Manzerolle, Vincent R. and Atle Mikkola Kjøsen. 2012. 'The Communication of Capital: Digital Media and the Logic of Acceleration'. *Triple-C* 10, no. 2. http://www.triple-c.at/index.php/tripleC/article/view/412.

Marchand, Philip. 1998. *Marshall McLuhan: The Medium and the Messenger: A Biography.* First Edition. Cambridge, MA: The MIT Press.

Marcuse, Herbert. 1991. *One Dimensional Man: Studies in the Ideology of Advanced Industrial Societies* [1964]. Boston, MA: Beacon Press.

Martin, Christopher. 2013. *Logistics and Supply Chain Management.* Fourth edition. Pearson UK: Prentice Hall.

Mattern, Shannon. 2015. *Deep Mapping the Media City.* Minneapolis, MN: University of Minnesota Press.

McCarthy, John. 1996. 'LISP Prehistory—Summer 1956 Through Summer 1958'. http://www-formal.stanford.edu/jmc/history/lisp/node2.html/.

McClelland, Mac. 2012. 'I Was a Warehouse Wage Slave'. *Mother Jones.* March/April. http://www.motherjones.com/politics/2012/02/mac-mcclelland-free-online-shipping-warehouses-labor.

McCulloch, Glenn. 2002. 'Heidegger, Augustine and *Poiesis:* Renewing the Technological Mind'. *Theology Today* 59, no. 1. 21-38.

McLuhan, Marshall. 1962. *The Gutenberg Galaxy: The Making of Typographic Man.* Toronto: University of Toronto Press.

—. 2003. *Understanding Media: The Extensions of Man* [1964]. Critical Edition. W. Terrence Gordon (Ed.). Berkeley, CA: Ginko Press.

Meany, Ken and Mike Barber. 2010. 'Guess Who's On The List? New Book Lists Canada's Top 100 Songs'. *Vancouver Province* (Vancouver, BC). 2 October.

Mersereau, Bob. 2007. *The Top-100 Canadian Albums.* Fredericton: Goose Lane.

—. 2010. *The Top-100 Canadian Singles.* Fredericton: Goose Lane.

Miller, Claire Cain. 2013 'Tech Companies Concede to Surveillance Program'. *The New York Times.* 7 June. http://www.nytimes.com/2013/06/08/technology/tech-companies-bristling-concede-to-government-surveillance-efforts.html?ref=global-home&_r=2&&pagewanted=all.

Monea, Alexander and Jeremy Packer. 2016. 'Media Genealogy and the Politics of Archaeology'. *International Journal of Communication* 10. 3141-3159.

Montford, Nick. 2004. 'Continuous Paper: The Early Materiality and Workings of Electronic Literature'. Presentation at the Modern Language Association annual conference. Philadelphia, PA. 28 December. http://nickm.com/writing/essays/continuous_paper_mla.html.

Morozov, Evgeny. 2013. *To Save Everything, Click Here: The Folly of Technological Solutionism.* New York: Public Affairs.

Morris, Jeremy Wade. 2015. *Selling Digital Music, Formatting Culture.* Berkeley, CA: University of California Press.

Morton, Timothy. 2015. 'They Are Here'. *The Nonhuman Turn.* Richard Grusin (Ed.). Minneapolis, MN: University of Minnesota Press. 167-196.

Mumford, Lewis. 1963. *Technics and Civilization.* New York and Burlingame: Harbinger.

Murphy, A.B. 1996. 'The Sovereign State System as Political-Territorial Idea: Historical and Contemporary Considerations'. *State Sovereignty As Social Construct.* T. Biersteker and C. Weber (Eds.). Cambridge: Cambridge University Press.

Nancy, Jean-Luc and Phillipe Lacoue-Labarthe. 1990. 'The Nazi Myth'. Brian Holmes (Trans.). *Critical Inquiry* 162. 291-312.

Neusner, Jacob. 1990. 'The Mishnah's Generative Mode of Thought: Listenwissenschaft and Analogical-Contrastive Reasoning'. *Journal of the American Oriental Society* 110, no. 2. 317-321.

Norman, Don. 2013. *The Design of Everyday Things: Revised and Expanded.* New York: Basic Books.

Nunberg, Geoffrey. 1996. 'Farewell to the Information Age'. *The Future of the Book.* Geoffrey Nunberg (Ed.). Berkeley, CA: University of California Press. 103-138.

Ong, Walter J. 1982. *Orality and Literacy: The Technologizing of The Word.* London: Methuen.

Parikka, Jussi. 2011. 'Operative Media Archaeology: Wolfgang Ernst's Materialist Media Diagrammatics'. *Theory, Culture, and Society* 28, no. 5. 52-74.

—. 2014. 'Cultural Techniques of Cognitive Capitalism: Metaprogramming and the Labour of Code'. *Cultural Studies Review* 20, no. 1. 30-52.

Parker, Martin. 1991. 'Reading The Charts—Making Sense With the *Hit Parade*'. *Popular Music* 10, no. 2. 205-217.

Parry, Milman. 1971. *The Making of Homeric Verse: The Collected Papers of Milman Parry.* Adam Parry (Ed.). Oxford: Oxford University Press.

Peters, John Durham. 1988. 'Information: Notes Toward a Critical History'. *Journal of Communication Inquiry* 12, no. 2. 9-23.

—. 1999. *Speaking Into The Air: A History of the Idea of Communication.* Chicago, IL: University of Chicago Press.

—. 2001. '"The Only Proper Scale of Representation": The Politics of Statistics and Stories'. *Political Communication* 18. 433-449.

—. 2008. 'Resemblance Made Absolutely Exact: Borges and Royce on Maps and Media'. *Variaciones Borges* 25. 1-23.

—. 2009. 'Strange Sympathies: Horizons of German and American Media Theory'. *Electronic Book Review: Critical Ecologies.* 4 June. http://www.electronicbookreview.com/thread/criticalecologies/myopic.

—. 2012. 'Becoming Mollusk: A Conversation with John Durham Peters About Media, Materiality, and Matters of History' in *Communication Matters: Materialist Approaches to Media, Mobility, and Networks.* Jeremy Packer and Stephen B. Crofts (Eds.). London and New York: Routledge. 35-53.

—. 2013a. 'Calendar, Clock, Tower'. *Deus in Machina: Religion and Technology in Historical Perspective.* Jeremy Stolow (Ed.). New York: Fordham University Press. 25-42.

—. 2013b. "Writing'. *The International Encyclopedia of Media Studies: Media History and the Foundations of Media Studies.* Angharad N. Valdivia and John Narone (Ed.). New York: Blackwell. 197-216.

—. 2015. *The Marvellous Clouds: Towards a Philosophy of Elemental Media.* Chicago, IL: University of Chicago Press.

Pitchfork online magazine. n.d. 'P2K: The Decade in Music'. http://pitchfork.com/p2k/.

Poletti, Anna. 2008. 'Where the Popular Meets the Mundane: The Use of Lists in Personal Zines'. *Canadian Review of American Studies* 38, no. 3: 333-349.

Poovey, Mary. 1997. *A History of the Modern Fact: Problems of Knowledge in the Sciences of Wealth and Society.* Chicago, IL: University of Chicago Press.

Quatronne, Paolo. 2004. 'Accounting for God: Accounting and Accountability Practices in the Society of Jesus (Italy, XVI-XVII centuries)'. *Accounting, Organizations and Society* 29. 647-683.

Quill, Greg. 2010. 'Start the Arguments, Music Fans: Canada's top 100 singles'. *Toronto Star.* 2 October. http://www.thestar.com/entertainment/music/article/869802--start-the-arguments-music-fans-canada-s-top-100-singles.

Quiñones, Marta García. 2007. 'Listening in Shuffle Mode'. *Song and Popular Culture* 52. 11-22.

Robinson, Derek. 2008. 'Function'. *Software Studies: A Lexicon.* Matthew Fuller (Ed.). Cambridge, MA: The MIT Press. 101-109.

Robischon, Noah. 2016. 'How BuzzFeed's Jonah Peretti is Building a 100-Year Media Company'. *Fast-Company.* 16 February. http://www.fastcompany.com/3056057/most-innovative-companies/how-buzzfeeds-jonah-peretti-is-building-a-100-year-media-company.

Rolling Stone Magazine Online. 2003. '500 Greatest Songs of All-Time'. http://www.rollingstone.com/music/lists/500-greatest-albums-of-all-time-19691231.

Rossiter, Ned. 2014. 'Logistical Worlds'. *Cultural Studies Review* 20, no. 1. 53-76.

Rotman, Brian. 1987. *Signifying Nothing: The Semiotics of Zero.* Stanford, CA: Stanford University Press.

—. 2008. *Becoming Beside Ourselves: The Alphabet, Ghosts, and Distributed Human Being.* Durham, NC: Duke University Press.

Sanjek, Russell. 1988. *American Popular Music and its Business, vol. 3.* New York: Oxford University Press.

Sans Soleil. 1983. Directed by Chris Marker. Paris: Argos Films.

Saramago, José. 1994. *The Gospel According to Jesus Christ.* Giovanni Pontiero (Trans.). San Diego, CA: Harcourt Brace.

Scahill, Jeremy. 2015. 'The Assassination Complex'. *The Intercept_.* 15 October. https://theintercept.com/drone-papers/the-assassination-complex/.

Schäfer, Peter and Shaul Shaked. 1994. *Magische Texte aus der Kairoer Geniza 1.* Tübingen: Mohr.

Schaffer, Simon and Steven Shapin. 1985. *Leviathan and the Air Pump: Hobbes, Boyle, and Experimental Life.* New York: Columbia University Press.

Schlager, Ken. 2006. 'Billboard History'. *Billboard Magazine Online.* http://web.archive.org/web/20060208224431/http://www.billboard.com/bbcom/about_us/bbhistory3.jsp.

Schmandt-Besserat, Denise. 1982. 'How Writing Came About'. *Zeitschrift für Papyrologie und Epigraphik* 47. 1-5.

—. 1996. *How Writing Came About.* Austin, TX: University of Texas Press.

Schmidt, Jeremy and Jacquelyn Ardam. 2014. 'On Excess: Susan Sontag's Born-Digital Archive'. *LA Review of Books*, 26 October. http://lareviewofbooks.org/essay/excess-susan-sontags-born-digital-archive/#.

Scott, Michael. 2013. *Making New Zealand's Pop Renaissance: State, Markets, Musicians.* Farnham, UK: Ashgate Publishing.

Serres, Michel with Bruno Latour. 1995. *Conversations on Science, Culture, and Time.* Roxanne Lapidus. (Trans.). Ann Arbor, MI: The University of Michigan Press.

Shakespeare, William 2002. *King Henry V.* Emma Smith (Ed.). Cambridge: Cambridge University Press.

Shannon, Claude E. and Warren Weaver. 1949. *The Mathematical Theory of Communication.* Champaign, IL: The University of Illinois Press.

Shapin, Steven. 1984. 'Pump and Circumstance: Robert Boyle's Literary Technology'. *Social Studies of Science* 14. 481-520.

Sharkey, Sabina. 1997. 'Irish Cultural Studies and Politics of Irish Studies'. *Cultural Methodologies.* Jim McGuigan (Ed.). London: Sage.
Shepard, Wade. 2016. 'China is Moving Mountains for the New Silk Road—Literally'. *Forbes.* 21 January. http://www.forbes.com/sites/wadeshepard/2016/01/21/china-is-moving-mountains-for-the-new-silk-road-literally/#376339bb6729.
Shumway, David R. 2007. 'Authenticity: Modernity, Stardom, and Rock & Roll'. *Modernism/Modernity* 14, no. 3. 527-533.
Siebel, Peter. 2005. *Practical Common Lisp.* New York: Apress.
Siegert, Bernhard. 2008. 'Cacography or Communication? Cultural Techniques in German Media Studies'. Geoffrey Winthrop-Young. (Trans.). *Grey Room* 29. 26-47.
—. 2011. 'The Map *is* the Territory'. *Radical Philosophy* 169: 13-16.
—. 2012. 'Doors: On the Materiality of the Symbolic'. John Durham-Peters (Trans.). *Grey Room* 47. 6-23.
—. 2013. 'Cultural Techniques: Or The End of the Intellectual Postwar Era in German Media Theory'. Geoffrey Winthrop-Young. (Trans.). *Theory, Culture, and Society* 30.6. 48-65.
—. 2015. *Cultural Techniques: Grids, Filters, Doors, and Other Articulations of the Real.* Geoffrey Winthrop-Young (Trans.). New York: Fordham University Press.
Softsky, Wolfgang. 1999. *The Order of Terror: The Concentration Camp.* William Templer (Trans.). Princeton, NJ: Princeton University Press.
Solomon, Rory. 2013. 'Last Out, First In: Network Archaeology and/as Stack'. *Amodern 2: Network Archaeology.* cris cheek, Braxton Soderman and Nicole Starosielski (Eds.). http://amodern.net/article/last-in-first-out/.
Spruyt, H. 1994. *The Sovereign State and its Competitors.* Princeton, NJ: Princeton: University Press.
Spufford, Francis. 1989. *The Chatto Book of Cabbages and Kings: Lists in Literature.* London: Chatto & Windus.
Srnicek, Nick, Levi Bryant and Graham Harmon (Eds.). 2011. *The Speculative Turn: Continental Materialism and Realism.* Melbourne: re.press.
Starosielski, Nicole. 2015. *The Undersea Network.* Durham, NC: Duke University Press.
Steele, Warren. 2011-2014. 'The Meaning of Technology'. Lecture series at The University of Western Ontario. London, ON.
Sterne, Jonathan. 2003. *The Audible Past: Cultural Origins of Sound Reproduction.* Durham, NC: Duke University Press.
—. 2012. *MP3: The Meaning of a Format.* Durham, NC: Duke University Press.
Straw, Will. 2015. 'Mediality and the Music Chart'. *SubStance* 138, vol. 44 no. 3. 128-138.
Suleiman, Summer. 2016. 'How BuzzFeed is Disrupting the Media and Changing the Way We Think About Content'. *The Distillery.* 15 January. http://blog.noew.org/distillery/2016/01/15/buzzfeed-disrupting-media-changing-way-think-content/.
Supreme Court of Canada. 1992. *Friends of the Oldman River Society v. Canada (Minister of Transport).* 1 S.C.R. 3 at paras. 88-89.
Swartz, Michael D. 2005. 'The Aesthetics of Blessing and Cursing: Literary and Iconographic Dimensions of Hebrew and Aramaic Blessing and Curse Texts'. *Journal of Ancient Near Eastern Religions* 5, no. 1. 187-211.
Terranova, Tiziana. 2004. *Network Culture: Politics for the Information Age.* London: Pluto Press.
The New World. 2005. Directed by Terrence Malick. Los Angeles: New Line Cinema.
Toffler, Alvin. 1971. *Future Shock.* Toronto: Bantam Books.
Turkle, Sherry. 2011. *Alone Together: Why We Expect More From Technology and Less From Each Other.* Philadelphia, PA: Basic Books.

Tzoref, Shani. 2011. '*Pesher* and Periodization'. *Dead Sea Discoveries* 18. 129-154.

Usher, Shaun. 2014a. 'The World's Most Intriguing Lists'. *The Telegraph*. 29 September. http://www.telegraph.co.uk/culture/books/11123049/The-worlds-most-intriguing-lists.html.

—. 2014b. *Lists of Note*. London: Unbound.

Velhuis, Nick. 1997. *Elementary Education at Nippur. The Lists of Trees and Wooden Objects*. PhD Thesis, University of Groningen.

Vonnegut, Kurt. 1976. *Slapstick, or Lonesome No More!* New York: Dell Publishing.

Virilio, Paul. 2006. *Speed and Politics*. Mark Polizzotti. (Trans.). Los Angeles: Semiotext(e).

—. 2007. *The Original Accident*. Rose Juile (Trans.). Cambridge: Polity Press.

Vismann, Cornelia. 2008. *Files: Law and Media Technology*. Geoffrey Winthrop-Young (Trans.). Stanford, CA: Stanford University Press.

—. 2013. 'Cultural Techniques and Sovereignty'. Ilinca Irascu (Trans.). *Theory, Culture, and Society 30.6*. 83-93.

Wasik, Bill. 2009. *And Then There's This: How Stories Live and Die in Viral Culture*. New York: Penguin.

Weber, Max. 1958. *From Max Weber: Essays in Sociology*. H.H. Gerth and C. Wright Mills (Trans. and Eds.). New York: Oxford University Press.

—. 2001. *The Protestant Ethic and the Spirit of Capitalism* [1930]. Talcott Parsons (Trans.). London: Routledge.

Werbin, Kenneth. 2008. *The List Serves: The Apparatuses of Security and Governmentality*. PhD Thesis, Concordia University.

—. 2009. 'Fear and No-Fly Listing in Canada: The Biopolitics of the 'War on Terror''. *Canadian Journal of Communication* 34, no. 4. 613-634.

White, Hayden. 1973. *Metahistory: The Historical Imagination in Nineteenth-Century Europe*. Baltimore: Johns Hopkins University Press.

Wilken, Rowan and Anthony McCosker. 2012. 'The Everyday Work of Lists'. *M/C Journal* 15, no. 5.

Williams, Raymond. 1983. *Keywords*. New York: Fontana.

—. 1991. *The Long Revolution*. Peterborough, ON: Broadview Press.

Winkler, Hartmut. 2010. 'Processing: The Third and Neglected Media Function'. Presentation at *MediaTransatlantic* Conference. University of British Columbia, Vancouver, British Columbia. 8 April. http://homepages.uni-paderborn.de/winkler/proc_e.pdf.

Winthrop-Young, Geoffrey. 2013. *Kittler and the Media*. Cambridge: Polity Press.

—. 2015. 'Siren Recursions'. *Kittler Now: Current Perspectives in Kittler Studies*. Stephen Sale and Laura Salisbury (Eds.). Cambridge: Polity Press. 71-95.

Woodman, Ross G. 1967. *Chambers: John Chambers, Interviewed by Ross G. Woodman*. Toronto: Coach House Press.

Young, Liam Cole. 2013a. 'Un-Black Boxing the List: Knowledge, Materiality, and Form'. *Canadian Journal of Communication* 38, no. 4. 497-515.

—. 2013b. 'On Lists and Networks: An Archaeology of Form'. *Amodern 2: Network Archaeology*. cris cheek, Braxton Soderman and Nicole Starosielski (Eds.). http://amodern.net/article/on-lists-and-networks/.

—. 2015. 'Cultural Techniques and Logistical Media: Tuning Anglo-American and German Media Theory'. *M/C Journal* 18, no. 2.

—. 2017 (forthcoming). 'Innis and Infrastructure: Dirt, Beavers, and Documents in Material Media Theory'. *Cultural Politics*.

Index

For Product Safety Concerns and Information please contact our EU representative GPSR@taylorandfrancis.com Taylor & Francis Verlag GmbH, Kaufingerstraße 24, 80331 München, Germany